WATCHING
THE DETECTIVES

Graham Nown

WATCHING THE DETECTIVES

The Life and Times of the Private Eye

Grafton Books
A Division of HarperCollins*Publishers*

GraftonBooks
A Division of HarperCollins*Publishers*
77–85 Fulham Palace Road,
Hammersmith, London W6 8JB

Published by GraftonBooks 1991

Copyright © Graham Nown 1991

British Library Cataloguing in Publication Data

Nown, Graham
    Watching the detectives: the life and times
    of the private eye.
    1. Private detectives
    I. Title
    363.289

ISBN 0–246–13650–2

Phototypeset by
Computape (Pickering) Ltd, North Yorkshire
Printed in Great Britain by
HarperCollinsManufacturing Glasgow

FOR SYLVANA & ROSIE
– and Darnell,
the smallest Sam Spadette of all

CONTENTS

INTRODUCTION AND ACKNOWLEDGEMENTS

The difference in outlook between private detectives in Britain and their counterparts around the world became more apparent as I researched this book. I approached private investigators in Europe, America, the Far East, and in Moscow and Leningrad. All of them welcomed an opportunity to talk about their work. Some provided confidential case records, others allowed me to sit in at client interviews and accompany them on cases. In Britain, all open-handedness evaporated. The initial reaction of most investigators was one of deep suspicion bordering on paranoia, a reflex strangely at odds with the popular image of PIs in drama and fiction.

I was accused of being an *agent provocateur* in the pay of other agents who wanted to destroy them professionally. As word of my interest spread like a bushfire, I received anonymous telephone calls, nervous excuses for not being interviewed and, on three separate occasions, attempts to tap into my telephone by computer. I was even discussed at a regional meeting of the respectable Association of British Investigators who dispatched an agent to run a check on my home and background. After making a few passes of the house in his car, he telephoned to enquire if he could call round to ask me some questions.

It would have been easy to interpret the world of the British private eye as one filled with dark corners and claustrophobic suspicion. Fortunately, this image proved not to be entirely true to life, despite an ingrained distrust of 'outsiders', especially the media, on the part of British PIs.

When suspicions abated, however, many turned out to be helpful and genuinely concerned about their bad public image. Behind the veil of unnecessary mystery lay a network of small businessmen with the attendant problems of cash flow and mortgages. They stressed that the life was decidedly unglamorous but admitted that it would be difficult to imagine earning a living any other way. The first point was undoubtedly true. Private eyes in America in-variably have one murder case, several kidnappings and a collection of confidence tricksters on their files. In Britain, bread-and-butter work is more likely to be serving writs, evictions if the agent is a certified bailiff, debt collection or repossessing cars. Yet despite the apparently depressing nature of the work, there exists an undeniable passion for picking over the economic debris of modern Britain.

'I get a buzz from it,' one investigator confided. 'Every time I knock on a door to serve a writ, it's like Christmas Day. I never know what to expect – should I be sympathetic, feign ignorance of what the papers are about or lean on them if they get stroppy? It's a powerful position because I am the arm of the judge who signed the process, and there isn't much they can do about it.'

Compared to the openness of private eyes internationally, including in Russia, British investigators were generally remote and guarded. It seemed that, collectively, a nerve had been scratched which ran deeper than a simple concern about bad publicity. They felt misunderstood for reasons which reach back several centuries and reflect a vastly different public attitude to PIs on each side of the Atlantic. In the UK an investigator will go about his business and hope that people are so unaware of his presence that they will not have an attitude; in the USA he may lecture to students about the dangers of crime and drug-taking, and hand you a leather-bound publicity profile, complete with press cuttings.

Reliable documentary material is not plentiful when trying to uncover the history of the private eye. The little that exists is often unattributed, lacking in dates, full names and places, or dramatized for a mass market of Victorian and Edwardian magazine readers. Private eyes' 'memoirs' make interesting reading, but in many cases were also dressed for an audience of voracious readers and perhaps equally unreliable. Despite the pitfalls, the history of private detection is a neglected story well worth telling.

All the accounts in the ensuing pages are to the best of my knowledge true and, where possible, have been verified. Names and locations have been changed in some for special reasons in the hope that the future of the survivors will remain undisturbed.

The book would not have been possible without the help, advice and good company of many private investigators and others. Special thanks must go to: Alex Agency; Jay J. Armes; Association of British Investigators; Fred Bates; Alan Cardoza; Vincent and Paul

Carratu; Peter Clark; Logan and Dona Clarke; Kathleen Cummings; Bill Dear; Bo Dietl; Shawn Donahue; Trevor Fishlock; Brenda Hanson; Peter Heims; Richard Jacques Turner; Richard Johnson; Marcus Joseph; Jane Judd; Tony Kinghorn; Valentin Kosyakov and interpreter Derek Aitken; Jim Lyness; C.M.; Robert Martin; C. J. Mastro; Kirby McCauley; Nancy McGuire; Steve McLoughlin; Tim O'Connor; Vincent Parco; Pinkerton; Tommy 'Gangland' Prior; George Pulley; Anthony Purbrick; Dick Riddle; George Rivers; Scott Schlenker; Cam Shaw; John Sheldon; Patterson Smith; Milo Speriglio; Jack Taylor; Martin, Pearl and Peter Tytell; Thomas Wathan; Larry Webb; Steve Weinstein; World Association of Detectives; David 'Kipper' Young; Al Zaretz; and my wife Sylvana.

Specialist manuals for PIs are available from Thomas Publications, of P.O. Box 33244, Austin, Texas, USA.

The author would like to thank the following publishers for permission to use quotations: Prentice Hall: *Incredible Detective* by Gene Caesar; University of New Mexico Press: *In a Narrow Grave* by Larry McMurtry; Crown: *True Detectives* by William Parkhurst; Macdonald: *Jay J. Armes Investigator* by Jay J. Armes; Robert Hale: *The Pinkertons* by James D. Horan; Souvenir: *But I Couldn't Do That* by Anne Summer; Playboy Press: *Super Detective* by B. W. von Block.

A special thanks must go to Channel 4 and Touch Productions.

While every effort has been made to trace publishers of works quoted, the author apologizes for any omissions.

PROLOGUE

On a warm, spring evening in 1988, as the sun sank like a great blood orange over the Rio Grande, the adobe homes clinging to the cracked mudflats assumed a soft pink glow. Half an hour later the sudden darkness of the desert had engulfed the Texan town of El Paso. Stars of cut crystal sparkled in the clear air above the sodium lights.

The headlights of Jay J. Armes's cream Cadillac Seville flickered along the chain link fence flanking Border Highway. Here and there, the mesh hung like torn grey curtains where 'wetbacks', illegal Mexican immigrants, had swum the Rio Grande and crashed through the frontier into the USA.

In the suburbs on the outskirts of town, beyond Fort Bliss Military Reservation and the low, bleached factories where the world's Levis are stone-washed, Jay J. Armes slowed to operate the remote control which opened the iron gates to his fourteen-acre estate.

The gates were ten feet high – the only break in a stout metal perimeter fence. Every few yards, the steel silhouette of a gun, emblazoned with Armes's initials, had been welded to the fence. Even the most unobservant passer-by could not fail to notice that this was a fortress designed to withstand the most determined invader.

Armes did not expect trouble. As a private investigator, he had survived sixteen assassination attempts, and took every precaution to safeguard himself and his family. As an active member of the El Paso Baptist Congregation he believed, perhaps with good reason, that God had clearly put him on earth for a purpose.

The Caddie was fitted with fax, radio telephones and state-of-the-art anti-terrorist scanners. From a distance of fifty yards, Armes could squeeze a button on his keyring to activate the on-board computer which checked the electrical circuits, lowered the windows, scanned the underside of the vehicle and, finally, started the engine.

As Armes navigated the first bend of the sweeping drive to his pillared front entrance, his son Jay, in the passenger seat, noticed a four-wheel-drive vehicle enter the main gates behind them and stop. In addition to the surveillance cameras and infra-red beams, the grounds were patrolled at night by what constituted perhaps the most efficient security force in Texas – a roaming collection of lions and lionesses, Siberian tigers, pumas and a mating pair of cheetahs.

Jay, also an investigator, touched his father's arm. 'I think someone's called to see us,' he said. 'Maybe they can't get out because of the animals.' He turned in his seat: 'The guy's trying to push them away with a stick or something.'

Armes glanced over his shoulder and saw immediately that it was not a stick, but the barrel of a pump action shotgun.

'For a split second I saw the gun metal gleam in the moonlight,' he recounted later. 'I threw myself on top of Jay as they blew out all the car windows around us.'

Armes's long experience of such matters told him that any hit man who knew his business would walk across from the 4 × 4 with an automatic weapon and strafe the Cadillac at close range, before finishing each of them off with a short burst of fire. Instead, there was a long silence. Finally, Armes cautiously raised his head and saw that the two occupants of the four-wheel drive were unexpectedly preoccupied.

The animals, agitated by the gunshots, had forced them to retreat into the vehicle. To add to their problems, the electronic gates had automatically closed on their four-wheel drive, like pincers. The driver gunned the engine and, with a tearing crunch of metal, reversed the vehicle free and swung on to the highway. With the gates open and a menagerie of nervous animals bounding round the grounds, the detective had no opportunity to pursue the intruders.

Next day, after working out how they had managed to follow him, Armes tracked one of the two men down and persuaded him to take him to the home of the driver, the man who had pulled the trigger. On the journey he also discovered why they wanted to kill him. The investigator had been working on the case of a kidnapped girl who had been murdered and buried in the desert. His attackers, both drug dealers, had seen him searching a remote area near their base of operations, and assumed he was investigating them. The easiest solution to the problem, they reasoned, was to kill him.

Armes pulled up outside a flat-roofed, cement-faced house in an El Paso suburb and locked his travelling companion in the car. When he walked up the short garden path and rapped on the door, the triggerman opened it with a look of complete surprise. Armes handed him some lead shot, gouged from the bodywork of his Cadillac.

'I believe you left these at my place last night,' he said unemphatically.

Despite the incriminating sight of his colleague locked in Armes's car, the hit man broke into a disarming smile and denied any knowledge of the incident. His confidence visibly returned.

'I'll even take a lie detector test and prove it,' he offered.

Armes studied the drug dealer's reactions carefully. He knew that he had taken twelve previous lie detector tests and managed to beat the machine on every occasion. With tablets to reduce blood pressure, or the simple device of pressing the foot against a tack placed in a shoe, it was no great achievement to disrupt the needle readings.

'Fine,' Armes shrugged. 'Get in the car now, and we'll go downtown to my interrogation suite.'

'Sure,' grinned the triggerman. 'Why not?'

On the way to his Montana Avenue headquarters in El Paso, Armes explained that his lie detector was not the standard model.

'If I were you,' the detective advised as they drew up outside his office, 'I'd tell the truth right now. The lie detector I have is infallible. It works by sensing adrenalin secreted through the pores when you lie. I think you ought to know that.'

Inside the small, wood-panelled waiting room, the man was still grinning.

'I'm giving you one last chance,' the investigator cautioned him.

'C'mon,' the dealer said impatiently, 'get the damn thing on.'

Armes left the room and was gone for some time. He returned leading a 600-pound Siberian tiger named Gemini on a chain. Gemini's paws, the size of soup plates, sank into the soft pile of the carpet. The tiger exuded a pungent musk-like odour which pervaded the room. The more the hit man inhaled it, the more he stiffened and froze, like a rabbit caught in a headlight beam.

Gemini caught the scent of fear, raised his enormous head inquisitively and took a step forward, almost pulling Armes off balance. The investigator, tough and wiry, strained to hold back the beast on its 28-pound neck chain.

The drug dealer's tanned face turned the colour of veal. He jerked out of the hypnotic state the tiger had imposed upon him and backed to the wall with such speed that his body hit the panelling with a loud crack.

'You're crazy,' he gasped thinly. 'What's this?'

'I told you,' Armes said evenly. 'My lie detector's a little different to the rest.'

By now Gemini was showing heightened interest in the stranger pumping the smell of panic into the small room. The man pressed himself to the wall, his instincts trying to achieve the impossible and press him into the adjoining room. He had pushed himself on tiptoe, and with each roll of his eyes Gemini's curiosity became the tunnel vision of the predator. Armes had to dig his heels into the carpet. Unsurprisingly, it was only minutes before the triggerman confessed and was under citizen's arrest to face the courts.

The story, which would appear bizarre even in the fantastic realms of detective fiction, rates as fairly mundane in the strange world of Jay J. Armes. What is perhaps not so unusual is that someone decided to use violence against an investigator.

Seven hundred and fifty miles away, at about the same time as the El Paso incident, a Los Angeles private eye named Logan Clarke was woken by someone ringing at his front door. Clarke raised himself from his pillow and saw that it was a little after 3 a.m. He was cautious, but not unduly worried. As someone who preferred to work from home among the palms and manicured lawns of Hollywood's showbusiness community, he was used to clients calling with all kinds of problems.

Clarke padded downstairs into the hall and saw, framed behind the glass of his front door, a gorilla of a man. 'When I say this guy was big,' Clarke recalls, 'I mean he had an eagle tattooed on his upper arm – with the wings outstretched.'

Clarke recognized him immediately as an organized crime armbreaker and hit man who had killed thirteen people. 'I had put him away three times before,' the investigator said. 'On the last occasion it had taken five bullets to slow him down. What kind of worried me when I saw him through the glass was that he was in prison uniform. There was no doubt that he was on the run and looking for me.'

Clarke, unshaven and wearing pyjamas, opened the door. The man was built like a Mack truck and clearly edgy.

'Logan,' he said, grinning. 'I've come to tell you something . . . '

'What's that?' Clarke asked him warily.

'I've found religion,' he said excitedly, with more than a trace of a mad gleam in his eye. 'I've been looking for Jesus.'

From behind the leg of his pyjamas, Clarke raised a heavy .357 'Dirty Harry' Magnum and pointed it without a tremor between the big man's eyes.

'Buddy,' said Clarke. 'I've got good news for you. In two seconds you're gonna meet him.'

The escapee computed his chances and wisely took off into the night. Logan phoned the police and the man was arrested three hours later.

On the basis of such dramatic stories, anyone would be forgiven for assuming that private eyes have few friends. Investigation, by its nature, lifts the hem of private lives to expose secrets which, for a variety of reasons, many would prefer to keep to themselves. The Philip Marlowe image of the private eye, received through books, TV and movies, is that of a hard-nosed agent-for-hire moving on the underbelly of society, gathering information by means which are often dubious. Spying, snooping, shadowing are words which spring to mind, but today's gumshoe is more likely to do his groundwork by telephone or computer before wearing out shoe-leather. The traditional picture has become so firmly fixed in the common imagination that it comes as no surprise to discover that, from time to time, the PI attracts enemies like sharks to bait.

Some investigators have been less fortunate than the vigilant Armes and Clarke. Violent times breed violent reactions: recently a 37-year-old private detective from Thornton Heath, Surrey, was found gruesomely murdered in a pub car park.

Daniel Morgan, a thick-set, bearded man, was killed minutes after leaving the bar of the 'olde worlde' Golden Lion in Sydenham High Street, South London, where he had been sharing a drink with his partner. He was found in the darkened car park alongside the pub, hacked to death and with an axe buried up to the hilt in his head.

Murder squad detectives found more than £1000 in his pockets and reasonably concluded that the motive was unlikely to have been theft. At first it was thought that Morgan might have accidentally uncovered information about his killer, who may have been connected with the divorce and debt collection cases he specialized in. Later, other leads were investigated and the field of motive widened. The case remains unsolved, but the reporters enjoyed the allegations made at the inquest.

Peter Heims, of the Association of British Investigators, the professional body to which British PIs belong, is resigned to newspaper stories of this kind. 'The only press we get is a bad one,' he says. After years of tabloid exposés, balanced by sensational stories which rarely reflect the true nature of the profession, British private eyes feel beleaguered by the media. From its earliest days, the profession has never received a great deal of public sympathy.

Investigators walk a curious tightrope fulfilling, on the one hand, an insatiable need for information and, on the other, attracting understandable resentment from those under observation. For historical reasons, the British public equates private eyes with the romance of Social Security investigators and traffic wardens. The antipathy is not shared by their counterparts in America, where the press and TV view them almost as a kind of renegade hero.

The difference is quite marked. Alan Cardoza, an unmarried PI from California, for instance, is almost embarrassed by the extent women are attracted to the private eye image. 'Before I had a steady girlfriend, I used to get so many women hanging around me at parties that it just became too much,' he laughed.

'The guys I hung around with couldn't take the attention anymore. Today, I tell girls I work in dairy produce. Then I point out a friend of mine, who really does work in dairy produce, and tell them: "Don't let on you know, but the guy over there is a PI. He doesn't talk about it too much, though." They all move over to say hello. I'm very popular with my male friends.'

Even in Russia, with its dark bureaucratic pedigree of secret police and invasion of privacy, the handful of private eyes who have been in business since *glasnost* are warmly received. Valentin Kosyakov, deputy director of the 'Alex' agency founded in April

1989, was pleased with public reception and conscious of creating the right image.

'People have a positive attitude,' he told Trevor Fishlock of the *Sunday Telegraph*. 'From films and novels I have heard of Philip Marlowe, of course. And I am trying to build the picture of a good private detective. He is professional, strong and helps people. A man of moral purity.'

1   BLOOD MONEY

The Strange History of the Private Detective

No one is precisely sure when the first private investigators began to operate. The profession of snooping goes back to Roman times, and perhaps earlier, when individuals would be paid to gather information for political purposes. Agents-for-hire were retained by rent-gathering feudal landlords of the late Middle Ages and were among government spies in the reign of Elizabeth I.

The few early accounts of private detection from the eighteenth and early nineteenth centuries concerned, not the forces of law and order, who were considered either universally incompetent or criminals themselves, but gifted amateurs who solved cases for a fee. As lawyers or court officials, they were not poor, so the driving force appeared to be enthusiasm rather than money. More importantly, their successes were the result of pure detection, in sharp contrast to the phoney enquiries of investigator/confidence tricksters who preyed on the public at the turn of the eighteenth century.

Perhaps the most engaging example was the Berkshire lawyer Edward Wise, who in the 1740s spent two years painstakingly solving a fraud case. Wise, a kind of Lord Peter Wimsey of his day, was retained by the villagers of Sunning when Thomas Chandler, an attorney's clerk, claimed to have been robbed in the neighbourhood.

Chandler had been travelling on foot between London and Reading a few hours before sunset on a March evening when, he claimed, three bargees jumped him and stole his fob watch and £960 in banknotes. The clerk testified that he was then tied up and thrown into a roadside ditch, where he lay trying to attract attention for more than three hours. The highway was well used, and he could hear carriages and horsemen passing by but was unable to call for help.

'At length he got out of the pit unaided,' according to the Victorian criminologist Major Arthur Griffiths, 'and, still bound hand and foot, jumped rather than walked for half a mile uphill, calling out lustily for anyone to let him loose. The first passer-by was a gentleman, who gave him a wide berth, then a shepherd came and cut his bonds, and at his entreaty guided him to the constable, or tything-man of the Hundred of Sunning, in the county of Berks.

'Here, he set forth in writing the evil that had happened to him, with a full and minute description of the thieves, and at the same time gave notice that he would in due course sue the Hundred for the amount under the statutes. All the formalities being observed, process was duly served on the high constable of Sunning, and the people of the Hundred, alarmed at the demand, which if insisted upon would be the "utter ruin of many poor families", engaged a certain attorney, Edward Wise of Wokingham, to defend them.'

Wise, whose reputation was well known locally, was asked to represent the impoverished villagers as a detective rather than a lawyer. Their investigator was an astute observer, with outstanding deductive powers. From the opening of his enquiry he was unhappy with the victim's story.

It struck the lawyer as odd that a clerk should be strolling at dusk with almost £1000 in his pockets. He was curious, too, about the length of time he claimed it took to free himself, especially when only a length of linen tape had been discovered at the scene. There was also Chandler's attitude to being robbed – not shock or anxiety, as one might expect at losing a small fortune, but a certain coolness and unconcern.

Wise made enquiries and found that when the clerk made the written complaint he was able to reel off the statutes which gave him authority to sue, almost as though he had looked them up beforehand. Bar staff at the local inn told him that, after reporting the incident, Chandler ordered a hearty supper and drank copiously until the small hours. The following day he slept in before riding in a leisurely fashion to London. Hardly the action, Wise concluded, of a man anxious to contact the bank and stop payment on his notes.

The country lawyer, in the manner of a modern private investigator, began painstakingly to research Chandler's background and financial affairs, in addition to reconstructing his movements the day before the supposed attack. Chandler was employed by a Mr Hill, a respected attorney in Clifford's Inn, who had asked his clerk to finalize a property deal for a client the previous day. Chandler had negotiated a mortgage on a property in Devizes, Wiltshire, and asked the client to settle up his old mortgage in favour of the new. On the day of the 'robbery', Chandler was walking the ninety miles to Devizes with £500 of the client's money and £460 which he claimed to be his own.

The notes, Wise discovered, were all in small denominations and too bulky for the clerk to carry under his gaiters, which was a common hiding-place. He made two stops on the journey to change the money – £440 was exchanged for two notes at the Bank of England and £300 for three notes at a bank known as 'Sir Richard Hoare's Shop'.

Gathering information on horseback and by letter was a slow process, which made Wise's achievement all the more astonishing. He rode to London to see Chandler's employer and, during the interview, heard something which interested him. Hill recalled that, on returning to town, his clerk seemed anxious to obtain a list he had made of the numbers of the original banknotes. Chandler had explained that he needed it to notify the bank, so that no one could cash them. Wise suspected a different motive and asked if he could examine the list.

When he scrutinized it closely, it appeared that several numbers on the list had been cleverly altered, a point which Mr Hill had clearly not noticed. By changing the numbers, Chandler was free to cash the original notes which he had hidden after the fake attack. The country lawyer deciphered the authentic numbers from the list and contacted Sir Richard Hoare's bank to find out if they had been returned as cashed. A £200 note had been presented to Hoare's by a gentleman who had accepted it in part payment for a captain's commission in the dragoons. When Wise traced the man, he confirmed that the note had been given to him by Chandler.

Tired and saddlesore from his journeys, Wise began to piece together the evidence he had collected. His methodical, terrier-like approach to detective work had earned him a solid reputation in the shires of south-east England. While he was away tracking down witnesses who may have handled the other banknotes, the court hearing took place, and Chandler won his case.

The verdict, based largely on the strength of his employer's honest character, was in favour of £975 – a sum which the village of farmworkers could ill afford. Fortunately, however, the hearing was adjourned on a point of law. Chandler's writ against them required a full description of the stolen banknotes, and he had failed to file one.

The clerk, fearing that the decision might ultimately go against him, that Mr Winter the mortgagee might sue for his lost money and that his employer might suspect trickery, took stock of the situation and fled. The decision was a timely one. While the case was being adjourned, Wise discovered that some of the missing notes had been cashed and returned to the bank by an Amsterdam broker.

The indefatigable detective eagerly followed this new lead and learned that the broker had bought them from an Englishman named John Smith, a man who happened to answer Chandler's description. Smith had been in Holland with a trader called Casson and, after a lengthy search, Wise succeeded in tracking him down.

Mr Hill, Chandler's employer, was now understandably anxious to contact his former clerk. He had written to him at a forwarding address which Chandler had provided when he joined the law firm – the Crown public house in Colchester, Essex. Wise set off on horseback with Mr Winter the mortgagee and Casson the trader, to confront the fugitive and, he hoped, make an arrest.

At the Crown they found one of Hill's letters lodged behind a display plate on a dresser, awaiting Chandler's collection. The landlord told them that he called about once a fortnight. With no guarantee that their man would return, the trio decided to put up for the night at a local inn before making the long journey back.

They had heard that Chandler had been seen in the inn several weeks before, and asked the landlord if he remembered him. The man appeared particularly vague and unhelpful. What Wise and his companions did not know was that he was Chandler's brother-in-law and owned the inn jointly with him. In addition, the very man they were closing in upon was hiding in a back room throughout their visit.

Soon after their departure the next day, Chandler sold off his belongings and moved to Coventry, where he bought another pub under his favourite pseudonym of John Smith. Some months later, worried about the warrants still out for his arrest, the former clerk sent Mr Winter £130 of his missing money, in the hope that things would cool down. It was the break Wise had been hoping for. The lawyer traced the letter and finally, two years after being hired by the villagers of Sunning, brought back his man.

Chandler was sentenced to an hour in Reading pillory at noon on market day before being transported for seven years. Wise, of whom nothing more is known, was presented with 'a handsome testimonial' by the grateful local people.

In 1692 the haphazard nature of investigation had changed when the Highwayman Act opened new opportunities in Britain for bounty hunters, thief-takers and criminal chasers. The inducement of £40 in cash for anyone who arrested and brought to justice highway felons created a new field of employment for freelance law-enforcers. The job carried authority, and a certain prestige. However, in an England where mainly the wealthy suffered from the attentions of highwaymen, outlaws were often seen as popular heroes. We are still accustomed today to viewing the Robin Hoods and Dick Turpins of folklore as legendary figures pursued by dubious forces.

Frank Morn, Assistant Professor of Criminal Justice at the University of Illinois, has made the point that the rich in the Middle Ages would form their own *posse* at the first sign of a hue and cry, and draw up rotas for night watches. With the rise of capitalism they looked around for others to carry out such time-consuming civic duties. *Posse*, incidentally, is now associated with the Old West, but the term was borrowed from the Latin *posse comitatus*, a group of men, aged fifteen upwards, assembled by the local sheriff to tackle crime. *Posse*, the short form, has been used since the sixteenth century.

'One of the earliest inconveniences was crime fighting,' Morn says in *The Eye That Never Sleeps* (1982), a study of early policing, 'and already by the 17th and 18th centuries a sub-class of professional ne'er-do-wells monopolized the ancient constable night watch.'

Morn, in fact, was generous in his description. The task of freelance crime fighting for many years attracted the type who mingled too closely with criminals. When 'blood money' was offered by the authorities and private property owners to combat rising crime, a raggle-taggle battalion of characters stepped forward. Criminals and men who rubbed shoulders with rogues, cheats and petty robbers were attracted by the lure of a bounty to make easy money.

Thief-takers – private agents hired to catch criminals – were not regarded as lone heroes seeking justice for society. They were distrusted by the public at large because of widely-held suspicions that they were in league with the outlaws they were supposed to pursue. It is possible that, instead of reducing crime, early investigators-for-hire stimulated it.

They were known to be shifty, dishonest and prepared to make deals with criminals for financial gain. The man who helped more than any other to give the profession its notoriety was Jonathan Wild, who set out from his office each day carrying a short, silver-topped staff to recover stolen property and catch felons. In 1718 he flamboyantly declared himself 'Thief-Taker General of Great Britain and Ireland', with a flair for self-advertisement still employed by a few private investigators today.

Wild enjoyed his power and position largely because of a loophole in the law. In 1691 pawnbrokers were regulated, making it illegal for them to deal with thieves or to become clearing houses for stolen goods. Tightening controls on this popular method of fencing did little to alleviate crime but forced criminals to find alternative ways to dispose of stolen property. The word 'fence' first crept into the English language as criminal slang around 1610, but after 1700, when the Act had taken hold and receivers were springing up everywhere, it became commonly used. It is thought to have derived simply from 'to fence', meaning to screen or protect the thief from the risks of openly disposing of his goods.

Fencing was, and still is, a risky occupation. Today, on the 'Costa-del-Crime', it curiously mirrors the methods pioneered by Jonathan Wild almost 300 years ago. Criminals sheltering under Spain's non-retrospective extradition laws employ middlemen to offer stolen property back to insurers. The difference, however, lies in the reversal of roles. Today's investigators, like specialist Peter Clark of Essex, are on the side of the insurers, not the criminals. Clark, whom we shall meet in Chapter Five, has been offered both art treasures and stolen bullion by British 'brokers' operating in Spain.

In Wild's day stolen property was 'recovered' and offered to its original owner for a fee. The Thief-Taker General then divided the sum with the burglar or pickpocket and moved on to his next client. Wild covered his true activities by making about 120 arrests – many criminals who were not in partnership with him, or petty thieves sacrificed to lend respectability to his business.

Unfortunately for Wild, the British public had an affection for the underdog. To enhance his career he pursued the robber Jack Sheppard, who was idolized by the public for his daring prison escapes. Each time Wild arrested him, Sheppard picked his cell lock, slid down ropes, or dug and chiselled his way to freedom. He was eventually captured in a public house, too drunk to resist arrest. In Newgate Prison Sheppard became a celebrity, and, according to *The Trial of Jack Sheppard* (1933, edited by Horace Bleakley and S. M. Ellis) in the *Notable British Trials* series, was 'visited by great numbers of people, and some of them of the highest quality'. Sir James Thornhill, the eminent portraitist, painted his picture and well-known aristocrats joined the queues to have audience with him.

When Sheppard was sentenced to death by the stern and un-sympathetic Mr Justice Powis in 1724, he still believed his popularity would save him. The robber hid a penknife in his pocket, planning to cut the ropes tying his hands and leap from the cart into the crowd at Little Turnstile, where the alleys were too narrow for the Sheriff's officers to follow on horseback. The public would undoubtedly have helped him to escape. Unfortunately, the knife was confiscated on a routine search in the prison press-yard.

Sheppard, who was 23, 'behaved with great decency at the place of execution, and confessed to having committed two robberies for which he had been tried and acquitted. He died with difficulty and was much pitied by the surrounding multitude,' Knapp and Baldwin reported in *The Newgate Calendar* (1824), a popular compendium of eighteenth- and nineteenth-century broadsheet crime.

'No public robber ever obtained more notoriety, no violator of the law had more hair-breadth escapes than Jack Sheppard,' they recalled with grudging admiration. 'He found employment for the Bar, the pulpit and the stage.'

Despite many attempts to bring Sheppard to justice, Wild never managed to eclipse the acclaim of the public's favourite desperado.

As early as the sixteenth century, thief-takers had been cursed and reviled from the gallows by condemned men. Wild, more than any of his predecessors, brought his dubious calling into disrepute by flaunting his success. Early in his career he ran a pub in Cock Alley, opposite Cripplegate Church in the City of London, which became notorious as a thieves' kitchen and clearing house for stolen goods. At the time, the law was vague about fencing. By 1718, Wild was clearly doing so well that a competitor, Charles Hitchin, tried to put him out of business by exposing him in a pamphlet called *A True Discovery of the Conduct of Receiveiers and Thief-Takers in and about the City of London*. (Hitchin, a former Marshall, had also made a fortune as a thief-taker turned fence.)

Wild responded 'with great bitterness' in a counter-pamphlet and an acrimonious, highly-publicized quarrel grew between them. A direct result of the mud-slinging was an Act which made receiving stolen goods an offence punishable by fourteen years' transportation. Wild was forced hastily to adjust his working methods.

'He called a meeting of all the thieves known to him,' the *Newgate Calendar* related, ' ... and informed them that he had devised a plan for removing the inconveniences under which they laboured and recommended them to follow his advice ... He would restore the goods to the owners, by which means greater sums would be raised, while the thieves would remain perfectly secure from detection.'

Wild quickly became wealthy enough to open what was probably the first private investigator's office, opposite the Old Bailey. He was soon besieged by the victims of burglars, robbers and pickpockets, begging him to recover their stolen goods, account books and personal papers.

'When persons came into his office,' Knapp and Baldwin related, 'they were informed that they must each pay a crown in consideration of receiving his advice. This ceremony being dispatched, he entered in his book the name and address of the applicants, with all the particulars they could communicate respecting the robberies, and the rewards that would be given providing the goods were recovered. They were then desired to call again in a few days, when he hoped he should be able to give them some agreeable intelligence.

'Upon returning to know the success of his inquiries, he told them that he had received some information concerning their goods, but that the agent he had employed to trace them had appraised him that the robbers pretended they could raise more money by pawning the property than by restoring it for the promised reward; saying, however, that if he could by any means procure an interview with the villains, he doubted not of being able to settle matters agreeably to the terms already stipulated; but, at the same time, artfully insinuating that the safest and most expeditious method would be to make some addition to the reward.'

Other private investigators, or thief-takers, were misusing 'blood money' to such a degree that the profession was now widely seen as a refuge for rogues. Eventually, in 1718, Sir William Thompson MP, Recorder of London, proposed a Bill which made it a capital offence to obtain reward for recovering stolen goods without prosecuting the thief.

Wild swiftly reorganized to avoid arrest: 'He now declined the custom of receiving money from the persons who applied to him; but, upon the second or third time of calling, informed them that all he had been able to learn respecting their business was that, if a sum of money was left at an appointed place, their property would be restored the same day.

'Sometimes, as the person robbed was returning from Wild's house, he was accosted in the street by a man who delivered the stolen effects, at the same time producing a note expressing the sum that was to be paid for them.'

Wild, inevitably, was caught and charged with a variety of offences. An investigation revealed that he had set up a vast international network of fences, selling stolen goods in Holland and other European countries.

On the day of his execution Wild knew the reception that would be awaiting him on the streets of London. When the Thief-Taker General was finally led to the gallows, thousands turned out to jeer him to his execution. Wild epitomized the people's view of private investigators as rogues and villains, a feeling which persisted into the nineteenth century. He tried to take his own life with an overdose of laudanum, but failed. On his way to Tyburn the crowd pelted him with stones and even threatened to kill the hangman if he was too slow at his work. To calm the mob down, the executioner was ordered to hurry his preparations.

* * *

There were other law enforcement agents from the lower classes who were more trusted than the thief-takers, among them the Charlies, employed by the parish as nightwatchmen in the reign of Charles II, and, soon afterwards, the Bow Street Runners. Despite their successes, old feelings persisted and suspicion occasionally surfaced. At the heart of the problem lay a deep unease about privacy, liberty and the idea of hired spies.

In the late eighteenth and early nineteenth centuries, social unrest and demands for parliamentary reform, sparked by the success of the French Revolution, led the Home Office to employ private investigators as *agents provocateurs* to infiltrate radical groups around the country. At the height of the troubles, in the 1790s, the Habeas Corpus Act was suspended, public meetings banned, reading rooms ordered to be licensed and pubs and coffee houses boarded up if they were thought to be used by agitators. During this severe bout of government hysteria, as often occurs when established power is threatened, underhand methods of restoring control were employed.

Among the most hated and vilified was the use of paid spies. The most notorious were three freelance investigators, Castles, Oliver and Edwards, who posed as campaigners for political reform to undermine the radical movement. They were so successful that magistrates all over England were encouraged to hire their own private agents to infiltrate the working men's movement in industrial towns. As a result of their efforts, executions, long gaol sentences and transportation of radicals became common. Like the thief-taker, the spectre of the private spy became universally detested.

Charles Lamb, the essayist, distilled popular feeling in a dark poem of death and surreal destruction, in which Satan digs three graves, surrounded by rivers of blood and headless ghosts. It concluded:

> I asked the Fiend for whom these rites were meant.
> 'These graves,' quoth he, 'when life's brief oil is spent,
> When dark night comes, and they're sinking bedwards,
> I mean for Castles, Oliver and Edwards.'

Oliver was hired to travel the country trying to stir working men to insurrection, with the intention of having them executed for treason. To conceal his identity, his name was at first kept out of court records, in the way that private investigators sub-contracted by the Security Services are still protected today. However, newspapers in 1817 were aware of the trio's activities and Oliver was finally exposed in the *Leeds Mercury*. There was public outrage, especially in towns where men had been executed or deported, and Oliver was no longer able to operate with the same confidence.

The idea of blood money took on a new meaning which law-abiding citizens found disturbing. Whenever officialdom required 'dirty tricks' performed on the populace, there were always disreputable elements ready to step forward and offer themselves for hire. As political and social climates changed, the private agent shifted the stance of his business accordingly, setting out his stall to cater for the greatest demand.

When London's crime rate climbed steadily in the nineteenth century, the Bow Street Runners were superseded by an organized police force in 1829. Many of the old Runners retired to set up in business as private investigators, offering to take on cases the new police were unable to cope with. But even the heroic Runners had not escaped reproach from a public which remembered past betrayals. The antics of Jonathan Wild had left a wake of suspicion which finally swirled around the feet of the Runners. Some people were concerned that they mixed a little more freely with criminals than was necessary. In 1828 an official inquiry into the Runners' activities heard evidence of bribes, corruption and working partnerships with villains. Today's Metropolitan Police Commissioners are equally sensitive to allegations of detectives mingling closely with criminals, and several officers have been censured for allowing their social lives to overlap with work.

Dickens offered a close look at the Runners at work when the aptly named Blathers and Duff investigated a burglary by Fagin and Sykes in *Oliver Twist*, published in 1838. 'The detective work carried on by officers of the Blathers and Duff kind was of very loose and often very immoral character,' the critic George Augustus Sala noted. 'The Bow Street Runners had to work hand-in-glove with highwaymen and burglars, coiners, cheats and receivers of stolen goods; and on the morrow, perhaps, of their carousing with these scoundrels, they would have to arrest them in the King's name, and slip handcuffs over the rascally wrists of their boon companions of the previous night.'

The detective's defence, of course, is that if he does not get close to criminals, he has no valuable intelligence or working knowledge of their plans. The dividing line between front-line detection and active villainy has always been brittle.

After their experiences with private investigators, ordinary people were extremely wary about the introduction of plain-clothes police detectives. The first House of Commons Select Committees into the police in the early 1830s were concerned solely with complaints about plain clothes agents, mainly about an officer known only as Sergeant Popay who had infiltrated a revolutionary group known as the National Political Union around 1830. Popay successfully posed as an anti-police agitator – until he was spotted through the windows of a police station, relaxing with his colleagues.

The outrage of the National Political Union was ignored. 'But it was a different matter,' wrote Belton Cobb in *The First Detectives* (1957), 'when parochial officials and other respectable and fair-minded citizens seethed with righteous indignation over such abhorrent practices. Attention necessarily had to be given to a strongly-worded complaint to the Government about "policemen disguised in clothing of various descriptions, sometimes in the garb of gentlemen, sometimes in that of tradesmen or artisans, sometimes in sailors' jackets, and sometimes in ploughman's frock".'

Cobb, incidentally, made the interesting point that there was such a bizarre variety of undercover clothes because detectives were not provided with them – they simply wore the working clothes of their last job before joining the force.

The Select Committee deliberated for several days before supporting the police commissioners. With an organized detective squad, the government was now in the safe position of no longer needing to depend on the services of freelance agents, and righteously agreed with the electorate that they were a deplorable species. The Select Committee made a solemn about-face and denounced the idea of private spies – 'a practice most abhorrent to the feelings of the people and most alien to the spirit of the Constitution'. If private investigators had felt themselves social outcasts in the past, they could now justifiably consider themselves disliked by everyone.

By mid-Victorian times, however, the climate had lightened a little and a lucrative outlet for their talents was found in the rising divorce rate. As the law demanded proof of marital infidelity, private investigation became a booming business. Although today's marriage laws are more liberal, private eyes are constantly asked to make 'peace-of-mind' inquiries by clients who suspect their partners of unfaithfulness. In Hong Kong, this kind of work outstrips any other and some agencies simply do not have the staff to cope with the demands of suspicious lovers and spouses.

In Victorian times, private investigation was not considered a gentleman's occupation. Indeed, by the end of the era, there were so many opportunists setting up shop to ride the matrimonial bandwagon that investigators were considered a public nuisance. A typical newspaper personal column carried sixteen advertisements placed by agencies offering 'secret watchings' to follow husbands to the club, or wives on shopping trips. One agency, with an eye to business, even offered a service checking out prospective partners before the wedding, supplying 'matrimonial details as to the social position, past character, future prospects, general habits and temper of the intended partner for life, in order to make marriage a success'.

Such specific lines in inquiry are still occasionally used by prominent families. One branch of Pinkerton's, the world's biggest detective agency, established in Chicago in 1855, had a request from a wealthy couple in Alabama in 1989 to screen a Latin lover who had proposed marriage to their daughter. He claimed to come from a wealthy family and that he travelled the world playing for the Argentinian polo team. He was eventually traced by a Brazilian agent to a Rio shanty, where he lived with a wife and small tribe of children. The detective, posing as a housing inspector, said it would help their application for better accommodation if they answered some questions about themselves and assembled for a group photograph. The results of the survey were despatched to the stunned millionaire in Alabama.

The Victorian journalist George Sala deplored the proliferation of private eyes in his weekly magazine *Sala's Journal*, in 1892. 'There is no reason to suspect private detective agencies of the slightest tendency to bad faith or corrupt practices,' he stated cautiously, 'but the mere fact of their existence leaves an exceptionally offensive taste in the mouth. The idea of the private detective will continue, I should say, to be unsavoury in a great many thousands of English mouths until the Divorce Laws are altogether revised and reformed. It is only the blundering, one-sided and, in many cases, cruelly unjust operations of these laws, as they are at present administered, that make a domestic spy system not only justifiable, but in its miserable way serviceable.'

As few insights into the early profession remain, it is interesting to allow Sala to vent his spleen at length. His editorial began:

'Let us take a glance at a class of people who, so far as I am concerned, make my gorge rise very disagreeably indeed, and who leave the most odious of tastes in my mouth. I mean the private detective. This individual may be of either sex; indeed, so widely have the ramifications of the English spy system been extended within the last few years that I should not be surprised if, in the course of some *cause célèbre*, evidence on one side or the other were given by a smoothfaced youth in a very large, shiny white shirt collar and a round jacket, who looked for all the world like an Eton or Harrow boy; or by a maiden of fourteen, with a pigtail, short skirts, and black silk pianoforte legs, who, in cross-examination, owned to the soft impeachment that he or she was in the employ of a firm of private detectives.

'These detectives, whom I ruefully confess to be, under the present conditions of our social scheme, all but indispensable, are ubiquitous. The sunburnt gentleman whom you meet in a boarding house, and whom you have reason to believe is H.B.M. Consul at Alcochafada, in the Spanish Main, may be a detective. So likewise may be that fascinating Marchesa Truffatore, the black-eyed beauty whom you met at that nice little dinner at the Hotel Lucullus, and who sang those little Venetian songs so sweetly after dinner.

'Your acquaintance with the Marchesa ripened into friendship at Monte Carlo; yet be not surprised if you come across her some day in the witness box at the Royal Courts of Justice, and if you find her acknowledging, while she is being forensically dissected by Mr. Bullybrook QC, that she has long been engaged by a private detective agency, and that her real name is Jane Runt.

'So distractingly numerous seem to be the private professional spies who encompass us, that I often ask myself, half despairingly, whither a man can go, with the positive certainty that he is not being "shadowed", and that "gimlet" eyes are not continually watching his movements, or nimble hands purloining sheets of blotting paper on which he has been writing. On board an ocean steamship you are obviously by no means free from the male or female detective's invisible but sedulous attentions. Among hotel waiters and chambermaids, he or she may be often found; and to me there would be little that was astonishing in discovering in church that the pew opener, or the sexton, or the clerk, was an employee of some occult detective organization.

'Now I ask you, is this a pleasant state of things? Is this an English state of things? ... The business of the Scotland Yard detective is to "worry out" the circumstances of a crime and, if possible, hunt down the criminal ... The main object, however, of the private detective, male or female, is neither the prevention nor the discovery of what we ordinarily term "crime" – I mean offences punishable by criminal law. The private detective, man or woman, is radically the outcome and the body-servant or the hand-maiden of the Court for Divorce and Matrimonial Causes.'

Sala's blustering attack reflected the views of his readers. There was clearly a stigma attached to private detection, and even the most reputable operators felt a certain public disdain. Herbert Marshall, the 'doyen of private detectives', retired in his seventies in 1924 and reflected on a working life which began in the late Victorian period. Despite a noteworthy career, he felt moved to open his memoirs with an apology: 'It is unfortunate that the profession of private detective has always been held in disrepute. There are black sheep in every fold, but I consider it monstrously unfair that a whole profession should be branded for the sins of a few of its members. I can truthfully say that I have never, during thirty years, been guilty of any action of which I might feel ashamed, nor have I done anything which I am afraid to disclose.'

Marshall concluded his reminiscences on a note of embarrassment: 'In bidding my readers adieu, I can but hope that they have felt amusement in these incidents of true life and will be charitable enough to believe that there are worse people in the world than the private detective.'

Curiously, even today, with their own respectable professional body and code of conduct, many British private eyes appear to compensate for the past by emphasizing how 'legitimate' they are.

A popular decoration in the foyers of many agencies is floor-to-ceiling framed certificates, shields, badges and other paraphernalia of membership and authority, to convince visitors of their reputability. They are felt by some detectives to be a necessary front-of-house feature in an industry which has long campaigned for regulation.

The integrity of the industry, however, has improved on its performance in the past. The upright Herbert Marshall, who wandered South America before becoming a private detective in Victorian times, was almost a monument to virtue alongside operators who sprouted like weeds around the Matrimonial Causes Act. The high cost of legal representation made divorce a privilege of the rich, and unscrupulous private investigators found the unworldly well-heeled easy prey.

One of the first agents to make a lucrative income from divorce work was Harry Benson, an illiterate investigator of uncertain background who carried all his case files and accounting in his head. Benson saw the opportunities divorce provided when he was released from prison after serving twelve months for theft. His first business venture, taking advantage of an inept and overworked police force, was to hire himself out as a security guard to protect the homes of the wealthy. Before long, in the manner of Jonathan Wild, Benson was faking burglaries and stealing from his employers.

The wily Benson saw clandestine promiscuity as the Achilles heel of the upper classes and developed an interest in collecting below-stairs gossip while carrying out his security work. Before long he was encouraging friends and employees to pick up scraps of interesting information and pass them on to him. When several strands of evidence came together, suggesting beyond doubt that someone was having an affair, Benson would pay them a visit and offer to keep his silence for a price.

Blackmail in the guise of security work became the mainstay of his business and he was soon able to open offices in Liverpool and Norwich. But perhaps the rich were not ultimately as gullible as he supposed. Benson's dirt-raking increased with his greed until he became regarded as a dangerous nuisance. His murdered body was discovered, badly beaten, lying in an open sewer and his assailants were never found.

Finding discreet and loyal household staff was a problem in any Victorian household where the master or mistress was concealing illicit affairs. Many servants were supplied by a long established domestic agency, Besson and Hemming, who had around 400 clients on their books. Staff were recruited from Scotland and Ireland to meet demand, but many from far-flung regions did not appreciate the agency's philosophy that working long hours for the wealthy was a privilege. Domestics increasingly complained about their low pay until word spread along the belowstairs network that Besson and Hemming were to be avoided.

'Between 1858 and 1860 the agency fell on very hard times indeed, due to a series of rumours put about by servants who objected to being forced to pay an exorbitant percentage of their wages for the pleasure of keeping their jobs,' Frederick Oughton related in his portrait of private detection, *Ten Guineas a Day* (1961). 'The principals of the agency maintained a far more powerful autocracy than the aristocracy itself. The reign of coercion ended when all the worms turned, refusing to register at the end of the working year. The number of people on the books was reduced to an alarming extent. The remedy, concluded Besson and Hemming, lay in additional and allied business of some kind.'

By a stroke of good fortune, their dilemma happened little more than a year after the Divorce Act was passed. It occurred to the now desperate Besson and Hemming that they had a ready-made network of spies in the homes of the rich to gather information on their sexual activities. New staff were recruited to spy on employers under the cover of working for them. Honest domestic staff, of course, would never have stooped to such low behaviour, so inevitably their searches produced a collection of dubious characters. Some had prison records, others had eked out a living on the streets. What united them was the attraction of easy money and a general lack of intelligence – a factor which became increasingly obvious as Besson and Hemming's business progressed.

A typical agency 'investigator' was an argumentative Scot named 'Scandal' Dougall, who had a reputation for being fired from domestic work for gossiping and impertinence. Besson and Hemming saw him as the perfect combination of experienced man-servant and incurable nosy-parker.

It became clear, however, that discretion was not one of

Dougall's strong points. When a German baroness approached the agency in the 1880s trying to find grounds for separation because of her husband's unfaithfulness, Dougall was given the case. He was not the ideal candidate as he had actually been fired from the house in Hatfield previously, but the woman persuaded her husband to take him on.

Dougall, unfortunately, shared the baron's eye for the ladies and was soon hiring prostitutes for his master and sharing them himself on the side as a form of commission. By all accounts, he became so engrossed in the pleasures of domestic employment that he forgot to file reports for the baroness's benefit. She became so frustrated by the excuses of Besson and Hemming, who had failed to deliver anything for her fee, that she decided to use her own resources. The baroness cornered Dougall in the house and seduced him. With the promise of sex, the Scot told her everything he knew. It was presumably a long story, because the two were still passionately locked together when the baron arrived home. The outraged aristocrat attacked Dougall's exposed parts with a boar-hunting knife and chased him from the house.

Besson and Hemming were not alone in seeing the potential of the domestic staff as paid snoopers. A rival London agency was run by an Irishman called Stephen Comer who, in addition to having been arrested for arson, had owned a failed tea shop and several other unsuccessful businesses. He was said to be an unfrocked priest, largely on the grounds that he quoted so freely from the Scriptures when drunk. He was also alleged to genuflect to policemen when he encountered them. A thin, sharp-faced individual, he occasionally went for midnight swims in the Thames and had to be rescued by boatmen on several occasions. Despite a reputation for idleness, he spoke several languages and was an accomplished musician.

Among Comer's many ventures was a domestic agency in London's Barbican area, staffed largely, it seems, by disgruntled employees who had deserted Besson and Hemming. By 1857 word reached him on the belowstairs grapevine that Besson and Hemming were no longer in the domestic business as everyone believed, but making a lucrative living from divorce. Comer was wondering how he could employ his own agency in this growing field when, by chance, he ran into a duchess with marital problems.

Her husband was spending the season in the South of France quite openly with his lover yet, despite having a Besson and Hemming investigator among his personal servants, the agency had reported that nothing untoward was happening.

Comer persuaded her to take on an attractive but very un-worldly Irish country girl as her personal maid, guessing that, when the duke returned from the Riviera, he would be unable to resist her. Comer posed as a footman to give himself free access to the house. Within days his perception of human nature paid off and the girl came to him, dishevelled, announcing that she had been seduced.

The work of private investigators has moved with the times and divorce no longer plays a prominent part in the activities of British agencies. The caseload of the average private investigator is like a social barometer which shifts according to fluctuations in pressures of modern life. Manchester private eye Stephen McLoughlin, for instance, was recently hired by a client who was having an affair with a married man and suspected him of two-timing with another girlfriend.

One aspect of divorce which has seen little change is the fierce battle between parents for child custody. One Victorian private eye, employed by a firm of London solicitors in 1896, went beyond his brief in a way which no one anticipated.

'It was the sequel to a divorce case,' according to a contemporary account. 'The decree *nisi* had been granted, and against the wife, who had been refused custody of one of the children born of the marriage. The husband was anxious to secure possession of the child, but the wife, like so many more of her sex, was much too sharp to be forestalled.

'She had a friend waiting at the court who, directly the decree was pronounced, started off in a hansom to the lady's residence, where the child was, laid hands on it, and brought it down to Victoria station just in time for the night mail to the Continent, by which the lady and child travelled together to the South of France. A detective was at once despatched in pursuit by the husband's lawyer, and his orders were at all costs to recover possession of the child.

'He soon got upon the lady's track. She had not gone further than Monte Carlo. The detective found it impossible to kidnap the child, so he managed to make friends with the mother, gradually grew very intimate, paid her devoted attention and eventually married her. When he was her husband he had no difficulty in completing his commission, and – possibly with the lady's full consent – he soon sent the child home.'

Unfortunately we have no account of how the marriage turned out.

It must be said that, among the plethora of Victorian opportunists, there were private detectives who were both reputable and efficient. Sadly, most were eclipsed by the antics of their fictional counterparts, whom the reading public considered more interesting. The twentieth century brought similar shady operators who surfaced with regularity in the popular press. More recently investigators have been exposed for bugging private telephones, paying police computer operators for information or carrying out undignified dirty tricks for the security services.

British investigators have pressed since 1913 for some form of official recognition which would give them a standing comparable to accountants, solicitors and other professional advisers. Their lack of success has not helped them achieve the public image they would like and, in most cases, deserve. Some members of the Association of British Investigators are outstanding detectives whose work amid outmoded restrictions on information makes them probably more resourceful and enterprising than their glamorous American counterparts.

The British Detectives' Association was formed by Harry Smale, an ex-Scotland Yard detective inspector, in 1913. The First World War decimated its numbers, but not the determination of members to pursue a royal charter. A vigorous lobbying of MPs followed; members of the legal profession were invited to meetings and views exchanged. In the early 1950s, progress appeared to be made: a delegation was received at the Home Office but, after talks, an appeal for licensing was abruptly turned down. Eight years later, in 1958, the presentation of a petition to Her Majesty's Privy Council for a Charter of Incorporation met with a similar lack of success.

In 1953 the British Detectives' Association became the Association of British Investigators by merging with a smaller body, the Federation of British Detectives, retaining Smale's original principles of Character, Competence and Integrity. Parliamentary sympathizers surfaced in the intervening years.

Tony Gardner, MP for Rushcliffe, proposed a Private Investigation Bill under the Ten Minute Rule in 1969. It was the first of its kind, advocating that agents should operate with a certificate from a County Court judge, declaring them to be fit and proper persons. However, it failed to win the required support. A year later, Sir Kenneth Younger's Committee on Privacy recommended a licensing body to control the activities of private investigators. When the House debated it, twelve months later, it was interpreted as 'a licence to snoop', and turned down. Labour's Les Huckfield followed with a Control of Personal Information Bill in 1972. Private eyes welcomed it as a blueprint for regulation, but that too failed to materialize.

The following year not one but two Bills for the Control of Private Detection came from Bury MP Michael Fidler. The first was limited to disqualifying anyone with a criminal record from describing himself as a private detective; the second set out the framework for a licensing authority and a Code of Conduct for PIs. The Association of British Investigators helped in preparing the Bills, but neither of them found approval with the House. All efforts have dissolved in the same soup of uncertainty which has surrounded the issue for almost eighty years. As a body, British private eyes seem condemned to this cycle of dismay. Whenever an operator is convicted of malpractice, the image of the industry deteriorates, but government fails to recognize it as logical grounds for legislation.

In September 1979, Peter Heims of the Association of British Investigators published a reply to a Home Office discussion paper on the private security industry. His view of the state of private investigation in the UK remains essentially unchanged.

'Private investigators like to think the legal world at last recognises the fact that they follow an honorable profession where the majority of investigators adhere to a code of ethics. It is, however, possible in the United Kingdom for a person to be released from prison today and for him to commence business as a private investigator tomorrow. Experience has shown that if such a person circulates all solicitors in the Yellow Pages with a well-worded letter printed on expensive notepaper, he will be guaranteed that a certain number of those solicitors will instruct him without checking his antecedents. There is, unfortunately, no legislation to control or license the private investigator in this country to stop this happening.

'A private investigator, by virtue of the nature of his profession, has probably more opportunities to commit crime than the normal person or businessman. Should he be dishonest then he could succumb to many temptations. He could take bribes to report to his client incorrectly, he could extort money from people whom he was watching so that he would not divulge to his client the true facts, he could bribe people to obtain information. He could commit burglary to obtain information. He could enter into a conspiracy to pervert the natural course of justice by falsifying the evidence. He could commit perjury.

' ... he has many opportunities to commit crime and surely this must, in itself, be adequate reason for him to be controlled in the public interest. The majority of private investigators are just as ethical and businesslike as solicitors but, unfortunately, there are some private investigators who do commit crimes and, due to headlines that the media give to these people's activities, the majority have to suffer.'

The American private eye has enjoyed a very different climate of public opinion. In the mid-nineteenth century, when America had its own fledgling police force, private detectives were regarded as having more integrity, professionalism and seriousness of purpose than their counterparts across the Atlantic.

Even American bounty hunters, who may not have been particularly popular, were held in great respect for their efficiency and impartiality, unlike Jonathan Wild and his cronies. Over the years, the image has remained unchanged. Despite their dwindling numbers, the romance of the dedicated, incorruptible hunter has been enhanced by recent movies such as *Midnight Run*, starring Robert De Niro, and Steve McQueen's last film, *The Hunter*.

Professional bounty hunters still exist in the USA, the most professional and feared being the quiet, methodical Peter Castillo, based in Arlington, Virginia, who rarely fails to get his man. He collects information on his targets from bond bailsmen – brokers who loan money to provide bail – and doggedly tracks them across every state. Castillo's authority has its origins in the 1692 Highwayman Act and English Common Law procedures 'imported' by early settlers. In America, the bounty hunter has the legal powers of a police officer, or local sheriff, in capturing and holding an escaped prisoner. Castillo, and others like him, work for around ten per cent of the bail posted on a no-prisoner-no-pay basis. They move discreetly, following leads, and carry a formidable collection of firearms. The job, which is not without its dangers, is viewed with subdued admiration, particularly by journalists who write about them.

This is due mainly to the nineteenth-century American private detectives who laid a foundation of public confidence in their profession. Indeed, the working methods of pioneers like Allan Pinkerton, originally a political refugee of radical persuasion from Glasgow's Gorbals, largely inspired the creation of the FBI. Today, most of the big surviving agencies in America, such as Pinkerton and Burns, derive their income from security work but still maintain the investigation arms on which their reputation was built.

In the 1840s, when the first urban police forces were established in America, officers wore civilian clothes. British colonization had left a profound suspicion of anything which looked vaguely military to the minds of democratic Americans. It took New York police eight years to obtain permission to wear uniform and, even then, many officers were vigorously opposed to the idea. By the 1850s, other major cities cautiously followed suit. The main function of the emerging US cop was to patrol the streets to keep down crime. At first there was little detection, and no criminal investigation departments. Much of the work of efficiently tracking down criminals, or recovering property, was carried out by private agents.

'Faith in private enterprise over public enterprise meant that private police were logical counterpoints to public police,' Professor Frank Morn observed in *The Eye That Never Sleeps* (1982). ' ... There were some areas in which the private detective agency enjoyed a natural monopoly simply because fears of a police state haunted America.'

Many of the agencies were small and provided property protection services in addition to detective work. When Allan Pinkerton set up in business in Chicago in 1850 the role and image of the private detective changed dramatically. He took it out of the bedroom and into the boardroom, creating popular confidence in the wide capabilities of private detectives.

Pinkerton, the son of a poor handloom weaver, was born in a dilapidated third-floor Glasgow tenement in 1819. He was eight when his father died, and left school to work as an apprentice in a pattern-making shop. After three years of what he called 'this dreary existence', Pinkerton left to sign up as a cooper's apprentice. When he qualified as a journeyman, his travels around Scotland made him aware of a changing political mood and growing support for the radical reforms of the Chartists.

He returned to Glasgow to make barrels and was soon elected Glasgow Coopers' representative at a Chartist convention in Birmingham. By the time he reached twenty, Pinkerton was probably the most ardent hard-line Chartist in Scotland, addressing rallies and preaching the six sacred principles of equal electoral areas, annual parliaments, universal suffrage, payment of MPs, abolition of property qualifications for MPs and election by secret ballot.

Pinkerton was a militant supporter of the impatient, violent arm of Chartism. In 1839 he led a Glasgow contingent in an attempt to free the radical orator Henry Vincent from imprisonment in Monmouth Castle. An army of thousands of supporters, many barefoot and wrapped in blankets, marched on the castle armed with iron bars and sledgehammers.

Word of the plan had leaked out and the King's 42nd Foot Regiment were lying in ambush behind the shuttered windows of a hotel in the town square. When the marchers rounded the corner, the soldiers fired volley after volley into the crowd, leaving many dead and dying as the Chartists fled.

The bloody incident increased Pinkerton's determination to campaign for reform, writing letters to newspapers, inviting prominent speakers to Glasgow and organizing meetings in his tenement room on Muirhead Street. The Glasgow Chartists, more enthusiastic about street fighting and physical force than their English brothers, stirred up so much trouble that warrants were issued for their arrest. Pinkerton went to ground and hid for months in rooms around Glasgow.

In 1842, still on the run, he secretly married Joan Carfrae, a member of the local Unitarian choir. Soon after, as the Glasgow police net tightened, the couple were smuggled aboard a ship bound for America. Pinkerton signed on to the crew as ship's cooper, while Joan travelled steerage as a passenger. Off Nova Scotia the vessel struck an ice floe and began to sink. The newly-weds took to the boats and managed to land safely, taking with them enough money to book a passage aboard a packet steamer to Montreal.

After a few months the Pinkertons settled near Chicago, where Allan found work as a cooper and ultimately stumbled into detection almost by accident. During a timber shortage he rowed to a deserted island in the Fox River to scout for wood for his barrels and came across a counterfeiting den. Pinkerton summoned the law and helped to arrest the gang when they returned. His efforts led to requests from local shopkeepers to investigate petty crime and he was soon appointed deputy sheriff.

Pinkerton's methodical approach and natural talent for observation quickly reduced local crime figures, and he was offered the post of deputy sheriff of Cook County, Chicago. The bluff Scot's energetic style of crime fighting earned him a healthy respect in the neighbourhood. There appeared to be no limit to where his career might take him. In 1850 he was appointed Special Mail Agent by the United States Post Office and, again, the number of unsolved robberies began to diminish.

A year later, aware of the growing clamour for his services, the former fugitive resigned and set up the grandly titled Pinkerton National Detective Agency. From the start, his approach to recruiting staff was curious. Pinkerton selected men who were immigrants with no previous experience of law enforcement. He looked solely for qualities of honesty and loyalty and hired several for no other reason than that he liked their faces.

Pinkerton had his own firm views on detection and wanted his first eight agents unencumbered by preconceived ideas. Today, the average Pinkerton recruit is expected to take about nine months to 'unlearn' techniques learned in the police or armed forces, and to study the agency's approach. Ethical guidelines for every Pinkerton detective are still based on the *General Principles* drawn up by Allan Pinkerton for his original staff.

The new agency adopted an open eye as its logo, with the motto: 'We Never Sleep'. The powerful symbol became widely known across America, earning Pinkerton detectives the nickname 'Private Eyes'. Pinkerton ran his office with military precision. He was belligerent and egotistical, but the agency won a reputation for being more efficient than the police.

Pinkerton became internationally famous, not only for his success in solving cases, but for pioneering methods of detection which are widely used today. Among them were the first criminal records – a Rogues' Gallery which began as crude drawings and progressed through daguerreotypes to photographs. On the back of each picture was a neatly written description and personal details of the wanted man.

Years later, in 1902, the agency's obsession with intelligence led to the final showdown between Butch Cassidy and the Sundance Kid and a heavily-armed contingent of Bolivian troops. Pinkerton's sons, William and Robert, who took over the business after Allan's death in 1884, followed the trail of the Wild Bunch from the early 1890s until the turn of the century, when Butch and Sundance fled to Bolivia to pursue their bank-robbing career in a more conducive climate. Out of sight, however, was not out of mind.

Pinkerton agents unearthed possibly the only photograph of the pair and printed thousands of 'wanted' posters for distribution throughout Bolivia. The result was the famous last stand in San Vincente, when the duo were shot to death by Bolivian militia after holding up a pay train.

Allan Pinkerton fine-tuned his intelligence methods when the American Civil War broke out. In 1861 he placed his entire squad of hand-picked detectives, together with their exhaustive files and invaluable experience, at the disposal of Abraham Lincoln. The Pinkerton agency became the North's military intelligence arm and carried out numerous undercover operations. In one of the most successful, agents working deep behind Confederate lines headed off a plot to assassinate Lincoln at Baltimore. They included Kate Warne, the first woman detective, recruited by Pinkerton in 1856.

Peacetime brought a huge increase in business from banks and express companies blighted by train robbers, hold-up artists, counterfeiters and safe-blowers. As the agency expanded across the continent, Pinkerton organized it along corporate lines, following the example of the giant companies who employed him. One of the main keys to his success was that, unlike the police, Pinkerton men were not restricted by State and city boundaries. They were free to travel anywhere across America, and even abroad when necessary, responding quickly to new leads. It was this flexibility and ability to circumvent bureaucracy to bring criminals to justice which drew attention to the need for an official agency along the lines of the FBI, which developed between 1908 and 1924 when J. Edgar Hoover assumed directorship.

Pinkerton's rapid climb to power and prestige was not without setbacks. He worked long hours and drove himself to his physical limits. In 1869 the pioneering detective paid the inevitable price and suffered a serious stroke. For a time he issued orders and charted his agents' progress from a wheelchair. With characteristic stubbornness and disregard for medical advice, he was back behind his desk within three years.

Pinkerton had barely resumed his office routine when his head-quarters, along with its famous Rogues' Gallery, were destroyed in the Great Fire of Chicago in 1871.

Pinkerton men, backed by their employer's insatiable hunger for publicity, established an image of the American private eye as efficient and unstoppable, but there was criticism of the agency when it became widely used for strike-breaking – an ironic turn of events for the man who was once the Gorbals's foremost radical.

One major incident during Allan Pinkerton's tenure, in January 1875, cast a shadow over an almost unblemished record. The Missouri brothers Frank and Jesse James led a gang which plundered banks and trains, constantly evading capture by Pinkerton agents. They had become folk heroes and Jesse, a natural leader, was regarded as the Robin Hood of the Midwest. They were eventually trailed to a remote cabin in Clay County, Missouri. Detectives surrounded it and a home-made flare was tossed in to flush the gang out. Unfortunately, someone in the cabin picked it up and threw it onto the fire, where it exploded. James's mother Zerelda lost an arm in the blast and his eight-year-old half-brother was killed – the gang were nowhere near the cabin at the time. The newspapers eagerly seized upon this terrible blunder and, although Pinkerton's issued a statement explaining what had happened, it was lost in a torrent of editorial abuse.

After Allan Pinkerton's death in 1884 the agency mushroomed into an international organization. By all accounts, Pinkerton himself was a determined rather than gifted detective. He was opinionated and difficult to work with, and encouraged the myth surrounding himself by courting the press and publishing pulp books about his successes. Nevertheless, his work created a foundation for national law enforcement in America and elevated the public's view of private eyes to the level of heroes.

The image of the tough private eye who never gave up was further confirmed by a pugnacious redhead called William Burns, who was perhaps the nearest America came to producing a detective genius. He was a man with a photographic memory, impressive forensic skills and a talent for intricate reasoning. Like Pinkerton, he also had a natural flair for showmanship.

Burns was born of Irish parents in 1858. When his father was elected police commissioner of Columbus, Ohio, his teenage years were spent hanging around the detective office and listening to the twenty-man squad spin stories of their exploits. He enrolled on a business course and was working in the family tailoring business while dropping in at the police precinct in his spare time. Finally, the lure of detection won. Seven years after his marriage to a local German-Irish girl, Anna Maria Ressler, he was offered his first amateur case. Columbus prosecutor Cyrus Hurling suspected Democratic ballot-rigging in a local election, but the police were too nervous to investigate for fear of upsetting their political masters. Burns readily took the job on and uncovered a complicated plot to forge election tally sheets.

The case attracted wide publicity and, in 1888, he left the tailoring business and set up as a private investigator. At first most of his business was passed on by Tom Furlong, a veteran detective who ran an agency in Ohio. For three years Burns travelled the Midwest, sleeping on trains and in cheap hotels, following small-time swindlers and missing husbands. The work placed a strain on his marriage. His young son died from diphtheria when he was away and a second son was born during another trip. In 1891 he decided to regularize his income and took a job as an assistant operative in the United States Secret Service for the handsome sum of three dollars a day.

The Secret Service in those days was an arm of the US Treasury and most of Burns's work involved tailing counterfeiters. However, it did little to stabilize his family life. His wife accompanied him on one stakeout when they rented a flat in Cincinnati to watch a nearby house. The weeks ran into each other and it was four months before Burns was able to break the case. As the first of the Secret Service's six General Orders stated: 'Each man must recognise that his service belongs to the government through twenty four hours of every day.'

Burns's star ascended briskly in government employment. In 1906, at the invitation of President Theodore Roosevelt, he temporarily left the service to head an independent investigation into graft and corruption in the city of San Francisco. His success, which brought coast-to-coast newspaper coverage, gave him a taste for returning to private work. Fifteen months after the case, Burns resigned to open his own agency, taking with him the hand-picked team of agents who had worked closely with him for the past six years.

Alongside Pinkerton, Burns was a minnow. But within three months he landed the country's biggest security contract, protecting the 11,000 banks who were members of the American Bankers' Association. Pinkerton's had held the contract for fifteen years and when it was suddenly snatched from them an enormous row erupted.

The move took Pinkerton's completely by surprise, particularly as Burns had advertised his new agency with the promise that he would never accept divorce or strike-breaking cases. The bold statement caused some mirth in an industry in which most small operators relied on divorce work and giants like Pinkerton on strike-breaking.

The bank contract made front-page news. Burns's biographer Gene Caesar noted in *Incredible Detective* (1968): 'The Pinkertons accused Burns of underbidding their rates, and Burns answered with a straight-faced promise not to infringe on the Pinkerton-dominated field of racetrack protection. But to fulfil his contract, and similar agreements that followed with the National Retail Dry Goods Association and with various chains of hotels, Burns had to expand his firm almost overnight into an organisation that would rival the Pinkerton agency in more substantial ways than glib press releases. For several winter months his life was a dizzying rush of train rides.'

At the same time, Burns was immersed in detective work. A

typical example of his methodical approach was a bomb blast in Wall Street in 1910, when a driverless wagon exploded outside the offices of J. P. Morgan, killing 29 people and injuring 300. Burns had a post-mortem performed on the remains of the horse and found that its stomach contained fresh grass. He deduced that it may have come from out of town as only hay was available in New York for fodder. His hunch was confirmed when he reconstructed the cart wheel from fragmented remains and saw that it had a wider rim than those used in the city. New York carts had narrow iron tyres to fit special rails laid in the street. The remains of the horse's shoes led him to the blacksmith who had fitted them and, six months of painstaking investigation later, he discovered the identity of a Polish anarchist who had sailed for Europe shortly after the incident.

In 1921, at the request of President Warren Harding, Burns was appointed Director of the newly formed FBI. The President referred to him as 'the only detective genius the country has produced'. During his short tenure he introduced the revolutionary idea of a National Fingerprint Bureau and broke the powerful grip of the Ku Klux Klan on the South. Burns, however, was by instinct a detective and had little appetite for the ruthless political in-fighting which surrounded the new bureau. He relinquished his post to his young assistant, J. Edgar Hoover, and went back to building his investigative empire.

'Personally, he was a man of strong opinions, with no hesitation about expressing them,' Gene Caesar wrote. 'Flamboyantly self-confident and totally extraverted, he was warmly loved and hotly hated, but never treated with indifference. Burns bore little resemblance to the classic storybook detectives, and still less to the heroes of detective fiction.'

Burns died in 1932 from heart failure, leaving – like Pinkerton – a legacy of experience in the field of private detection which official law enforcement agencies were quick to follow. More importantly, the image of the private eye created by two giants of the business who never ceased to promote themselves made a deep impression on Americans. Generations later, the public would have no hesitation in turning for help to a private eye when trouble loomed, rather than to the overworked police. In newspaper terms the romantic figure of the private detective always made a better story than the faceless police officers who seemed to trail so far behind them. Burns, and other agencies who saw the value of publicity, promoted an impression of resourcefulness, ingenuity and, above all in capitalist America, value for money.

In terms of public acceptance, British private detectives have found the American act a hard one to follow and one which no amount of parliamentary lobbying for recognition could hope to make up for. In Britain the investigation industry has struggled to overcome an unfortunate history and the setbacks of bad publicity. Across the Atlantic there have been rotten apples, too, but the foundation built by pioneer private eyes proved strong enough to support the belief that they could not contaminate the barrel.

2   SIZZLE

The World of the Homicide Investigator

Generally, it takes a team of experienced specialists, drawn from several disciplines, to gather and assess the details of a suspicious death. Homicide detectives have become the movie stars of murder investigations – making TV appeals for witnesses and issuing progress statements to the press. When a conviction is finally secured, newspapers and magazines often elevate them to the level of popular heroes.

From the public's point of view, it is unusual – perhaps unthinkable – that anyone other than the official arm of the law could undertake a murder investigation. The police would wholeheartedly agree; private inquiries in parallel with their own are interpreted, in Britain especially, as unwelcome interference. Unwanted, unwarranted poaching on a manor which has long been regarded as undisputed territory.

The perimeters of British murder investigations are carefully marked. With the possible exception of UK private eye Brian Wiggins who recognized a wanted man alighting from a Reading bus in 1986 and boldly stepped in to execute a citizen's arrest, and the Crumbles Murder in 1924, British private investigators have rarely been involved in homicide cases. The Crumbles file involved a private eye who was hired to shadow Patrick Herbert Mahon to obtain evidence for a divorce. He found a bloodstained suitcase which he promptly handed to Scotland Yard and abruptly dropped his inquiries. Mahon was later convicted of murder.

In America the perspective is slightly different. Homicide squad officers often resent the intrusion of private investigators, but the attitude of the public is more appreciative. Rising murder levels have made it logistically impossible for the police to pour all their manpower into every suspicious death. Homicide departments are overstretched and overworked, leaving bereaved relatives to face the unpalatable fact that, in some cases, the chances of bringing the guilty to justice are slight.

William C. Dear, a private investigator with a taste for Hart

Shaffner three-piece suits and extravagant diamond rings, has spent most of his career trying to put the balance right. His cases often take two or three years to resolve and are invariably homicides in which the police have failed to make any headway.

Dear is six feet three inches tall, with a moustache, horn-rimmed glasses and a dry sense of humour behind his sleepy Texas drawl. He never advertises – all his cases come to him by word of mouth or personal recommendation. His caseload is so heavy that he works through all the usual public holidays, including Christmas, managing on four or five hours sleep a night. When he detects the warning signs of burnout, he disappears without announcement to his house in the Florida Keys to sleep the clock round for days. His staff note his absence and make no attempt to contact him until he returns.

The police are often uneasy about Dear's presence on a murder enquiry, and a little restless at the sight of rings on his fingers which could buy a condo in a retirement community or take care of them comfortably for the rest of their lives.

Dear is phlegmatic. 'I see them looking,' he says, 'but they know I work damned hard for what I get. When I take a case, I meet the detectives handling it and suggest we work together. They look me up and down as if to say: "Who is this guy?" If they want to do it their way, it makes no difference to me. I tell them I'm not going anywhere. They have to learn to live with me.'

Many of his clients are families traumatized by suicide who refuse to believe that a relative could have taken his own life. Initially, Dear's staff make every effort to confirm the autopsy conclusion, but his methods are so thorough that there is no certainty which way an investigation may turn.

On occasions, clients have run out of money but Dear, sensing a miscarriage of justice, has refused to abandon the case. At other times he has been a hairsbreadth from obtaining evidence to convict a killer, but with no means of succeeding other than confession. At this point, many PIs would concede defeat and move on to more profitable pastures. Dear prefers to turn up the heat. He drives straight to the killer's home and knocks at the door. When the subject opens it, the surprise is presumably unnerving.

'I look them right in the eyes and tell them I know what they've done. "Wherever you go, I'll be there, watching you. I don't care if it takes years. If you go away, I'll follow you. I will never give up until you tell me what I want to know. See, I know you know. And one day you're going to tell me."' Dear shrugs: 'That's the way it's done.'

Guns, like stetsons, chewing tobacco and tooled leather boots, are part of the Texan way of life. Pick-up trucks fitted with rear-window shotgun racks are a common sight on Dallas freeways; handguns can be bought on production of a driver's licence, and victims of Saturday-night shootings are routine for hospital staff.

Bill Dear has a formidable knowledge of firearms and practises regularly. The walls of his office display a small arsenal of weapons, from lightweight Uzis to cumbersome Thompson sub-machine guns – some purchased, some confiscated from would-be assailants. Within easy reach of his glass-topped desk are a loaded Walther PPK, of James Bond fame, and a 'Dirty Harry' Magnum, in case of intruders.

He makes it clear that he would not hesitate to use them. 'There have been times when I woke up in a cold sweat,' he says, sipping from an ever-present bottle of Evian water, 'but the bad guys don't really frighten me. I take the view that you either kill me, or make your best shot, because if you don't, I'll kill you. The first time you raise that gun to me, and I know you're going to kill me, I'll shoot you just as quick as I possibly can. And I won't be playing games – I'll shoot to kill you.

'That's the other side of the coin with me. Let's just say I'm prepared to defend myself to a point where justice prevails. If anything happens to me, there are people who will take care of business. It's a standing rule. People can say, well, that's not the way it should be done. Some people might not like that to be said. But that's the way I feel.'

Texas's 4000 registered private eyes inhabit a twilight society which is particularly violent and unpredictable. State law prevents most of them from carrying a weapon and, perhaps as a result, many have moved into the less dangerous world of corporate clients or investigating claims for insurance companies.

'I don't even like to tail people,' confides Dallas private eye Paul McCaghren, who typifies the trend. 'I don't want to carry a gun, and to tell you the truth, I don't see that many private eyes running round trying to trick people.'

While such investigators may have found a haven of safe and profitable ventures, there is no shortage of Texan clients seeking swashbuckling solutions to their problems. *Dallas Magazine* ran a survey of private eyes in 1985 and found that McCaghren, like many of his colleagues, has at least one unwanted caller a week:

'Some man with fiery eyes and a fat wallet will drift into his office and ask the 52-year-old sleuth to burglarize his estranged wife's apartment, or a forlorn mother will beg him to hop a plane to Houston and steal back her kids from their father. Maybe the visitor will be an angry boyfriend who will want McCaghren to plant an electronic bug in his female companion's telephone or a sleazy-looking character offering a tidy sum to rough someone up.

'Sure, McCaghren would be the first to admit there are a handful of Dallas gumshoes who would accommodate such requests if the money was right. But most PIs tell such would-be clients they've been watching too much TV. In the real world most private investigators say the threat of going to jail far outweighs the lucrative fee for doing illegal work. And in the real world, the average sleuth misses out on Hollywood scenarios that include romantic encounters with attractive women, high-speed auto chases through crowded city streets, fistfights in dark bars and shootouts in penthouse suites.'

Dale Simpson and Associates, of Dallas, have fifteen agents throughout Texas, of whom all but one are former FBI agents. 'For the most part, we're briefcase investigators,' says bureau chief Don Schonhoff, whose company portfolio describes their work as: 'ascertaining financial responsibility, bond claims investigations, business intelligence, character and fitness investigations, computer security, electronic countermeasures, inventory shortages and protection of proprietary information.'

The list reads like a private eye's guide to steady profitability. Despite the fact that for every staid Texas corporation there are perhaps a hundred individuals prepared to pay high fees for Hollywood-style results, investigators shy from the TV image of the fearless crusader for justice, running on a mixture of guts and intuition.

The pattern is similar among successful Dallas private eyes who have turned to corporate work. Michael Grimes, who comes from a long line of New York City cops: 'I just don't have the temperament for defence work. In my opinion, most of the people charged with a crime are guilty. I spent too many years putting people in jail. I'd rather hang 'em than help 'em.'

Robert Sadler, a former Dallas policeman and vice-president of the North Texas Association of Private Investigators: 'I don't work with people I can't control. I don't get into fistfights or shootouts, and I don't get the girls.'

There are a few, however, who still do – and make a highly successful, if dangerous, career out of it. Bill Dear has become something of a legend in murder investigation.

His methods are so meticulous that he rarely moves unless he is sure of his ground, yet trouble has a habit of following him around. The American media dubbed him 'The Real James Bond', an image he finds both flattering and amusing. Dear became a maverick by taking cases others were reluctant to touch. His success with difficult murder investigations has built him an international reputation many investigators would envy, but demanded a price few would be prepared to pay. Dear has been shot, tossed into a ravine with his throat slit, and stabbed in the back. His work also cost him two marriages and presented problems of bringing up his son Michael single-handed in a world where threats of kidnap and violence are commonplace. Along the way, Dear learned that carelessness does not produce results and can cost an investigator heavily. In a high-risk field the best survivors are those with the longest experience.

In his 25-year career, precaution has become second nature. He has half-a-dozen serious telephone death threats a year and several contracts have been taken out on his life.

'There was one for $10,000 out on me,' he smiles, 'and I thought that was very cheap. So I sent word back to the people and told them I was worth more than that. I continued until I caught the guy who put the contract together. He's serving thirty years now.

'The most recent was when I was pulling out of my house and I saw a car make a pass in front of our area. Where I live, I know pretty much who's in and around, and I noticed it was a rental car. I went back to the house for a minute and saw it make a second pass.

'Somebody was with me so we opened the remote control gates and pulled out to see if he was watching. When I slowed down and saw him behind, he passed. Everywhere I went, he went. I felt like having some fun, so I pulled down this neighbourhood and, sure enough, he pulled down it, too. I went through a couple of streets to lose him and then waited where I knew he'd have to come out. When he appeared I followed him. He realized I was behind him so I moved over into the next lane and pulled up alongside.

'I honked the horn and reached over and waved at him. He looked at me and realized that I knew exactly who he was. I veered off then and picked up the radio and checked his tag number. I found he had a criminal record and was from Ohio, where I was working a murder case. There was no doubt that he was going to hit me, but he would not have been foolish enough to have a go in those circumstances.' He shrugs: 'I expect they'll wait for a while and try again.'

Unlike most Texas investigators, who operate from office suites or ground-floor premises with large billboards outside, Dear's headquarters are in rural DeSoto. Visitors have to travel dusty Texas roads, flanked by white ranch fencing and fields of palomino horses which wheel and canter at the sound of approaching cars. It is big sky country, with the water towers of farming communities marking the landscaping like coloured pinheads on a map. Off the road, a ten-foot-high glass fibre horse stands on a rich expanse of lawn, hoofs pawing the air, in front of a 17,000 square foot former warehouse – the nerve centre of Dear's operations. A Western-style wooden porch runs along the front of the building, with a traditional swing bench suggesting that the owner enjoys sucking straw or whiling away the hours whittling sticks. The impression is dispelled by the bullet-proof glass entrance doors and high security beams which ping when visitors step inside. Radio communications crackle from distant rooms, punctuating the dull clack of word processor keyboards operated at high typing speeds.

The walls of the reception area are covered with framed photographs of Dear on cases around the world – in snow-covered Swiss streets, against London backdrops and Florida poolsides. They are outnumbered by cuttings extolling his investigations, citations and letters of thanks. A wide foyer leads from the lobby, lined almost floor to ceiling with shelves containing devices which might have been used in a dozen Bond movies. Rows of metal filing cabinets bear intriguing labels, such as 'ash tray microphones', 'artificial blood' or 'miniature cameras'. Alongside, a run of perhaps a dozen expensive briefcases, all well-used, contain a variety of built-in weapons and recording equipment. The impression is that of a film studio props store in heavy demand for a detective series. The difference is that all the hundreds of items of equipment, regularly checked and serviced, are actively carried in the field. Those with signs of wear have newly-boxed replacements next to them, in case of failure.

At the end of this strange hall of surveillance, the foyer takes an abrupt left turn into an area with a well-stocked bar and man-size fridges crammed with food. Through an alcove, refectory tables and chairs are arranged in a room the size of a small restaurant. A covered chuck wagon for hors d'oeuvres is parked in the corner, overlooked by buffalo heads peering from the high walls and framed examples of early American frontier art.

A staircase and ground-floor doors lead to lecture rooms where Dear has opened a detective training school. 'I got tired of people picking my brains,' he smiles. 'I thought they could pay to learn the job, instead.' The first two-week course, which opened in the summer of 1989, was advertised only by word of mouth and fully booked within weeks. Among the students were working private eyes, anxious to learn the Dear approach to crime investigation. Elsewhere, workmen were about to start constructing fake murder scenes and automobile crashes. There was already a replica Texas courtroom, complete with American flags, where lessons are given in handling cross-examination and the presentation of evidence. The court was authentic down to wooden public benches and a stenographer's chair.

Curiously, it was the restrictions of police work and courtroom appearances which persuaded him to turn freelance in the first place. 'I started out as a policeman when I was seventeen years old in the uniform division of the Highway Patrol in Florida,' Dear said. 'I learned an important lesson there. They taught me "How, When, Where, Why?" But then I saw how a lot of those guys ended up. When I left the department because of a transfer and later moved to the Sheriff's Office in Florida, I saw the way the law really was. During those times there were people we could arrest, and people we couldn't arrest. I didn't like that. I felt the law was for everybody.'

Dear crossed his grey ostrich-skin boots on the table and smiled. 'The other thing that bothered me was that I was starving to death. I worked all day as a policeman and part of the night parking cars or being a bodyguard to drunks or people who had all the money. I resented the fact that I had to eat free food round the back of restaurants.

'The major restaurants would give you food either free or at half price, if you ate it back in the patrol car in the garage pit. After that, I made a promise to myself, "One of these days," I said, "I'm going to go in the front door." I set myself that goal, and when I quit being a policeman, that's exactly what I did. It gives me a kind of kick to walk into one of those places and order a fine meal.

'What hurt me most back then was the way the law worked. Every time I arrested certain people, I'd be put on punishment tour. They'd never tell me why, but I'd be moved down to the airport where I'd have to walk the line. But even down there I arrested Jimmy Hoffa. When any of the big mob figures flew in, I'd stop them.'

Frustration at being unable to follow cases through and the realization, when he roped off the scene of a crime, that it would take eight years in the promotion system to make detective grade, led Dear to quit the force. He moved to Texas and set up on his own as a private investigator. In Dallas he drove a Colombo-style car, had a limited wardrobe and handled a variety of small cases. Until, one day, a successful investigator took him to one side and told him to take a close look at himself: 'Son,' he said. 'We're all in this business to sell steak. But if you're gonna sell good steak, then you've got to have sizzle, too.'

Dear took his advice. He changed his car, bought a suit and attracted cases which became more complex and demanding as his reputation grew.

As William Parkhurst put it in his study of the industry, *True Detectives*: 'Enterprising PIs know how to look, talk and speak corporate, or they hire those who do. Clients who shell out six and sometimes seven figure retainers … don't warm to the rumpled, wisecracking stereotype with a day's growth of beard and a flask of bourbon in the hip pocket. Anyone with an office on the bad side of town gets bad-side-of-town clients.'

'I learned a long time ago,' Dear says, 'that it is fine to put out the sizzle, but you have to produce a damn good piece of steak. I enjoy the excitement but I know that I have to deliver at the end of it. I've been in the business in excess of 25 years. It's tedious and dangerous but I have to produce results in cases. I know who I am and what I am. I have to live up to the image, but the public enjoys it. Many police officers are envious, I know how they feel, because I was there once. Unlike them, I can jump on a plane at a moment's notice and fly anywhere in the world. I can interview anybody. When I'm working a case I can do what I want, when I want and exactly how I want to do it.'

What few of them realize, however, is the price Dear has paid for it, in terms of two broken marriages and the problems of bringing up his son single-handed. When Michael was younger, Dear turned the sizzle – the public image of the wealthy PI – into a means of protecting him. He bought 28 acres of wild scrub in rural DeSoto and built a home which became a hilltop bunker. Dear installed attack dogs, a helicopter pad, sensors which could determine the height and weight of an intruder (and thereby even work out their sex). Inside the house he constructed a hidden room as a refuge for his son in case of attack or kidnap, with a secret escape tunnel into the safety of nearby trees.

As Michael grew older, and eventually went to college, the sizzle outlived its usefulness. Dear sold up, moved to a home in a solid suburban community and commuted daily to his new headquarters. The dogs, the bodyguards and the private pilot have disappeared, but the James Bond image refuses to go away. He is in constant demand from publishers, TV chat shows and lecture circuits to talk about his life. Occasionally he accepts, but his determination to break cases always keeps him immersed in detection.

'I've been in my swimming pool twice in three years,' he says. 'And just once on my tennis court in the same period. I belong to a major athletic club which I haven't even been to in three-and-a-half years. I have a house on the Keys which I adore but only get to about twice a year. I have to slow down a little. The trouble is, I'm a perfectionist. I holler a lot, I demand a lot from people around me. I always want to see that little extra they can give me. I eat fast, think fast, my mind works faster than my voice comes out.

'When I'm after somebody in a case, I can be very violent. I have no hesitation if it's my life or theirs. I take more chances than anybody. People keep telling me to slow down. They're afraid I'll have a stroke or something.'

The pressure to solve long, complicated cases is intense, and the outcome is often unpredictable. When James Dallas Egbert III vanished from Michigan State University campus in 1979, it took the PI almost a year to track him down. Dallas, as he was known, was a computer genius with an IQ of 180 plus, and a passion for playing Dungeons and Dragons. Dear's search for him took him through a labyrinth of rooms and tunnels beneath the university, along passages which even ran within the walls themselves. The hunt became a Gordian knot of rumours of homosexuality, witch-craft and drugs. Bill Dear finally out-manoeuvred the brilliant games-playing mind of Dallas and returned the boy to his parents. Some time later, despite renewed efforts of support from his parents and Dear's continued interest in his welfare, Dallas Egbert, unable to cope with life, finally put a .25 automatic to his temple and pulled the trigger.

Occasionally the much-travelled detective is called upon to investigate a death on his own home ground. Familiarity with the terrain is no guarantee that the case will not be as complex and demanding as any other. The mysterious death of Glen Courson was a perfect example.

Despite embracing culture with a broad Texan hug, Dallas has made no secret that the love closest to its heart has always been a well-stuffed billfold. When the oil business began to skid a little in the mid-eighties, and stores in the prestigious downtown area went out of business and were boarded up, Dallas felt the same kind of awkward embarrassment it experienced when Kennedy was assassinated. There was an uncomfortable tension in the air. Today, the latest status symbol comes not gift-wrapped from Neiman-Marcus but in a manilla envelope from a process server. A man is measured by how many lawsuits he receives when his business hits the rocks.

The average visitor does not have to look far for telltale signs of recession today – acres of 'for sale' ads, a proliferation of cut-price stores and pawnshops, and a rising incidence of petty crime. There are those who blame the increase in hold-ups and murder on the drug problem or on social conditions, but Dallas carries a unique wound which is proving hard to conceal and slow to heal.

Businessman Glen Courson sensed the inevitable in the mid-1980s and had a shrewd idea which way the economic pendulum was swinging. Courson was well known in Irving and a familiar figure throughout Dallas. He had raised money and taken part in the planning of a popular piece of Texas flag-waving – the reconstruction of a wagon-train drive to celebrate the State's 150th anniversary in 1986. Channel 8 news bulletins had shown the wobbling covered wagons trekking along straight, shimmering Texas highways, crossing urban flyovers and dwarfed by Dallas's downtown skyscrapers. People would nod and say hello when they ran into Courson around town. He had Texas spirit and everyone liked that.

Dallas's declining fortunes had made the shops at the intersection of Story and Rochelle a target for chancers and small-time thieves. Courson's sporting goods store had been broken into twice. On another occasion, Glen had followed a suspicious character into the alley and, as one neighbour put it, 'popped him' with a flurry of punches. He was regarded as friendly and generous but, at times, a man with a short-fuse temper. 'He was a sweet guy,' a friend said, 'but you sure as hell didn't mess with him.'

He planned to open a pawnshop in Irving, a working-class Dallas dormitory suburb of 7-Eleven stores, tyre discounts, pick-up trucks and roadside diners. Unfortunately, the opening never took place. Courson's life ended with a fist-size hole punched in his chest by the close-contact blast of a Winchester pump-action shotgun. He died in an alley behind his store at around midnight on 11 February 1987. Irving police arrived on the scene, turning the bleak serviceway into a kaleidoscope of flashing lights. Within twelve hours of opening the investigation, they announced a verdict of suicide. Two of the dead man's family, however, were serving police officers. They were disturbed by the speed of it all and decided to call on a friend, private investigator Bill Dear. Just to take a look around, they explained, so that there was absolutely no doubt.

The police in Irving, just half-an-hour's drive from the detective's $3 million home in rural DeSoto, were perhaps a little puzzled when Dear agreed to resurrect a case which had officially been closed.

According to the police, Courson, perhaps because of business debts, had walked down the alley behind his shop carrying his Winchester and positioned himself between his pick-up truck and the wall. There, he had placed the barrel of the gun against his chest, then probably lifted the heavy weapon horizontally and somehow reached forward to squeeze the trigger. The recoil from the blast threw him on his back and sent the gun flying 30 feet, where it was later found by patrolmen.

Dear established that Glen Courson had accumulated business debts, but no more than any other local shopkeeper in a time of regional recession. He had shown no inclination to worry, or suicide, and was known to care deeply for his wife, Marianne. He would have been aware that by taking his life in such an obvious way she could not have benefited from his $1 million insurance policy with US Life.

Around dawn on the day of Courson's funeral, the family met Bill Dear in the long, litter-strewn alley behind the row of shops. Suppressing their grief, they walked to the rear of a cheap jeweller's, an army and navy surplus store, Courson's own sporting goods store and the pawnshop he planned to open. Half-way along, they pointed out the spot where Glen had been blown onto his back, coming to rest with his head a few inches from the wall and feet beneath the rear of his pick-up truck. As Dear poked around, sifting the garbage with manicured hands, two things immediately caught his eye. The first was that the holes gouged in the brick wall by the heavy shot had not been circled by the police. The second was that some of the big, pulverized lead balls, which had torn through Courson's body, were still lying on the ground at the base of the wall. It perhaps meant little, but it was enough to make Dear's instinct nudge him to take the case.

The family shook hands with him in the alleyway on a fresh February morning and dispersed to prepare themselves for Glen Courson's funeral.

Dear watched the simple ceremony from his black Corvette, parked beneath the leafless trees surrounding the Garden of the Cross section in Dallas's sprawling Restland Cemetery. Away from the roar of trucks on the distant highway the arrival of the funeral cortège was preceded by the traffic of local wildlife. Squirrels ran in ripples between the graves while straight-tailed mockingbirds called scornfully from the branches at crows hopping heavily below.

When the last of the mourners had paid their respects to the widow, Marianne Courson, and made their way to waiting limousines, Dear picked up his radio and made a call. A white stretch hearse appeared, bouncing slowly along the cemetery pathway on its air suspension as though crossing a pontoon. It cruised in and out of the shadows cast by oaks and mountain ash and halted alongside the green canopy above the grave. Two men climbed out and opened the rear doors. One of them pushed the button operating the electronic winch which thirty minutes earlier had lowered the casket into the grave. Little by little the coffin inched into view again until it was high enough to be lifted and discreetly slid into the rear of the hearse.

A few days later a video camera was set up to record a private autopsy conducted in Dear's presence by an independent pathologist. 'It is not the kind of thing I enjoy,' Dear remarks, 'particularly when the guy is someone you know. It doesn't make the whole thing easy.'

The incident prompts him to recall autopsies when, unlike Glen Courson's, the bodies were in a state of severe decomposition. After one, the pathologist treated him to lunch and, to Dear's dismay, ordered spare ribs and tucked into them voraciously. When the detective presided over the exhumation of the remains of Lee Harvey Oswald, there was a nightmarish moment in the post-mortem theatre when someone knocked the operating table and the head fell off and rolled across the floor.

After making detailed studies and measurements of the angle of entry of the wounds in Courson's body, Dear tried to re-enact with pathologist Dr Maralyn Cebelin how the shot might have been fired. With each reconstruction, he found it increasingly difficult to believe that Courson could have held the long, heavy Winchester to his chest and shot himself.

Rifle and shotgun suicides are unusual in Texas, perhaps because the sheer length of such firearms makes the feat next to impossible. A common form of accidental death occurs when a gun owner, usually out hunting, snags the trigger on barbed wire while climbing a fence. Some suicides have capitalized on this, using a fence barb to squeeze the trigger and make death seem accidental, so that relatives still benefit from life insurance. Others, less concerned about their survivors' welfare, have improvised a stick, or fishing-rod rest, to reach the trigger and make the job easier. Courson was said to have used his thumb – a difficult operation, and one not guaranteed to end his life painlessly.

According to gun experts it is highly doubtful, if not impossible, for a shotgun to recoil 30 feet on firing. Dr Vincent Mayo, an expert in gunshot wounds at Bexar County Medical Examiner's Office, San Antonio, believes that two feet is a more reasonable distance. The impression of an independent pathologist, Dr Linda Norton, was similar. 'The gun could not have travelled the distance claimed by police,' she said later. 'I think it is more likely that an assailant, or assailants, dropped the weapon on their way from the scene.'

The police saw it differently. Courson's weapon had a rubber shock absorber at the end of the stock, which led to a hasty theory that it could have landed some distance away, then bounced end-over-end until it came to rest. The only thing certain was that the gun was fired at body contact into his chest. In such circum-stances, a vacuum is created as the shell discharges, causing internal tissues to be sucked to the surface of the body.

When Dear approached Irving police and asked if he could view the official scene-of-crime photographs, they were uncooperative. Eventually he obtained copies by serving a subpoena. The results were revealing – at least one of the pictures showed a cigarette and cigarette lighter near the body of Courson, who was lying on his back with his arms thrown above his head. It suggested that, rather than shooting himself, he might have been in the act of lighting up when the blast of the gun floored him. It was a theory worth con-sidering, and Dear decided to pursue it.

When Bill Dear interviewed the witnesses, a picture quite differ-ent from the police version of suicide began to crystallize in his mind. In addition, the dead man's friends and other people he had last spoken to were all adamant that suicide was the last thing on Glen Courson's mind that evening.

The chief witness was Clarence Mayberry who had worked for Courson for many years until the night of his death. Clarence was a tough, slow-talking man who wore a battered baseball cap and the pugnacious expression of a pit bull terrier. He was a close friend of Glen Courson and an intensely loyal employee. The death shook him emotionally and, even two years on, demonstrating how he found his boss in the alley, Clarence was almost moved to tears.

On the evening of his death, Glen Courson's store suffered a power cut, an event which was not unusual and one he was equipped to deal with. He had a portable generator bolted to the bed of a flat-back truck which could be plugged into the store's mains supply from the rear alley. Courson ran his emergency lights and power in this way until the evening when he decided to close the shop.

Worried that the generator might attract thieves, he asked Clarence Mayberry and a workmate to move the truck and lock it up for the night. The generator was screened by boards, but the noise of it running for several hours would have alerted anyone with a mind to steal it. Once the bolts were loosened, it would take only two men to carry it away. Generators are regarded by Dallas petty criminals as extremely pawnable items, and Courson's model could well have raised something approaching $2000.

Clarence Mayberry and his partner took the truck keys, but decided to stop off at a local go-go bar for a few drinks before moving it. Courson, realizing what they had done, was angry. He was unable to move the truck himself and was forced to hang around until they returned.

About two hours before his death, he passed some time chatting to Barbara Barclay, manageress of a 7-Eleven store around the corner. In the course of the conversation, Glen mentioned two suspicious characters who had earlier been hanging around his store. He had chased them off, but he had later seen them loitering again.

Barbara, a slight, nervous woman with a quiet voice and vulnerable demeanour, had been worried, too. She had noticed the same two men, of dirty appearance and possibly driving a green pick-up, acting suspiciously in her own store earlier the same evening. They were strangers to Barbara – she had seen them neither before nor since.

The last known person Glen Courson spoke to that evening, while keeping an eye on his generator, was a close friend, James Harris. Glen telephoned him to see how he was getting along, and happened to mention the two strangers. 'A couple of scuzzas,' a derogatory term Courson was fond of, was the way he described them. Then, in the middle of the conversation, Glen exploded: 'There they are again.' Harris cautioned him to take his gun if he was planning to go after them – and the conversation ended.

By the time Clarence Mayberry returned from the bar, with several beers under his belt, the alley was dark. He parked his pick-up and walked to the generator truck, feeling a little guilty about not moving it sooner. It was then that he found Glen Courson dead with a gaping gunshot wound to the chest. In the half-light, Clarence noticed Courson's Winchester lying about twenty feet from the body, near the end of the alley.

Clarence called Irving Police Department to report a shooting, and the alley was soon alight with patrol cars and fire-trucks. Their lights, flashing intermittently, picked out the perimeters of the scene – the stark brickwork of the rear of the shops on one side, and a long broken picket fence on the other. Behind it, in the darkness, the winter fingers of gnarled trees reached skyward in nearby gardens.

It is standard procedure in Dallas for the fire brigade to accompany police on a homicide call. They were requested by officers at the scene to place ladders against Courson's flat-topped sporting goods store and check the roof area. Within a short time, the sirens, lights and rattle of climbing equipment alerted the neighbourhood that something had happened.

Clarence, despite reporting the incident, was immediately taken downtown in an Irving black-and-white and treated as a prime suspect. He was read his rights and had his hands subjected to swab tests to see if he had recently fired a gun. After being closely questioned and asked to make a statement, he was given a lie detector test to check its veracity.

Still anaesthetized from his night of drinking, Clarence was bewildered both by the shock of his discovery and the stone-faced suspicion of the police. When they appeared satisfied that he had cleared the polygraph, they escorted him to a patrol car and drove him back through the cold and empty early-morning streets of Irving to the scene.

Two years on, intrigued by a Channel 8 news report on the mysterious death of Glen Courson, Jack Taylor, veteran hard-news reporter of the *Dallas Times-Herald*, decided to dig into the case.

He interviewed Bill Dear's witnesses and found them all to be genuine. What he also found, long after Courson had passed from most people's memory, was that some of them were very edgy. Bill Dear had suspected the reason for some time, and it made him more determined than ever to break the protracted case and bring those responsible to justice.

To Dear, an ex-police officer well-schooled in the dos and don'ts of homicide investigation, Clarence Mayberry's statement left him almost lost in disbelief. One of the first patrolmen on the scene, Clarence recalled, picked up the gun. He ejected three shells, two live and one used, then picked them up and strolled closer to the body. About ten feet away, he put the Winchester down on the concrete floor, with the shells alongside it, and continued with whatever he was doing. No one challenged him, or even appeared to think it unusual.

Jerry Nichols, a good-humoured fireman from Irving Fire Department, arrived with the tender about fifteen minutes after the first police officers and occupied himself putting up a ladder for them to search the rooftops. Three or four officers were combing the area for possible suspects and the scene in the dimly lit alley was alive with activity. Nichols, preoccupied as he was, could also not help noticing one of the patrolmen pick up the gun. He could not remember what happened to it, as he was busy with the ladders, but he had no doubt about what he saw.

'He just bent down and picked up the shotgun,' Nichols recalled. 'I couldn't believe it. I've been to enough crime scenes and watched enough TV to know that it should not have been touched.' He shook his head in amazement, 'It was picked up by an Irving police officer, and whatever they say nothing can change that.'

When Clarence Mayberry arrived back in the alleyway in the hours before dawn, more people were there, including detectives examining the area. Glen Courson's truck, with the generator aboard, was still there as the dead man had left it, along with Clarence's own pick-up, which he had left in the alley when he discovered the body.

As he walked to the vehicle, he was surprised to see Courson's shotgun in the cab. Someone had placed it leaning against the middle of the seat, with the barrel down on the floor and the stock upwards. Clarence scratched his head and went to look for one of the detectives to ask him what it was doing there.

The detective beckoned him over to the pick-up and climbed into the driver's seat. He motioned Clarence to join him on the passenger side. They sat there in the darkness, watching the flashing lights of the patrol cars, with the gun still untouched between them. It seemed to have a presence Clarence was unable to ignore.

Later, in a statement, the detective explained the strange scenario by saying: 'I didn't believe Mayberry intentionally killed Courson, but he could have easily killed him at night, not realising who he was ... I thought maybe it was an accidental shooting.'

By complete chance, and probably because he was still shocked, Clarence did not touch the Winchester. As they sat there with the cab doors open, another Courson employee approached the pick-up to see what was happening, but was brusquely ordered away by the detective. At this stage, the police were still looking for a suspect and, if Clarence's prints had been discovered on the gun, he would have had a lot of explaining to do.

The incident, however, came to nothing. A few minutes later, another Courson workman, Michael Bailey, saw a uniformed patrolman take the gun from the cab of the pick-up and carry it to a police car.

Bill Dear studied the statements he had taken and wondered just how many sets of fingerprints were now on the Winchester, obscuring the fingerprints of the killer, or those of Courson himself.

Jim Kitching, now retired as a certified fingerprint examiner after a lifetime of service with Dallas County Sheriff's Department, later recalled his own job as scene-of-crime instructor at police training school. Officers, he said, each received forty hours instruction on how to pick up a murder weapon and leave evidence intact. Normally, suspicious weapons had to be carefully lifted with sheet plastic or paper, to prevent the officer's hands smudging them. Only in very unusual circumstances was a gun permitted to be unloaded at a crime scene, and then only with the highest authority. Some small Texas police departments, he explained, had investigation rooms next to the jail. When there was overcrowding, it could be inadvisable to have loaded guns unattended around the building, but these were rare occasions.

Bill Dear, of course, was aware of all this; he had received similar training many years before as a young policeman in Florida. What interested him most was how many sets of prints the tests at police fingerprint laboratory would reveal. The answer proved to be astonishing, and cast a new light on his enquiries.

In the early hours of the morning of 11 February, Glen Courson's Winchester arrived at Dallas County Sheriff's Department for fingerprint processing. The man who carried out the task was Lieutenant James Cron, head of the Physical Evidence Section, and a former pupil of Jim Kitching. The two still keep in touch and Kitching remembers him with affection as an outstanding student with a keen eye for accuracy and procedure.

Lt. Cron supervised the fingerprint check as the twelve-gauge shotgun was placed under a highly sophisticated laser scanner, an expensive piece of hardware which has made huge advances in the field of fingerprint technology. The chances of a print being over-looked by the laser are almost negligible. When he surveyed the results, Cron found the gun completely clean, with the exception of 'one faint partial print of insufficient quality for comparison'.

Jack Taylor of the *Dallas Times-Herald* put this curious point to Irving Police Chief Benny Newman.

'Forensic specialists could find no fingerprints on the shotgun, possibly because the weapon had been wiped clean after police mishandled it at the scene,' Taylor reported in 1989. 'Chief Newman has given conflicting answers when asked by the *Times-Herald* if police might have inadvertently erased any fingerprints from the weapon. When first asked, Newman acknowledged that police might have destroyed any fingerprints when they wiped away dew that had formed on the weapon in the early morning chill. Asked about the fingerprints again, Newman would say only that police had dried off the weapon to prevent it from rusting.'

Lt. Cron's reaction, as a highly-trained professional, was under-standable. Taylor interviewed him and wrote: 'He told the *Times-Herald* that when he received the shotgun, "I expected to get better than we got. This was pretty devoid of prints."

'Chief Newman says: "It's not all that unusual not to get fingerprints off a weapon. It's more common not to find identifiable prints, even using a laser, which we did."

'Not so, according to Cron.

'Cron said while chances of finding fingerprints on any weapons are only thirty to forty percent when using standard dusting techniques, the chances are significantly increased and are "better than fifty-fifty" when using laser technology.

'When told of Newman's acknowledgement that the weapon might have been wiped dry, Cron was shocked.

'"That might explain our lack of prints," he said. "If they wiped the dew off, that really hurts the chances of getting prints."'

Lt. Cron was perhaps even more shocked when Taylor's piece appeared in print. He contacted the newspaper to say he had been misquoted and was upset by the article. Dear and Taylor reacted philosophically. The veteran reporter and the seasoned private eye both knew that Irving Police Department was a regular fixture on Cron's lecture circuit.

When the truth dawned on Clarence Mayberry that he could have spent the rest of his life in jail by accidentally leaving his fingerprints on the shotgun in the pick-up, he was angry and emotional.

With witnesses prepared to state that the gun had been moved, a question mark hung over the way in which the investigation was conducted. Within twelve hours of Glen Courson's death Irving police presented scene-of-crime evidence to medical examiner Dr Mary Gilliland which led her to conclude that the death was by suicide.

At that point, the officers involved could be forgiven for thinking the case was neatly wrapped up and closed. But Dear was still pursuing his enquiries, and events which rapidly followed made him more determined than ever to follow them to their conclusion. US Life, acting on the official suicide verdict, refused to pay out on Glen Courson's $1 million insurance policy. In the months that passed, Marianne Courson was forced to give up her late husband's business and then her home to survive financially.

Attorney Gary Richardson talked the matter over with his client in the light of evidence Bill Dear was amassing, and decided to sue the insurance company for $3 million. Ironically, Mrs Courson was working behind a bank counter at the time, handling other people's money to make ends meet, because she was unable to claim what was due to her. The pre-trial discovery phase of the case, held in November 1988, gave Dear and Richardson an opportunity to subpoena witnesses, both police and civilian, and interview them in depth. Their testimonies gave an interesting insight into police working methods in a small Texas town.

Why, for instance, in the face of strong evidence that Courson was murdered, did the police conclude it was suicide? As J. Frank Dobie observed in his 1943 *Guide to Life and Literature of the Southwest*: 'I should probably have been a wiser and better informed man had I spent more time out with the grasshoppers, horned toads and coyotes ... ' An officer talked to Barbara Barclay, manageress of the 7-Eleven store, who had seen the same two suspicious characters as Courson had, and to the dead man's friend, James Harris, who recalled the dramatic interruption of his telephone conversation. The officer concluded that Courson had introduced the subject as a ploy to make his intended suicide look like murder.

'It's just, to me, too obvious that Glen was trying to show that this is going to be a suicide – I mean, I'm sorry, is going to be a homicide,' he testified.

Dear and Richardson faced a difficult problem, as the *Times-Herald* reported: 'Although Marianne Courson's attorneys and investigators have offered a $25,000 reward for information leading to the arrest and indictment of the person, or persons, responsible for the death, both Dear and Richardson concede that any prosecution would probably be difficult because of what they consider a botched crime scene investigation.'

Over at Irving Police Department, where the single phone in reception was besieged by Mexicans trying to raise attorneys, and the clerk of the court's parking slot at the courtroom next door was filled by a pick-up truck, the mood was bullish.

'Chief Newman hotly denies that Irving police botched the investigation,' the newspaper reported. '"I don't need to defend this department. We did a super job on this thing. We haven't done anything wrong."'

While claim and counter-claim volleyed back and forth, Dear was breaking new ground. He had long arrived at the conclusion that the only way for Marianne to have a hope of success against the insurance company would be to produce her husband's killers.

Bill Dear's office is at the end of a short corridor off the main reception area of his headquarters. It is furnished in a glitzy mixture of Japanese lacquer and chrome-glass Americana. It was here, surrounded by loaded guns and trophies, that he received a telephone message in the middle of the Courson inquiry. The caller was anxious not to give his name, but said he had vital information on the killing. Dear had time only to reach for a pen before the man gave a vehicle registration number and hung up.

Dick Riddle, one of Dear's associates, immediately checked the tag number against computer records and found that it belonged to a green pick-up, similar to the one driven by the two men loitering around the 7-Eleven store on the night of Courson's death.

The address was about thirty miles away and an investigator was sent to check it out. The two construction workers who lived there had moved out and had been so determined to erase any trace of their existence that even the mail box had been ripped from the wall. Neighbourhood enquiries – the mainstay of any good PI – revealed that one of the men had been living for some time within six blocks of Courson's sporting goods store.

Dear's ten-year-old bronze surveillance van, heavily curtained behind tinted windows, was despatched to watch the house. It looks like any second-hand vehicle found parked in a Texas neighbourhood. Riddle kept watch for hours, a stone-faced man who resembles Hollywood's idea of a Bronx detective. The temperature inside often climbed into the nineties, as he took still photographs and videoed everyone who called at the old wooden house. Among the most frequent visitors was the second construction worker. Both men fitted the loose description given by Courson and the manageress of the 7-Eleven store.

It appeared to be a tremendous breakthrough – but Bill Dear's problems were only just beginning.

He telephoned Irving Police Department to offer the officer concerned the information, but was told he was out. Dear claims he rang again and again to tell the police he had addresses and photographs of suspects who matched witnesses' descriptions, without success.

'He was repeatedly ignored and rebuffed,' Jack Taylor of the *Times-Herald* wrote in his critical report of the pre-trial lawsuit hearing.

'Chief Newman says Dear never told police he knew the names of two potential suspects. "I don't think he ever showed up with these names."

'That's not how Dear and Richardson remember it. And their

recollections are supported in part by sworn testimony, ironically by the officer and Dr Gilliland, who acknowledged in their depositions that Dear had attempted to contact police on the point.

'"I called and they never returned my calls," Dear said. "I left word that I had very important information about possible suspects."

'The officer acknowledged in his deposition that Dear had left telephone messages for him and once, when Dear did contact him, he couldn't meet with him because his mother was ill.'

Finally, on 17 December 1987, more than ten months after Courson met his death, Dear, out of sheer frustration, contacted Dr Gilliland, the pathologist who had ruled suicide, and asked her to help. Dr Gilliland, who has since resigned from her post, found the new evidence significant enough to try to contact Irving police herself.

As she testified at the hearing, she had little success: 'When I got the information from Mr Dear that he knew who the people were that were seen around the shopping centre and that he knew their names, knew their addresses, had photographs of them, I tried to get that information to the police department, either by asking Mr Dear to do it, which he declined to do, or by asking the police to talk with Mr Dear. And through a series of apparent miscommunications, that all had a tendency to fall through.'

The death of Glen Courson was still officially recorded as suicide. Dear, however, refused to accept it. His search for evidence had taken him to prison to interview an inmate offering to identify the killers, and to New Mexico to examine Courson's pick-up. The vehicle had changed hands several times, but still showed signs of forced entry made on the night of Courson's death. Attempts to lever open a quarterlight were noticed by witnesses who made statements to Dear.

Two years after the killing, as the PI amassed trunks of statements and evidence, there was a flurry of activity among certain Irving police officers. Barbara Barclay, the 7-Eleven store manageress, was visited by detectives without warning one night and asked if she could identify photographs of certain men. The detectives, she claimed, were brusque and gave no explanation for their behaviour. Officially, the department was not investigating what was claimed to be an open and shut case of suicide. Barbara felt unsure of herself and telephoned Dear. His reaction was typical of the man: 'I'm an irritation to certain people. They know me particularly well because I'm working close to home, so they know I'm not going to go away.'

While Dr Gilliland did not retract her suicide verdict, she admitted in a deposition that one of the key factors which led her to her conclusion was 'the fact that the gun was near the body'.

Others, however, became less sure as Dear's evidence accumulated. Dr James Weiner, a pathologist who added his signature to the autopsy verdict, later moved to a post in Pecasset, Mass. When Dear sent him new evidence, Weiner replied: 'It is my view that the manner of Mr Courson's death be reclassified as undetermined.'

Dr Linda Norton, a pathologist in private practice who worked for many years for Dallas County Medical Examiner's Office, went further. 'At the risk of over simplification,' she said in a statement, 'the case seems to boil down to two theories. Those in favour of a suicide ruling opine that Mr Courson, motivated by severe financial difficulties, chose a long-barrelled shotgun, over the many other firearms available to him at his gunstore, to be the instrument of his own death. He then drove his pick-up truck into the alleyway behind his store, exited the truck, leaving his motor running and the parking lights on, walked to the back of another truck parked in the alleyway, stood between the truck and the wall of the building, pressed the gun to his upper abdomen, lifted the gun up and to his right, and fired it.

'The proponents of this theory further opine that some combination of recoil and effort on the part of the then fatally-wounded victim propelled the weapon a distance of at least 10 feet from the body. This theory is a little far-fetched at best.

'Those who would call this case a homicide theorize that Mr Courson drove into the alleyway behind his store armed with a shotgun to make sure that two suspicious characters seen earlier in the evening were not tampering with a truck parked there ... One of these individuals gained control of his shotgun and, during a brief confrontation with Mr Courson, shot him in the upper abdomen at contact range.

'All of the evidence is either consistent with, or very strongly supportive of this theory, and it is my opinion that this case is homicide.'

Perhaps even more worrying to the Irving police was evidence of discomfort at the verdict within its own ranks. At the pre-trial hearing one of the first officers on the scene, 34-year-old Thomas Hudspeth, was asked for his view of what happened by Marianne Courson's attorney, Gary Richardson.

Hudspeth: 'I can only tell you … what my opinion would be.'

Richardson: 'O.K.'

Hudspeth: 'If it was me, you need to be looking for the guy that did it …'

Richardson: 'You do not, I take it then, feel that there's enough evidence there to conclude that it's suicide?'

Hudspeth: 'I don't know … I've never come to a good conclusion myself whether it was suicide or murder.'

Unlike many murders he had worked on, Dear's time was not unlimited. A date for the insurance lawsuit had been set for October 1989 and, with only four months to go, the detective had to produce conclusive evidence that Glen Courson was murdered.

In mid-June he persuaded Clarence Mayberry, the loyal Courson employee who discovered the body, to undergo deep hypnosis. Dick Riddle, Dear's associate, felt particularly pleased, because he had been nursing a private theory throughout the case.

'I'd like to find out exactly what Clarence really knows,' Riddle said, stuffing an old briar pipe with a tobacco blend he has specially made up for him. 'I think he may know more about the whole business than he can remember – or than his mind is allowing him to remember.

'It reminds me of a traffic accident I investigated many years ago. A guy was decapitated when he ran into the back of a truck. His head just flipped off and rolled into the back seat. I tracked down a woman who saw it all happen. She was so shocked that, from the time of the accident to the moment she drove into her own garage, she could remember nothing. Clarence still gets very upset about Glen Courson's death. Two years have passed by since he was gunned down in the alley, and it makes me wonder why. I know they were close, but it's kind of strange.'

Dear had noticed the cigarette and lighter on either side of Courson's body in the police photographs, which indicated that he may have placed his Winchester on the flatbed of the pickup to light a cigarette when someone snatched up the weapon and killed him.

The thought had even crossed Dick Riddle's mind that Clarence, returning to move the truck, may have been frightened by the sudden flare of the lighter, grabbed the gun and fired into the shadows in panic. Grief and guilt have been known to block such devastating traumas from the conscious mind. Dear thought it unlikely, but was nevertheless curious what the session would reveal.

Clarence turned up for the appointment at the surgery of Dallas psychologist and hypnotherapist Dr Harry Davisson, in mid-June. Dear had mulled over the idea of asking Clarence to agree to an injection of sodium pentathol, the so-called 'truth-drug', but from previous experience decided against it.

'It's a very expensive process,' he explained, 'and I believe I could get the same results for my client with hypnosis. Besides, pentathol has several drawbacks. It has to be administered in hospital under the strict control of an anaesthetist in case anything goes wrong, and only the doctor in charge is allowed to ask the patient questions. Under hypnosis, both the doctor and I can put questions and, if there are any which are better not coming from me, I can write them down and get the doctor to put them on my behalf.'

Clarence proved a perfect subject and rapidly succumbed to the soothing commands of Dr Davisson. Once he was under, both Dear and the doctor took him back to the period leading up to the Courson killing and gently guided him through it. In the quiet of the surgery it was like experiencing a strange, direct communication with the past. Clarence lived each moment as it had occurred, describing people in places in the present tense as he was coaxed into recalling his employer's violent death.

Clarence emerged from the 45-minute session looking pale. His testimony left Bill Dear convinced that he had played no part in the killing of Glen Courson. Two valuable pieces of information, however, had emerged.

Under hypnosis, Clarence had entirely retraced his steps, through a thicket of painful memories, to the night of Glen Courson's death. As he sat drinking in a bar instead of moving the pick-up and generator to safety, he described an Irving police patrolman calling in for a meal around 2.30 a.m. A short time later it was the same patrolman, Clarence recalled, who picked up the shotgun at the murder scene and moved it. He not only relived each incident in great detail and clarity, but positively identified the officer.

The second vital piece of evidence hidden in Clarence's dark substratum of memory concerned the two suspects Courson had chased from his store. He described the two men who had been hanging around the gun shop earlier on the day Courson died and also identified them as the same two men who had been cruising the neighbourhood several days earlier.

What delighted Bill Dear was Clarence Mayberry's detailed description of the men, which matched the two construction workers Dick Riddle had already followed and photographed.

A month before Clarence's hypnosis and after several unsuccessful efforts, Bill Dear had finally handed the police information about them. One lived near Glen Courson's store with his wife and mother-in-law. The dilapidated frame house had been under regular surveillance by Dear's agents since the tip-off.

Irving police found themselves in a growing dilemma. The more evidence Dear offered them, the greater was the pressure to re-open the Courson case. It was rather like being held in the steel jaws of a can opener – with every turn, the well-protected contents became more exposed. Finally unable to ignore the detective's offer of new leads any longer, officers picked up the two men for questioning.

What the police did not realize, however, was that they were not simply facing a determined player, but a strategist who was working several steps ahead of them.

By early August 1989, Dear was already putting the final touches to a multi-million-dollar lawsuit on Marianne Courson's behalf, charging Irving police with incompetence. The PI's offer of information on the suspects boxed them into a corner of the chessboard.

Bill Dear was giving the Courson file a lot of his attention, but other work was weighing him down. Various urgent cases demanded constant investigation, and a stream of new clients was calling the office daily. Two major cases had arrived in one afternoon. The widow of a bank vice-president desperately wanted him to look into her husband's death in their fume-filled garage. The police had decided it was suicide, despite the body being several yards from the car and the fact that two faint marks on the neck suggested a stun-gun. A telephone conversation with the woman made it clear that other executives from the same bank had also met with strange accidental deaths.

Two grandparents wanted Dear to snatch their granddaughter from her father, who was deeply involved in a particularly violent satanist cult and was preparing her for initiation. The owner of a wax museum had been found with traces of strychnine in her body, and Dear was also trying to break a long enquiry into the shotgun death of a top jockey who may have stumbled on a huge cocaine ring operating among the hierarchy of the racing world.

With the October deadline of Marianne Courson's lawsuit against US Life drawing nearer, the gaunt PI's working day lengthened as the summer drew on. To obtain results he would have to plan his moves in the Courson chess game well in advance to draw the players into the open.

He had two main leads – the construction workers confirmed by Clarence Mayberry's description, and another name offered by the prisoner he had interviewed in jail. The two did not match, but Dear was getting a clearer picture of how the jigsaw fitted.

Surveillance on the clapboard house where one of the construction workers lived revealed that, after being pulled in by Irving police, the two construction workers began to talk to friends about what had happened. They admitted that they were in the alley on the day of Courson's death to steal the generator from the back of the truck. Soon after being interviewed by the police, one of them – the man Dear privately suspected of pulling the trigger – left town.

The informant in prison hinted that a friend of his, whose rear garden backed on to the alley, was dealing drugs in an outhouse at the time. He had heard a shot and poked his head through a hole in the picket fence to see what was happening, possibly witnessing the murder from a distance.

Dear was interested in reports that one of the suspects had a lot of callers at his home and drug dealing was almost certainly going on there.

'We know that some of the people who are going there, and some of the suspect's friends, are on probation for drugs. We also know that some of them are hurting for money. We think that maybe if we approached them correctly, one of them might turn as an informant. The $25,000 reward will help to make it an airtight case. Let's say that we wire our informant and have sufficient people from the law enforcement agency listening to what is going on. If these two make a statement that we can record, and admit to killing him, then it won't make any difference whether there were prints on the gun, or not. The case will be difficult to try, but not to arrest.'

In Dear's opinion, each careful move he made was 'another nail in the coffin'. Each piece of evidence began to assume vital importance in the increasingly complex puzzle. In the summer of 1989, as the PI reviewed the information available, he received a surprise.

The empty case of the shotgun shell which had killed Glen Courson, plus the two full rounds found with it, were missing from the property room of the Dallas County Medical Examiner's Office. An examination of the records revealed that they had been removed by Dr Gilliland, on 18 February 1987, and never returned.

Dear pushed back the bridge of his spectacles with his forefinger and thought it over. 'I don't have any idea why she would have checked them out of the property room after Glen's death,' he said. 'But they were never returned, and she no longer works there. I think she took those shells for a real purpose. If she was pressed to return them, they would probably pop up. If they didn't we'd have a problem. There is a good possibility that, by examining the spent casing, or the two cartridges, we would find a double mark or indentation on them. Perhaps even an enlarged indentation, showing that maybe the hammer was pulled down a second time, which would definitely indicate that the police department handled the gun, and put the shells back in it.'

He sighed and looked thoughtful. Dear was resigned to long enquiries with twists and setbacks.

Two months later, the shotgun shells turned up in the property room as mysteriously as they had disappeared. Despite requests from Dear's office, officials did not disclose why they had been removed, or where they had been for a period of eighteen months.

In April 1990, Marianne Courson's action against the insurance company was settled out of court before the hearing took place. A condition of the settlement was that the sum paid to her was not to be disclosed. The *Irving News* reported, a month later, that 'sources close to Mrs Courson' put the figure at $800,000, plus interest. In the meantime, one of Dear's suspects had vanished without trace, while the other continued to be kept under observation.

On 9 May 1990, Bill Dear and attorney Gary Richardson filed a lawsuit on Mrs Courson's behalf at Dallas Federal Building. The papers sought to claim damages of between $10 million and $15 million on the grounds, as the *Irving News* put it, that 'Irving police had conspired to cover up a botched investigation'. The lawsuit was filed against the City of Irving, Police Chief Benny Newman, Dallas County Medical Examiner Charles Petty and former medical examiner Dr M. F. G. Gilliland.

Judge Mary Ann Robinson, of Amarillo, was scheduled to hear the action, which was expected to take 'several months' to come to trial.

Two years on from the death of Glen Courson, with thousands of words of witness testimony and exhaustive forensic tests, the mystery of what really happened in the alley that night was not finally resolved. Whatever the outcome, the long-held faith in the power of the private investigator, demonstrated by the Courson family, was once again upheld in America.

Dear, who displays infinite patience, was prepared to play a waiting game. 'I've got as long as it takes,' he said. 'I think I know who killed Glen Courson and there is no doubt in my mind that I will get them in the end.'

On Dear's formidable track record, the killers could not have slept easily in their beds.

3   DOUBLE INDEMNITY

Private Eyes in Fiction, Fantasy and Fact

On a still June night in 1989 Bill Dear arrived at his office to prepare for a raid on a satanist coven. He paused on the bleached boards of his porch and glanced at the heavy pudding-bag clouds gathering in the dusk. If it rained the ritual would probably be indoors. If the weather held it would be in the woods, and that's where the trouble would begin. He knew from experience that covens posted armed guards – some even had closed circuit TV in the trees – to protect against intruders.

Dear swung open the armour-plated front door and let it close behind him, abruptly silencing the buzzing of a thousand crickets outside. He walked down the floor-to-ceiling racks holding his equipment and immediately put his hand on a box containing a camera. The detective knew instinctively that it had been opened by one of his staff and not replaced properly. Showing mild irritation, he positioned it exactly as it should have been. In much the same way that a soldier can strip down a rifle blindfolded and know the feel of each component, Dear knew his equipment intimately, down to the position of each piece on the shelving. Before an operation he checked and rechecked it, aware that the slightest oversight could let him down.

Like many PIs, Dear is the first to admit that he is obsessive. The trait is not obvious, but it wriggles in the brain of investigators in both real life and fiction. On the opening page of Raymond Chandler's first novel *The Big Sleep* (1939), Philip Marlowe walked into a house and took in the detail. Over the ostentatious entrance there was a large stained-glass window depicting a knight in armour rescuing a lady. Our first insight into Marlowe reveals obsession: ' … [the knight] was fiddling with the knots on the ropes that tied the lady to the tree and not getting anywhere. I stood there and thought that if I lived in the house, I would sooner or later have to climb up there and help him.'

Unravelling knots, of course, was Marlowe's preoccupation. The interesting point is not Chandler's accuracy in drawing character –

realism, after all, was his stock-in-trade – but the extent to which life and art have overlapped again and again in the world of the private eye.

Both the public's perception of how an investigator works and the image he holds of himself have become a strange amalgam of fact and fiction. The origins of this curious blurring of reality occurred almost by accident and reach back to the first true detective and the way he portrayed himself to the world at large.

Eugène François Vidocq, born in 1775, was a thief turned detective, the mirror image of England's notorious Jonathan Wild. He killed a fencing master in a duel at fourteen, earned a living as a professional criminal, served his time as a convict in the galleys, became a freelance police spy and rose to head the Paris Sûreté, where he drew upon a wealth of experience, and became possibly Europe's first bona fide private eye.

His rightful place in the evolution of private investigation lies not in the fact that he is regarded as the father of private detection, but rather in the powerful influence fiction and fantasy have exerted on our cultural perception of the world of the private eye.

Vidocq's life needed little fictional embroidery. Physically he was a formidable figure, with a leonine head and powerful arms and shoulders. His build, however, owed little to the harsh life of the convict galleys – he escaped several times and served only a small part of his sentence. His wild life ran strangely at odds with his respectable background. He was the son of a God-fearing baker from Arras and the family were well regarded locally. After killing the fencing instructor, Vidocq forced open his father's safe with a crowbar, stole two thousand francs, and ran away to America. At fifteen he was back home penniless. To his parents' relief, he joined the Bourbon Regiment, but fought fifteen duels in the first six months, killing several of his opponents. His bravery in battle, at Valmy in 1792, however, drew attention and soon he was promoted to corporal.

After the execution of the King and Marie Antoinette in 1793, the revolutionary guillotine spread throughout France, but Vidocq remained unimpressed by the political fervour of the *sans-culottes* around him. He was jailed for stopping three dragoons who were dragging women to the executioner. Vidocq called them cowards and then took them all on in a ferocious swordfight. He was freed by his father's influence and finally, after a series of fights and altercations, banned from his home town.

After wandering around France, gambling and womanizing, he was sentenced to three months' jail in Lille for breach of the peace. Unable to stand the appalling conditions, he escaped several times and, for his pains, was sentenced to eight years in the galleys, a form of forced labour in the naval base at Brest. After hacking off his leg irons with a stolen chisel he went on the run again, only to be recaptured and sent to the worst brig of all, in Toulon. Vidocq even managed to escape from there, falling in behind a funeral cortège and walking to freedom.

His mother hid him several times on the run, but Vidocq had to fight hard not to be drawn into serious crime. On two occasions he ran into former convicts who threatened to turn him in if he did not carry out armed robberies for them. Vidocq refused and managed to move on undetected. Caught between crime and the police hunt for him, the chances of returning to a normal life seemed increasingly slim.

In desperation Vidocq arranged to meet a formidable officer called Henry, nicknamed the Bad Angel, who was head of the Paris police criminal department, and poured out his story. In exchange for amnesty, he offered to inform on the ex-prisoners who had propositioned him. Henry decided against it and had the fugitive arrested. He knew that the runaway could be valuable to the force, but wanted to be in a position to dictate the terms. He offered Vidocq a deal: either he could return to the galleys, possibly for the best part of his life, or he could become a secret police agent. Henry sensed that his man had broad knowledge of the underworld and that his nerve was cool enough to carry out the task. If Vidocq considered absconding, the threat of the galleys would keep him in line.

The runaway accepted the proposal and took to undercover work with a gusto which was both crude and melodramatic. Vidocq, like many great investigators, basked in public acclaim, but behind the showmanship lay careful and methodical detective work. He found the skills came to him quite naturally and soon became something of a legend both in the police and the underworld.

By 1811 Vidocq was the first full-time detective in the Paris police, and certainly the only effective one. He created a unique position of influence for himself and was already planning how his work could be expanded to form a complete department. His proposal for a Sûreté, or security division, was eagerly accepted. A century later the Police Judiciaire, or P-J, was born from the Sûreté and the thoughtful, pipe-smoking Inspector Maigret became its most celebrated fictional detective.

Vidocq headed the security division for seven years before he was finally granted a pardon in 1843. Even then, the pardon was not formally recorded. A decade passed before the old sentence was erased by the court at Douai. The Sûreté was a great success in fighting crime. Previously, police officers had an almost parochial outlook and tended to shelve cases if a suspect moved out of their area. The new system employed a central organization covering the whole of Paris, with twenty-four full-time agents and a network of former criminals employed as police spies.

The operation was impressive, but conditions were primitive. Because of resentment by the regular police at the Prefecture, the Sûreté moved into its own building, where Vidocq had rooms above the office.

'Some living accommodation for the agents was also provided, and Vidocq fed them, one of their wives seeing to the cooking,' Philip John Stead wrote in his 1953 biography of the detective. 'The agents were not paid a salary, but got such expenses as he saw fit to allow them, and a fee for every arrest. They signed no receipts, for fear of disclosing their identity, and were not issued with police warrant-cards until 1822. Vidocq ranked as a police officer; they were only agents, engaged at his discretion.'

Vidocq had a heavy-handed theatricality which ensured that their successes received maximum publicity. In 1953, Marshall Diston, writing in the magazine *Answers*, summed up his music-hall style: 'Vidocq had his own sense of the dramatic, a love of the spectacular coup. On one occasion he had to arrest a ruffian whose accomplices, already in custody, had informed against him. Vidocq found him at work and whispered that he had a message from his associates. The criminal took him to a tavern, ordered wine, and they sat down near a group of Sûreté men. Vidocq told him of his friends' arrest.

'"Who caught them?" he asked.

'"Vidocq," said the detective.

'"If he ever comes my way, I'll give it him," said the desperado.

'"You wouldn't. You'd do like all the others. You'd give him a drink."

'"I'd die a thousand times over, first," said the man, and filled the glass the detective held out.

'"Die when you're ready," said the Sûreté chief. "I am Vidocq and I arrest you." The criminal made no resistance as the agents closed in and seized him.'

In 1827, at the age of fifty-two, he retired on a pension and expected to live out his days in comfort. One of his dreams, based on his own hard experiences, was to form the first discharged prisoners' aid society to help rehabilitate men with criminal records. He opened a paper mill which employed both male and female former prisoners. In principle it worked well. 'Not one of the ex-prisoners I gave work to broke faith with me while he was under my orders,' Vidocq wrote afterwards. But he was not a business-man and the project was a financial disaster. Vidocq became insolvent and was forced to return to the Sûreté.

When he retired a second time in 1836, he set up in business as a private detective. His agency is regarded as the first in Europe specializing solely in the investigation of crime – almost twenty years before Pinkerton established his National Detective Agency in Chicago. The rooms of his Bureau de Renseignements – Infor-mation Office – were in Rue Cloche-Perce, near Place de la Bastille, and a stream of business and professional callers, attracted by his emotive advertising, began to call.

Among the services he offered was the chance to subscribe to a blacklist of convicted confidence tricksters, for twenty francs a year. 'Since leaving the public service,' Vidocq's publicity brochure read, 'I have collected innumerable documents which the multiplicity of my duties did not then allow me to gather. I shall have at my disposal the list of all who have been brought before the courts, accused of or condemned for swindling, during the last thirty years ... '

The agency was a tremendous success, building a reputation, in the best traditions of detective fiction, of beating the police at their own game. Unfortunately, everything did not go entirely smoothly. When a banker, Monsieur Delessert, was robbed, the police had little success in catching those responsible. Delessert engaged Vidocq, but concealed his real name because his brother was the new Prefect of Police.

Vidocq not only solved the mystery but also discovered the real name of his evasive client and sent the report directly to his home. The banker was delighted, and recovered his property, but Prefect Delessert was infuriated by the humiliation his men had suffered. Vidocq's offices were raided on suspicion of misappropriating police documents, and 3500 files seized – more than half relating to the Sûreté. He was arrested on charges of corrupting members of the civil service and, through information supplied by them, obtaining money by false pretences.

Vidocq was kept in jail for nine months awaiting trial. In the end he was convicted, but succeeded in getting the conviction reversed on appeal. The damage by that time had already been done, and the agency never recovered from the publicity.

Insolvent once again, Vidocq decided to try to restore his finances by writing *Memoirs of Vidocq, Principal Agent in the French Police*. Published in two volumes in 1828 by Hunt and Clarke of Covent Garden, London, the work was an enormous success. It was in this field that his influence on the myth of the private eye turned out to be more lasting and important than his contribution to detective work. Until Vidocq picked up his pen there had been virtually no detective stories, mainly because of a lack of authentic detectives. In an age of increasing literacy, popular taste was crying out for his larger-than-life exploits.

Readers had already enjoyed a brief taste of the potential of mystery and deduction in Voltaire's short philosophical novel *Zadig*, which appeared in 1748. The tale recounted the adventures of a young man with amazing powers of observation who lived in ancient Babylon in the reign of King Moabdar. Zadig applied the methods employed by Vidocq a century later so skilfully that he was able to describe the king's runaway horse and the queen's lost dog, even though he had seen neither, so accurately that he was thrown into prison accused of stealing them. Before he was sentenced, the animals were found and Zadig had an opportunity to explain how he had deduced his facts by examining the ground.

When he was originally asked if he had seen the missing dog, Zadig told the Chief Eunuch that he had not, but added that he knew the animal was a small spaniel bitch, which had recently had puppies; she had a lame left forefoot and very long ears.

'I saw an animal's tracks on the sand,' he explained to the court, and I judged without difficulty they were the tracks of a small dog. The long, shallow furrows printed on the little ridges of sand between the tracks of the paws informed me that the animal was a bitch with pendant dugs, who hence had had puppies recently. Other tracks in a different direction, which seemed all the time to have scraped the surface of the sand beside the forepaws, gave me the idea that the bitch had very long ears; and as I remarked that the sand was always less hollowed by one paw than by the three others, I concluded that our august queen's bitch was somewhat lame, if I dare say so.'

Zadig's reading of the horse tracks was equally intriguing: 'The dust on the trees in this narrow road only seven feet wide was raised a little right and left, three-and-a-half feet from the middle of the road. This horse, I said, has a tail three-and-a-half feet long, and its movement right and left has swept up this dust. I saw beneath the trees, which made a cradle five feet high, some leaves newly fallen from the branches, and I recognized that this horse had touched there, and was hence fifteen hands high. As regards his bit, it must be of twenty-three-carat gold, for he rubbed the studs against a stone, which I know to be a touchstone, and tested. From the marks his hoofs made on certain pebbles I knew the horse was shod with eleven-scruple silver.'

The style was closer to the sophisticated deduction of Sherlock Holmes than Vidocq's blatant showmanship. But, a hundred years on, the Parisian detective's audience was hungry for true crime adventure.

'Vidocq's life paralleled the transition from rogue to detective which was taking place in the literature of realism and low life, where the anti-hero had dominated in the preceding two centuries,' American publisher Patterson Smith concluded in an article called 'Sleuthing the Origins of the True-Detective Memoir' in the American book magazine *A. B. Bookman's Weekly* in April 1987.

The market may have been ripe, but the destitute detective was unprepared for the world of publishing. 'Vidocq was not the first notability to embark upon a book without any great notion of how it was to be done,' his biographer Philip John Stead explained. 'Nor had his vast experience of the underworld equipped him to deal with publishers. He produced his manuscript which, like nearly all amateur manuscripts, was much too short – for the publisher wanted three or four volumes to recoup the money he had laid out – and the publisher employed a literary man to give it more commercial form. As literary men do, when given a free hand with someone else's manuscript, he went too far.'

The ghost writer allowed his imagination to run wild and turned Vidocq's memoirs into an improbable blend of fact and bizarre fiction which, of course, was an enormous best-seller. Soon after its two-volume publication in Paris in 1828, two volumes were printed in London, followed by two more the following year. Almost overnight, the image of the private detective outsmarting police and bringing lawbreakers to justice fired the vision of fiction writers.

'His memoirs enjoyed immediate and widespread success,' Patterson Smith declared, 'and proved an immense influence on novelists and detective story writers to follow. He was the model for Balzac's Vautrin, Hugo's Javert as well as his Jean Valjean, Poe's Dupin, and Gaboriau's Lecoq; Dickens drew on him for *Great Expectations*, and Sue for *The Mysteries of Paris*; and Conan Doyle's Sherlock Holmes is in his debt.'

Vidocq's ghost writer, in lavishly adding what journalists call 'topspin', created a fantastic impression of private detection which fiction writers fed upon and which other private eyes, in turn, stretched their own reminiscences to emulate. To add to the confusion, works of fiction began to appear in the new school of realism which purported to be true detective adventures.

Patterson Smith, who is also a leading antiquarian bookdealer specializing in true crime, still shares a problem with many colleagues in separating the embroidered detective biographies from the true. The dealers' bible, Sir John Cummings's definitive *Bibliography Dealing with Crime* (1914), contains memoirs which are pure fiction, like *The Revelations of a Private Detective* written by A. Forrester in 1893, which deceived thousands of Victorian readers.

Some of the first books to jump on the Vidocq bandwagon were about police detection. William Russell, an English writer, produced *Recollections of a Policeman* (1852) and *Experiences of a French Detective Officer* (1861) under a pseudonym. Both were completely fabricated and such a success on both sides of the Atlantic that pirated editions abounded.

In America, where private detection enjoyed unrivalled esteem, Allan Pinkerton was quick to pick up the French baton. He saw popular books as a perfect vehicle to publicize his agency, and in 1874 published the first in a long line which proved to be the most successful series of private detective memoirs ever produced. He was so confident of his market that *The Expressman and the Detective* carried a page boldly announcing five further titles. The taut narrative style of his books was to influence writers of detective fiction for years to come. There was no doubt about their accuracy – all the stories were based on authentic Pinkerton cases and carried the famous eye logo gold-blocked on the cover.

Pinkerton's style has never been fully credited for its influence on crime fiction, but his brisk touch was recognized as a strong selling point by novelists. In *Bank Robbers and Detectives*, published in 1882, Patterson (no relation to Smith) is a Pinkerton undercover man posing as a fence for stolen bonds. Pinkerton's writings seldom referred to agents by their full names, either for security reasons or from a fear of removing the spotlight from the detective himself.

'Patterson's first move on reaching his room was to rush to the closet, secure a decanter of whiskey and glasses. Filling the latter for all, and without waiting for the others he gulped down a portion of the liquid, with the remark: "All's well that ends well. Now, to business, gentlemen." Taking a knife from his pocket, he next seized his valise and, bending over it, ripped the lining, saying: "What I have here is in United States bonds, Mr. Marston; I presume they will answer as well as money?"'

This first genuine, if melodramatic, insight into the working life of a private eye did little to dispel the mist of half-truth and mystique surrounding the subject. Pinkerton agents were always portrayed as cool and controlled, with an economy of style more associated with fictional heroes. The author may have run a true course with his cases, but he sailed close to the wind with his characters. The success of Pinkerton's books triggered a further spate of poorly written fiction purporting to be the real thing.

Three years after the appearance of *The Expressman and the Detective*, George S. McWatters, who claimed to have eleven years' experience as a New York City detective, wrote *Detectives of Europe and America*, with a golden eye deceptively similar to Pinkerton's on the cover.

'The first-person stories which McWatters relates are the experiences of a private detective working from an office never located, for clients never identified who are involved in incidents I have never been able to confirm by external evidence,' Patterson Smith evaluated. 'The work must be considered suspect.'

McWatters is thought to have earned himself a small fortune from this and other equally dubious titles. When Pinkerton published his first book in 1874, a rival was launched by John H. Warren Jr. called: *Thirty Years' Battle with Crime: or, the Crying Shame of New York, as Seen under the Broad Glare of an Old Detective's Lantern.* The weighty, 400-page work, laced with detailed descriptions of 'temples erected to lust' and stories of fallen women, enjoyed robust sales. Patterson Smith, however, could find no trace of an old detective in New York City Police records by the name of John H. Warren.

Such matters are perhaps best consigned to the capable care of bookdealers and academics. As far as the public were concerned, the more dramatic and intriguing the stories were, the more they wanted to read them. In the nineteenth century the cult of the private detective was built on foundations which no amount of reality could shake. Even those who came close to it, like Pinkerton, distorted the picture with storyteller's licence.

In Britain, the subject was approached more warily. There was certainly not the same plethora of publications, but one or two detectives saw a welcome opportunity to enhance their lowly standing in society by publishing tales of intrigue and adventure.

For the greater part, the world of the private eye was left to novelists to convey to the public and, as a result, the image of the industry sank a little lower. With few documented sources to compare fact with fiction, it became generally accepted that the private detectives of popular stories were a true representation of the real thing.

The confusion came to a head in 1929, when the Earl of Birkenhead, Britain's former Secretary of State for India, wrote an article for the mass-circulation magazine *Pearson's Weekly*, which launched an attack on the genre to remind everyone how ineffectual the British private eye really was:

'The detective novel is a gigantic system of imposture practised on a credulous public,' he wrote. 'I doubt if there are two private detective agencies in England, or ten in the whole world, whom one could trust with any more onerous or delicate inquiry than that of tracking a supposedly unfaithful wife.

'Anyone with experience of our courts knows how poor a figure the average private detective cuts in the witness box. Amazing with what diligence he follows the wrong person; with what persever-ance he waits outside the door of a room which his quarry has long since vacated; and with what lack of finesse he interrogates, and is deceived by, persons interested to lead him astray; with how little skill he disguises himself so that nobody can possibly mistake his calling and purpose.

'Such is the private detective in life. The amateur detective is even less admirable …

'I suppose that no crime takes place nowadays where there is the slightest doubt about the culprit and his whereabouts without at least half a dozen would-be Sherlock Holmeses endeavouring to take a hand in his detection. I do not recall that in a single actual case of which I have had direct knowledge, or of which I have read, these earnest busybodies have contrived in the very slightest degree towards the elucidation of the mystery. They have, on the contrary, often caused the police much extra trouble … The amateur detec-tive is, in short, a blundering ass, while the private detective agency is not, and does not pretend to be, an important factor in the detection of crime.'

Three years earlier, Herbert Marshall, 'the Doyen of Private Detectives', had published his memoirs *Memories of a Private Detec-tive* (1924). While most of his stories were probably authentic, the dubious hallmarks of vagueness and lack of detail which char-acterized private eye memoirs were recognizable. It may be that British private eyes considered their work dull and in need of some enlivenment, or that they simply saw the success of other semi-factual works and hoped to cash in.

Marshall's account of how he became an investigator is unquestionably woolly. His father was a 'well-known Devonshire clergyman' and after school he became apprenticed to a firm of millers. With little explanation, he claimed to have worked on a ranch in the United States and survived 'several revolutions' in

Central America before sailing for England. A suspicious vagueness then set in:

'I returned to England in 1893, and on the liner in which I travelled I became exceedingly intimate with a fellow passenger, with the result that on arrival we exchanged addresses. A short time later, I received a letter asking me to meet him, which I did. He asked me if I would care to undertake some work for which he thought me eminently suitable, for he was good enough to say that he thought I did not know what fear was.

'On expressing my willingness to assist him provided that every-thing was quite legal and he wouldn't land me in trouble, he arranged that I should dine with him and two friends a few nights later. His friends turned out to be foreigners, and obviously men of high position. During the course of the meal they told me that the daughter of a reigning prince on the Continent, who herself was married to a minor royalty, had eloped with an officer, taking with her a large quantity of jewels which were heirlooms in her father's family. For obvious reasons a scandal was unthinkable, and there-fore it would be better if the police were not brought into the matter. The lady and her lover were on the Riviera, and would I go there and endeavour to get possession of the jewels.

'The adventure appealed to me and I consented. Unfortunately, I am not at liberty to tell my experiences, but within a month I was back again with the jewels.'

The way in which Marshall conveniently drew a curtain of mystery across the incident was a common ploy among ghost writers with a flair for embroidering an otherwise uninteresting story. His memoirs are thick with dialogue, action, police outwitted and puzzles unravelled but thin on names, places and dates. However, they were considered to have a basis of truth.

If the world of books was unreliable in presenting a true picture of private eyes at work, popular magazines were even less con-strained by the truth. Readers loved the idea of private detectives, and magazines such as *Tit-Bits* advertising 'true stories' were guar-anteed good sales. Against this background of mostly fabricated thrills and mystery, real investigators worked hard to clean up their public image.

When two judges, Mr Justice Charles and Mr Justice Goddard, castigated private inquiry agents for their methods during their summing up of two unconnected cases in the summer of 1936, newspapers were quick to seize on the story. Investigators responded with renewed calls for a system of licensing and regulation.

Ronald Leach of Leach's Detective Bureau, a reputable agency, put his case to *Reynolds News*: 'The general public's impression of a detective,' he said, 'is a man with a bowler hat, big boots and a red nose, who goes snooping through hotel keyholes to secure evidence in divorce proceedings.

'Actually, I find on looking up my files that only about thirty per cent of the work done in our office is concerned with divorce cases. Commercial work is far more profitable to the reputable private detective, and far less objectionable.

'Fraudulent claims on underwriters and insurance companies give us a good deal of work. We expose innumerable faked accidents and burglaries.

'One case I call to mind is that of a firm of furriers who claimed several thousand pounds on the grounds of burglary, at which, so they said, stocks accumulated for their regular business trip to the provinces had been taken.

'Our men shadowed them on behalf of the insurance company, and brought to light such matters as contact with known receivers, a duplicate bank account, and a provable falsity in the statement of claim. The partners in the firm went to prison.'

Leach was a good operator and well aware of the distorted view of the profession. He believed in pushing back the frontiers of private detection and pioneered the use of technical equipment before the police did. The hardware was crude by modern standards, but reasonably effective. In the late twenties he planted a microphone in the office of a broker who was being blackmailed and trapped the culprit – though, if standard BBC microphones of the period were anything to go by, concealment must have presented problems.

In the early 1930s, Leach's Detective Bureau was also the first investigating agency to use film to solve a case. Armed with a clockwork cine camera, Leach and one of his operatives kept watch on a warehouse from which sides of bacon were regularly disappearing.

'We kept observation and noticed that whenever the commissionaire went off duty for his lunch, a number of bales of bacon were always brought out to a side door, which we understood was not in use, and loaded onto a waiting van.

'So we used a cine camera with a telescopic lens to photograph the proceedings and showed the film to the heads of the firm. They were able to say with certainty that the men shown in the film had no authority to load the bacon, and we were able to present the police with evidence for a conviction.

'When I add that a bale of bacon is worth between £6 and £8, according to quality, and that several bales were vanishing every day, it is obvious that the position of even a stable firm may be shaken, and that the private detective earns his fee.

'Inquiries into the stability and repute of business firms, which we can take several stages further than the often perfunctory inquiries of the ordinary business inquiry agency, are a big source of jobs.'

Ronald Leach was doing his best to improve the public image of British investigators, but his efforts to dispel the impression of private eyes relying heavily on divorce work were not quite honest. Even though the commercial side of the industry was steadily improving, divorce continued to provide the lion's share of the private detective's income.

In 1948, more than a decade after *Reynolds News* printed that interview, *New Review* ran a survey on the type of cases worked by British investigators. Divorce still provided the vast majority of cases undertaken, followed in descending order by investigating theft and fraud, dealing with blackmailers, checking business reputations, tracing missing people, escorting celebrities and guard work.

Security work has since branched out to become a multi-million-pound industry on its own account, while celebrity work is a highly specialized field. Hollywood, of course, had its own system of celebrity bodyguards to keep troublesome fans at bay. In Britain the star system was comparatively new, but not without its problems. Record companies, theatres and celebrities themselves made discreet but increasing use of private investigators from the late 1920s onwards.

The management of the London Coliseum consulted an unknown investigator in 1937 when the comedian and singer

Lupino Lane received a telephone death threat in his dressing room minutes before going on stage for a live BBC radio broadcast of his 'Twenty-to-One' show. In the best tradition of melodrama, the anonymous voice whispered: 'The blow will fall in the second act,' and hung up. Lane went ahead with the show, the detective (presumably summoned at extremely short notice) found nothing and life at the Coliseum returned to normal.

In 1938 *Radio Pictorial* ran an interview with an unnamed private eye under the headline 'Racketeers of Radio'. It summed up much of the forgotten magic of the era:

'There was a click as the last of the eight records was played through on the great walnut radiogram in the middle of the heavily-carpeted office. The automatic-change mechanism switched the instrument off. And the massive, immaculate managing director of a world-famous recording concern puffed at his cigar, staring at me in silence for a moment.

'Then he said: "What d'you think of them?"

'"They're eight very good dance records," I ventured. "Billy Cotton, Hylton and Carroll Gibbons, I should say. But I don't imagine you called me here just to judge a dance-tune contest."

'"I did not," he said tonelessly.

'"Then, who made the records?"

'"That is what I'm paying you to find out."

'He took one of the discs off the pile of eight and handed it to me. It was a perfectly normal gramophone record, bearing a disc and a label of a well-known gramophone concern. There seemed nothing wrong with it.

'"A pirate?" I ventured.

'"Yes," explained the recording chief. "I have checked up with the BBC and foreign programmes. These pirate records are simply recordings of actual broadcasts. As you can hear, there isn't the 'finish' that you get with a proper record. The acoustic qualities are bad, as most of these pirate discs were re-recorded from ballroom broadcasts. These labels are good forgeries."

'"Why haven't you handed the case over to the police?"

'He smiled. "I may do so later. But the man who's behind this racket must be a clever technician. If he straightens himself out he may be worth employing. See what you can do."

'It took me three months to bring forward vital evidence. I sent "scouts" out into various districts handling publicity material for this gramophone firm. Then one day the phone rang shrilly in my office. It was one of my men on the line.

'"I'm speaking from a call box in Bristol Road, Birmingham," he said. "I've found a man who's handling records which he says are genuine, but he gets them at forty per cent off. Of course they're not genuine. I'm checking up the source and will report."

'That hunt took us from Birmingham to Leeds, through the sub-branch of a wholesaler, then back to Camden Town, London. The ramp was discovered – and squashed.'

This bald magazine style was devoured by readers and added to the hotch-potch of mystique already fashioned by novelists and quasi-factual private eye 'memoirs'. In the war years which followed, 'true' detective stories provided welcome distraction through the long hours of the blackout. The format rarely varied, consisting of an endless stream of titillating reminiscences, but a noticeable change had occurred in the by-line.

Magazine articles were no longer written by 'a private detective', or 'as told by a secret agent'. A cult of personality emerged, with the hero at first illustrated by line drawings but soon afterwards by photographs so there could be no doubt as to his authenticity. In the magazines read on buses and tube trains, a handful of private investigators became popular heroes. It became a form of recognition which years of parliamentary lobbying had failed to achieve.

One of the first 'stars' to come out of the closet of anonymity was ex-Scotland Yard detective inspector Harold Brust, who resigned from the police in 1927 to open his own private detection agency. In 1938 Brust sold a series to *Tit-Bits*, a popular weekly of 'true life drama' and obscure information, and had the distinction of becoming the first investigator to be identified by name and photograph in a magazine. Dramatic studio pictures were staged of Brust, in dinner jacket and black tie, leaning from the side window of a taxi cab, pressing the barrel of an automatic against the driver's head. 'My Life As A Secret Agent' received enormous coverage in the magazine.

'In these articles,' ran the teaser, 'he explains for the first time the methods that enabled him to bring his most sensational cases to a successful conclusion, and describes vividly the adventures that befell him. Last week he dealt with the Casino Slaves in Havana, and how he fell foul of sundry shady characters in the sinister districts of that port.'

The story of Brust's interlude as 'a secret agent in Havana' began as he sauntered down the steps of the Casino at four one morning after a night at the tables to find his usual taxi-driver replaced by a strange Mexican. Within minutes the plot quickened in pace. Brust was offered drugged coffee from a nearby refreshment stall and bundled into the cab. For a moment, it seemed like the end of the Brylcreemed, overweight ex-detective inspector, but he summoned reserves of bulldog will.

'I sat in the corner of the cab and made a determined attempt to throw off the effect of the "hocked" coffee, and after five or six minutes, although I felt very tired and sick, I realised that I was not going right out, and I was also very pleased with the fact that I was carrying an old friend – my Webley Scott automatic – in the inside breast pocket of my overcoat.'

What exactly the detective was doing wearing an overcoat in the tropics quickly became inconsequential. The taxi pulled to a halt in 'one of the most sinister parts of the city' and, 'suddenly, from the window of a house there was a flash and a bullet drove through both windows of the cab, in one side and out of the other. I saw the driver give a start. He flung a hurried glance over his shoulder at me, put his foot on the accelerator and dashed off.

'I leant out of the window, pushed the barrel of the automatic into the back of his head and told him to pull up at the side of the road. I then got out of the cab and discussed the situation. The man, a Mexican – as usual – was in a terrific state of nerves. His knees were almost knocking together as he protested that he knew nothing of the attempt, that the cup of coffee he had brought me in the cab was exactly as he had received it at the coffee bar, and that he was as innocent as the babe unborn.'

From then on the reader waded knee deep in spineless Mexicans, full-bosomed girls called Juanita with flashing smiles that did not take in Brust for one instant, and playboys in tuxedos 'with more money than brains'. The reason for this Ealing comedy of errors was that a gang of cigar crooks suspected Brust of discovering their operation. Their plan, backed by a clandestine factory printing counterfeit cigar-bands, was to substitute cheap imitations for expensive cigars and foist them on unsuspecting smokers.

Why anyone would bother to steal cigars in pre-war Havana, where they were presumably as common as girls called Juanita with flashing smiles, was not fully explained. *Tit-Bits* readers, however, were not generally sticklers for detail.

The point, rather, was that the public's perception of private eyes was now approaching the realm of fantasy. Ex-detective inspector Brust was still going strong in 1940. But perhaps the *Tit-Bits* readership had tired of him; he surfaced further downmarket in an obscure publication called *Guide and Ideas*, which devoted considerable space to systems for winning the football pools.

Brust was this time on the Riviera, still in woollen overcoat and trilby, chasing jewel thieves. From the illustration of him supposedly arresting an attractive girl, he was the same stern, portly figure. One would have suspected that he might have lost some weight perspiring around the hottest parts of the world in unsuitable clothing, but the double chin and the clipped moustache were unmistakable. So, too, was the lack of detail:

'A titled woman, whom I will call Lady X, was travelling to France with her maid, and in her luggage was a strongly constructed case containing a valuable pearl necklace.

'When the case was opened in Paris by Lady X the contents were intact – save for the necklace. How and where it had gone the distraught woman could not imagine. The case had been in her cabin the whole way over the Channel and in her compartment on the trains both in England and France. And yet the necklace had vanished. I was called in to solve the mystery.

'I was rather suspicious of the fact that the maid had left her employ not long after the loss. I decided to check up on her. To my surprise I found her living in a nice villa in the Riviera, in a manner and style far above that of a lady's maid. I set watch on the villa.

'Next morning I saw her come out and get into a car to drive to the railway station, and into the back of the car a good deal of luggage was piled. To my amazement, I saw what appeared to be Lady X's dressing case from which the necklace had disappeared.

'I crossed the road, and asked the woman what she was doing with the dressing case in her possession. A look of terror sprang into her eyes. She burst into tears and poured out her story.'

That was more or less the last popular magazine readers heard of Brust. But as one private eye faded from the limelight, another was always standing in the wings ready to take over. In 1946 *Reynolds News* ran a series called 'Memoirs of a Private Detective' which, though anonymous, was one of the few accurate accounts of private investigation to appear in the popular press. Arnold Sutton, who conducted the interviews and ghosted the articles, was more concerned with lively stories than investigative techniques. However, readers gained a little real insight into private detection and began to draw a picture of how freelance investigators were frequently hired behind the scenes on famous cases.

The private eye's version of the celebrated Russell Baby Case of the twenties was particularly interesting because it revealed the extent to which lawyers were availing themselves of investigators' services.

The case first hit the headlines when the Hon. John Russell sued his wife Christabel for divorce in the most costly and prolonged matrimonial action heard in an English court. The marathon hearing began in July 1922, producing claim and counter-claim, and continued until June 1924, running up legal bills of £10,000, perhaps £250,000 at today's rates. The case then went to the House of Lords which reversed the previous verdict and established the legitimacy of Geoffrey Russell as heir to the barony of Ampthill. The cost of the second trial was said to be far in excess of the first.

'During the course of the case at least eight private inquiry agencies were employed on one side or the other,' the anonymous PI told Sutton. 'At one particular period I counted thirty "unofficial" detectives working for either plaintiff or defendant. They had been instructed by the solicitors with specific tasks, chiefly connected with the checking up on the integrity of the eighty or so witnesses who were to go into the box.

'Costs and expenses rose to astronomic heights. As each side wanted to keep an eye on the other's witnesses and learn all they could about them, they demanded from us a round-the-clock vigil with check-ups on the movement of witnesses and their companions. Then, as each side did not know what witnesses their rivals might call upon, they instructed the inquiry agents working for them to watch the inquiry agents on the other side.

'It became a tangle of watchers watching the watchers.'

'I was employed by solicitors acting on behalf of the Hon. John Russell,' the *Reynolds News* PI went on with his story. 'We had an important witness coming from the Continent and I received instructions that he was to be watched night and day until after he had been in the witness box.

'I was waiting for him to leave his hotel one morning when I became aware that two men whom I knew belonged to a rival agency were watching me. I guessed that they were not so much shadowing me as trying to find out who was our witness.

'When he left the hotel a few minutes later, therefore, I let him go and waited for a newcomer. About half an hour later an elderly benign old gentleman came out. I let him get about 100 yards away and then I started to stalk him. I had not gone far before I realised that not only were two men following me, but that they in turn were being followed by two others.

'Eventually my own personal shadowers, thinking I suspected nothing, passed me and went after the innocent old man. The others followed them and I faded away to a hard-earned breakfast. I learned a long time later that this unwitting victim of what happens when rich folk go to law, was watched for days before it was realised that he had nothing to do with the suit.'

Curiously, there have been other cases of private eyes watching private eyes. In 1950, the Federation of British Detectives mounted a mass observation on new applicants for membership in an attempt to clean up the industry. For nine months PI shadowed PI, eventually resulting in the rejection of 70 membership applications out of 220. Armed with the evidence, a delegation of eight FBD members travelled to London to lobby MPs to introduce a Bill regularizing their status. Most of their information related to disreputable agents who took up to £100 from clients, promising to produce divorce evidence but failing to deliver it. The exercise amounted to yet another abortive bid for regulation.

A more amusing story came from Chicago in 1970, when businessman Adrian Benstead hired private detectives to watch his apartment when he went away on a business trip. He was worried about attacks on women in the area and was fearful for his wife Lily's safety. The PIs watched his flat day and night from an empty apartment across the street.

Unfortunately, Lily knew nothing about her husband's concern. On the very first day she saw a man watching her through binoculars and phoned the police. They reacted immediately, thinking that a raid was being planned on a bank next door to the Bensteads.

Plain-clothes officers moved discreetly into Lily's home – and for nine days the detectives watched each other. Adrian was summoned back quickly after hearing reports from his private eyes that his wife was entertaining men around the clock.

Although couched in the same style as dubious 'memoirs', the *Reynolds News* series about the Russell divorce broke new ground by cutting through the manufactured myth of investigation with some interesting cameos. Unfortunately, its success resulted in another avalanche of semi-fictional round-ups of bizarre cases by nameless investigators.

'Hired Bodyguard When He Gave His Wife His Wages' trumpeted *Reveille*, a magazine, like *Tit-Bits*, said to be read mainly by soldiers on trains. 'I'm a private detective,' it began, 'but to look at me you'd never suspect it. I'm not tall. I haven't got big feet or a deep voice. My height is 5ft 3in. I am forty three years old.

'Those who think we chaps spend our time spying on people to obtain evidence for the divorce court, or checking up on hire purchase customers, would be surprised at the odd jobs which come our way ... '

The veneer of glamour attributed to the profession by publishers and journalists was particularly resented by the police. It was well known that many private investigators were retired police officers, but there were clearly others who were little more than confidence tricksters.

Police Review ran an editorial in 1949 by Owen Marris which was generally sympathetic to private eyes: 'In Britain many private detectives are ex-Police officers and conduct themselves with propriety ... Occasionally one falls from grace but, as with policemen, so rarely that the occasion makes news ... Provided they do not transgress the law, do not obstruct the police, and do not damage the flower beds with their ladders, they should not be discouraged. They do not have the opportunities of Sexton Blake or Paul Temple and the other amateur sleuths who regularly, in print and on the air, beat us at our own game, but they can tell some interesting stories.'

The editorial leaned heavily towards a licensing system and, significantly, pointed to historical differences between the industry in Britain and America, the standards set by Pinkerton and rigorous licensing regulations in New York State.

In the 1950s, when popular newspapers placed emphasis on exposés and competition for exclusive news stories reached a peak, it was inevitable that attention should be drawn to the widening gap between the image of the private eye and his working practices. It was not the first time that the media had turned on a creature of their own creation. As private eye series continued to be published and the hard news war heated up, the operator who happened to be caught in the crossfire was Charlie Chrystall.

There is some doubt whether this was his real name, but Chrystall was undoubtedly the last of the great magazine detective showmen. The *Daily Mirror* ran a series in 1954 entitled 'Secrets from the Casebook of Charles Chrystall'. *John Bull*, a mass circulation weekly magazine, gave Charlie another leg up the ladder of national fame a year later with a valued double-page spread. There were tales of hidden microphones, rummaging for secrets in waste baskets, bribing maids and eavesdropping in attics, but Lawrence Hanley's photographs told more. Charlie was pictured in the seediest of offices, six feet square, with a rickety gas fire, and a kettle on the floor. The walls were papered with newspaper cuttings about private eyes and a dog-eared map of London. Chrystall himself, a gross figure in an old overcoat with a trilby pushed back on his head, sat on the edge of an office chair which looked about to collapse under his weight. He faced a bank of ex-Ministry of Defence short-wave transmitters balanced on top of a filing cabinet, and appeared to be speaking urgently into a microphone.

The 52-year-old Yorkshireman, who called himself 'Britain's Number One Private Eye', operated from a rented second-floor office near Piccadilly Circus under several company names – Charles Chrystall International Detective, the Anglo-American Detective Agency, the Department of Special Investigation, John Smart's Private Investigation Office and the Anglo-Continental Detective Agency. The sign, which was almost bigger than his floor space, should have told journalists something, but no one seemed anxious to let the truth get in the way of a good story.

Newspapers loved the bulldog, larger-than-life character in belted coat and size eleven boots. When the phone rang and Charlie told them it was Rome, or New York, they nodded and wrote it down. Business boomed with every story as Chrystall stressed his wide network of contacts, the detective organizations of which he was a member (almost exclusively obscure and American), his radio equipment and his honesty.

'He normally asks for three guineas for eight hours' work, plus expenses for meals, car or taxi, and tips given to people who help him with information,' *John Bull* reported. '"Sometimes we get a wealthy client who insists on paying us a big fee," says Chrystall, who often speaks in the first person plural. "We always settle on a figure in advance. But I don't make a fortune. I live like an ordinary man."

'If he finds a client is in the wrong, he quickly returns the fee. Sometimes he refuses to take money at all. "We get problem adults," he says. "They create a monster in their minds, often about husbands or wives, and they bring the monster to life."'

The saint was not without his shortcomings. Bachelor Chrystall freely admitted to being a woman-hater: 'You can't trust 'em. If you'd seen the things I've seen … '

Inevitably, his downfall came a few years later when the man who specialized in hunting people down was busy dodging the *Sunday Pictorial*. By this time Chrystall, whom the *Pictorial* claimed was really called John Smart, had branched into security. A builder paid him £250 in an attempt to stop pilfering at a Bexleyheath site where 600 new houses were under construction.

The cheque was handed over in the late afternoon and early next morning Chrystall cashed it. 'Then,' according to Patrick Chapman's *Pictorial* report, 'his outfit – Plant Security and Protection Services – thundered into action.

'A man from Smart's turned up at the estate and asked the night watchman if he could sleep in his hut. Another man phoned and asked where the estate was.

'During the next week Mr R. A. Wendes, a director of the firm, made twenty-one unanswered phone calls to Smart's detective agency. He told me: "Nothing further has been done. They will not answer the telephone or our letters. We were told a number of men would be sent immediately."'

Chrystall went to ground and left his Piccadilly offices never to be heard of again. The great affair with the media was over. Charlie Chrystall was an example of the image at odds with the reality. The media created a role figure and, hungry for new stories, began examining its flaws. The fall was precipitated by private eyes who courted the media and made the error of believing their own publicity.

In America, on a different level, Jay J. Armes was, and probably still is, the best known and most instantly recognized private eye in the country. Armes, perhaps more than anyone in the history of private detection, took elements of the myth and fantasy which the public devoured and made them reality. His headquarters, home and lifestyle have more in common with a film set than the usual office chaos of a working investigator in London, New York or Los Angeles.

For years, television, magazines and toy manufacturers wooed him; the investigator continues to talk to interviewers about spectacular cases, television deals and ambitious plans for the future. When the media worm turns, however, it is never a welcome experience. And for Armes, a man who surrounded himself with all the paraphernalia of a James Bond, it must have been particularly ungratifying when a glossy magazine, *Texas Monthly*, published a long and uncomplimentary article about him in 1976, asking 'Is Jay J. Armes For Real?' The incident was seen by some members of the private detection community as a lesson in over-exposure.

The contrast between Armes's lifestyle and the image perceived by Texas journalist Gary Cartwright, who wrote the piece, is interesting.

The fourteen-acre estate surrounding Jay J. Armes's home is stocked with a collection of jungle animals more suited to a Tarzan movie than to the arid banks of the Rio Grande, in the frontier town of El Paso, Texas. The beasts are turned loose at night because America's self-made private eye legend has had many attempts on his life.

'They've tried everything from bombs to bullets,' he says. 'I've had booby traps in my car and the Mafia tried to throw me from a launch with a block of concrete tied round my neck. I survived them all, so I guess God must have put me on earth for a reason.'

Armes is the only private eye in the world who guarantees results, and what makes his confidence more remarkable is that he has no hands. They were blown off at the age of eleven when he picked up a stick of railroad dynamite. He mastered the use of two alloy hooks and can now slice a steak or sip a glass of wine as well as the next man. He recalls the childhood experience of losing his hands as a kind of religious experience. Armes tells the story of lying in hospital and watching the sky darken as he bitterly asked: 'Why me, God, why me?' The clouds parted as he realized that the infirmity was a result of his own action and he would have to struggle to overcome it. A determination to be the best pervaded the rest of his life.

The hooks are also Jay J. Armes's secret weapon. They have guns built into them which can be fired on a muscle reflex. A worrying thought, but he hastens to stress that they cannot be triggered by accident; it is mind over matter, Armes explains. He can carry out the most delicate tasks or, by flipping a customized gear switch, exert pressure powerful enough to crush someone's hand in the manner of a Bond movie villain.

At four-thirty each morning the light goes on in the master bedroom of Armes's sprawling white ranch house with its pillared entrance. The detective hitches himself up in bed and rests on one elbow to study a battery of TV monitors beside the circular bed. Cameras slowly pan the high electric perimeter fences. On the screens, the moonlight picks out his personal logo of a gun bearing his initials, welded to the iron gates.

The room is sparsely furnished and carpeted in flame red twist pile. There are lots of mirrors. His Chinese wife Linda is still asleep when he pads down a thickly carpeted spiral ramp to his gym. Armes's day begins on a Nautilus machine, followed by a daunting regime of press-ups and karate moves on a heavy bag suspended from the ceiling. Anyone who meets him quickly realizes that he has a driving energy and determination above that of the average person. On his way back upstairs, he takes the inside lane of the spiral ramp, which is steeper, to exercise his leg muscles.

Some years ago he had a basement firing range, where a computer triggered pop-up targets in random sequence to improve his reflexes. Unfortunately, it was inadequately ventilated, and a build-up of gases from the hundreds of rounds he fired daily made him collapse. Luckily, said Armes, his family found him in time and carried him into the fresh air. He has since practised out of doors.

When Ideal Toys ran a marketing survey on Jay J. Armes, 85 per cent of American adults and 75 per cent of children were said to be able to identify him immediately. A Jay J. Armes doll, with detachable hooks for a variety of tasks, sold eleven million models, according to the detective. His autobiography was translated into thirteen languages. *Newsweek* called him a super-sleuth – 'perhaps the best private eye in the country'.

Armes is a devout Baptist who donates a tenth of his income to his local El Paso church. In his work he sees himself as a crusader against crime and speaks of bringing criminals to justice with the earnestness and sincerity of a latter-day Bruce Wayne, Batman's alter ego. The church is presumably doing well – Armes claims to have charged several million dollars for successfully solving a case.

His tools of the trade appear to be an embodiment of the saying 'he who dies with the most toys wins'. There are thirteen custom cars and trucks, designed for surveillance and helping him to stay alive. A Corvette Stingray has a rearview camera which can pick up anyone tailing him seventeen blocks away. A small dashboard TV monitor allows him to take a closer look at his pursuers. The car also has revolving number plates and a smoke gun which can engulf a whole block at the touch of a button. A black stretch limo has video surveillance cameras built into the headlights. The cream Cadillac Seville, described elsewhere, has built-in fax and radio telephones, and an onboard computer which scans for hidden bombs.

Armes's cases have taken him all over the world. In Chad he solved the murder of a millionaire's nephew, and found himself the target of a government assassination squad. He fled the country on the only available plane – a Russian military transport bound for Moscow. En route, Armes charmed the crew into radioing ahead to arrange an entry visa for him.

He rescued Marlon Brando's abducted son within three days, when police investigations had drawn a blank. He is said to have whisked a millionaire from a Mexican prison yard by helicopter, and dived on behalf of his client General Franco to locate a US atomic weapon, accidentally jettisoned in the Mediterranean.

Clients generally have to make the journey to his El Paso office if they wish to meet him. It is difficult to miss, with its huge billboard portrait of the investigator soaring above the concrete bombscreen outside. The interior resembles something designed for a James

Bond film set. There is a choice of ascending to Armes's office by a spiral staircase with zebra-skin treads, or riding directly to the inner sanctum by leather-lined elevator. When the doors open, the first thing visitors see is a life-like wax dummy of Armes, sitting on a sofa reading a magazine. The aim of the effigy is to draw the first fire of anyone trying to kill him. Armes himself sits behind a 15-foot semi-circular desk on a raised podium at the other end of the room.

In front of him is an array of buttons arranged to spell the word 'investigator'. Some dim the lights, at the touch of a hook, or turn them up to the candlepower of a TV studio. Others activate a hum of machinery which turns a panelled wall into a revolving soft drinks bar (Armes is teetotal and does not smoke), or make a bookcase swivel to reveal racks of automatic weapons. Another bookcase swings away from the wall to display shelves of night-scopes, tracking transmitters and bugging devices.

Armes is a hi-tech devotee, because of its usefulness in his investigative work and also because of the obvious pleasures he receives in showing it off. The private eye and the carefully culti-vated image are extremely difficult to separate.

Behind him tower huge illuminated maps of the United States, with lists of distances between major cities, presumably for the purpose of calculating expenses. At the opposite end of the room, facing his desk, a four-foot TV screen constantly checks the exterior of the building and cars parked outside. The camera lens is powerful enough to home in on car interiors to check for concealed weapons as visitors alight. In front of the concrete bomb screen, jagged rocks set in the pavement prevent vehicles from attempting to bulldoze down the heavy front doors.

'They are sensible precautions,' he says. 'I guarantee my work, so I have to guarantee my own safety.'

All his cases are unusual and oddly reminiscent of the private eye magazine serials of yesteryear. There was a Saudi Arabian prince who asked him to keep an eye on a small tribe of desert nomads on their first visit to Las Vegas. When Armes saw that their head-dresses were encrusted with rubies and diamonds, he had to deploy a small army of bodyguards. At the Las Vegas Hilton there was panic when the desert people decided to roast a lamb in the hotel bath. His reported fee for the eleven-day nightmare – $11 million.

According to the novelist Frederick Nolan, who ghosted his

autobiography, Armes 'wears lightweight suits with shoulder epaulettes and turned-back cuffs. They look faintly military, somewhere between a uniform and a safari jacket, and he has seven hundred and fifty of them, all different materials cut to the same pattern, tailored to conceal the holstered .38. His way of speaking is soft, his vowels Texas-rounded. He comes on so much like a good ole boy that it is easy to miss the steel beneath the softness.'

But not for long. Armes makes it clear that he would have no hesitation in gunning someone down to save a client's life or his own. He talks of his religious convictions and, minutes later, demonstrates the battered leather briefcase he uses for ransom demands. It contains a sub-machine gun which fires through a luggage label.

A kidnap case in the early 1980s took him to St Ives, Cornwall, where a wealthy Pennsylvania doctor had absconded with his young daughter. The father had planned to snatch the girl from her mother's lawful custody for almost a year, concealing his trail by closing down his bank accounts and cutting himself off from his normal circle of friends. Armes discovered that regular transatlantic calls were being made by relatives to St Ives. Agents he retained in London soon discovered the whereabouts of the father and daughter and reported back to El Paso.

With a convoy of three limousines and the mother standing by, Armes snatched the girl from her school playground. Teachers who witnessed the incident thought it was a terrorist kidnap and alerted the police. By the time the cars had swept through the steep streets of the old town of St Ives into open country, a roadblock manned by armed police was in position. The first car managed to get through and drove on to London to alert a barrister. Armes and his clients, in the second car, were forced to a halt at gunpoint.

'Don't you ever believe those stories that British bobbies carry nothing but sticks,' he smiled. 'These boys had machine guns and automatic weapons, and they weren't playing around. Right in the middle of frisking us, one of the policemen waved to his boss and shouted: "It's Jay J. Armes, the famous detective." He told me later that he'd read my book.'

Armes's fame failed to keep him out of custody. The occupants of the two cars were locked up until lawyers arranged their release pending a court hearing. The judge concurred with his American counterparts and agreed that the mother had lawful custody of the child.

Armes said that his fee for that particular case was half-a-million dollars up front. In contrast he likes to uphold the image of the crime crusader who occasionally waives his fee. An example he cited was the parents of an El Paso man jailed for sexually assaulting a young boy; the parents pleaded with the detective to gather evidence for an appeal.

Armes became convinced that the man was innocent and began an investigation of the jury which had convicted him. He taped evidence in doorstep interviews that a girl on the jury had had an affair with the defendant and had been jilted by him. Other women jurors had become nervous when they heard that his attorney had a list of jurors' addresses. They convicted him, probably with the idea of securing their own safety.

On hearing the tapes, the appeal court judge overturned the verdict and released Armes's client. The man's family, who had little money, had mortgaged their home to pay for lawyer's fees. Armes says that, on discovering their financial plight, he charged them nothing.

Such stories made him an American hero fighting on the side of justice in a world of corruption. Many of the clients who contacted him must have been inclined to think the same. In 1976, Gary Cartwright, staff writer for the influential glossy *Texas Monthly*, had his doubts.

Cartwright accompanied a Canadian TV company, CTV, who were making a documentary about Armes and it soon became clear that the private eye was perhaps as keen on fantasy as on reality. At a corner table of Miguel Steak and Spirits in El Paso, Armes discussed the programme with producer Heinz Avigdor. The detective's bodyguard Fred Marshall sat at another table, between his boss and the door.

According to Cartwright, Armes told the producer he was a karate black belt and was keen to demonstrate his prowess: '"I want to show you what a black belt does, besides hold your gi [karate regalia] up," he smiled at the producer. "Look, I've been in a lot of films, I know what I'm talking about. Do it my way, I'll show you what it's all about."

'Armes had called ahead and cleared the plan with the Miguel manager. It would be a scene right out of *The Investigator*, a proposed television series which, according to Armes, CBS would begin filming right here in El Paso, right here at the Miguel, in fact, on January 20. CBS planned a pilot film and 23 episodes, all of the stories adapted from Armes's personal files. Jay J. Armes, of course, would play the title role of Jay J. Armes.

'This was the scenario Armes outlined for the CTV producer:

'As soon as the Canadians had positioned their lights and camera, a telephone would ring. Armes would be paged. Fred would presumably go on eating his steak and chili. As Armes approached the lobby he would be confronted by a large Oriental who would grab him by the collar and say: "You've been pushing around the wrong people, Armes." Jay would project his thin smile, inform the Oriental that he was a man of peace, then flip the startled giant over his shoulder with a lightning quick maneuver of his hooks. A second man would charge him with a pepper mill. Armes would deflect the blow with one of his steel hands, jump into the air; and paralyze the second assailant with a judo chop.

'"Uh, Jay," producer Heinz Avigdor said feebly, "I think that is a bit dramatic for the purposes of our show. We're doing a documentary. I think perhaps a workout in your private exercise room, wearing your karate outfit, then some footage in your shooting range downstairs, and maybe a shot in your library. Something from real life, you see."

'Jay Armes saw, all right: he saw that the producer was a fool.

'"I'm offering you something from real life," he said, that edge of impatience returning to his voice.

'"But, Jay, it's so ... so staged," Avigdor argued. "W-5 isn't that kind of show."

'"It's real," Armes snapped, and the pitch of his voice was much higher. "What you're talking about isn't real. There's nothing real about working out in a gym, with a body bag, wearing a stupid gi. This way, I'll be in a suit and tie in a public place doing my work, exactly like real life."

'Avigdor protested that his crew didn't have the manpower or equipment for the scene Jay was suggesting. Jay sighed, adjusted his hooks to the fork and knife. He changed the subject abruptly: he began telling the two magazine writers about his secret code, and about his dissolvable stationery that you could stir in a glass of water and drink.'

Fascinated, Cartwright followed the journalists and TV crew on the standard Armes tour, listening to stories and watching demonstrations of his gadgetry. Back in the office he began checking them out and claimed that some of the statements Armes made to publicize his agency were difficult to substantiate.

In 1981 Tom Zito of the *Washington Post* wire service had a similar encounter with Jay J. Armes and received more or less the same impression as Cartwright. *Texas Monthly* publisher Mike Levy told Zito: 'Armes got an injunction to stop publication while we were on press. I spent three days hiding from process servers while we got the thing mailed, and then we got the injunction lifted. He never even tried to sue. We stood by our story.'

In 1989, Armes talked about another TV series about to be made featuring his cases, starring Jay J. Armes and shot on location at his El Paso headquarters. Armes's son Jay joined us for lunch and, riding around in the Cadillac later, confirmed some of the stories. The impression was that business was good. I was told about the worldwide scope of his operation, with a bustling turnover of cases and agents in almost every country of the world. What struck me as strange was that, apart from a secretary in the front office, the whole building was as silent as a tomb.

If Jay J. Armes goes down in history it might not only be for his detective exploits, but also for the fact that he reached the furthest extremity of one curious branch of the private detection family tree. Eugène François Vidocq's love affair with publicity nearly 200 years ago sowed the seeds of a powerful image which grew through books, magazines, movies and finally into television. The fanciful might see its origins in Jung's archetype of the Shadow – the romantic in the figure of the lone hunter entering the mists of the collective subconscious.

Television, as might be expected, has supplied our most enduring impressions. Series about British private eyes have been a mere trickle compared to the torrent from America. Apart from amateur sleuths, such as Paul Temple, who made his TV debut in 1969, Miss Marple or Lord Peter Wimsey, one of the first bona fide British small screen private eye series was *Shadow Squad*, starring Rex Garner, which appeared in 1957. Although technically interesting in its use of close-ups, it bore little resemblance to reality. *The Protectors*, a 1971 ATV glossy starring Robert Vaughn, Nyree Dawn Porter and Tony Amholt, had its operatives jetting around the world on unconvincing assignments. *Shoestring*, starring Trevor Eve in 1980, was an enormous success in terms of international sales. The private eye operating from a local radio station was novel and entertaining, but more a figment of producer Robert Banks-Stuart's agile mind than anything akin to reality.

Strangely, the most enduring figure also happened to be the seediest. *Public Eye*, in which Alfred Burke starred for 33 episodes as the threadbare Frank Marker, was first transmitted in 1965. It touched a chord with British audiences and summed up their impression of private detection. Realism was one of the series' strong points, with Marker in his grubby mackintosh working small cases for small returns. He was low on style but high on tenacity and many British private investigators still cringe at the memory of comments they received during the original transmissions.

In the USA the idea of the slick, infallible investigator also lacked long-term appeal. The image of the American PI as a mixture of hero and misfit led to a strange assortment of popular characters who made big box office – the overweight, gourmandizing *Cannon*, starring William Conrad; *Harry-O*, which featured David Janssen working from a dilapidated Californian beach hut; beleaguered Jim Rockford of *The Rockford Files*, wryly played by James Garner, who lived in a rented trailer and was beaten up more times than any screen investigator; *Longstreet*, the blind gumshoe portrayed for twenty-four episodes by James Franciscus assisted by his guide dog Pax; and the freeloading *Magnum*, launched in 1980 and starring Tom Selleck as a PI living on Hawaii in borrowed style beyond his means.

Hollywood brought some of the great detectives of literature to life, but perhaps none so convincingly as Dashiell Hammett's Sam Spade and Raymond Chandler's Philip Marlowe. The hard-boiled school which reached its peak in the mid-forties was a reaction against all that had gone before. As William K. Everson pointed out in *The Detective in Film*: 'The tough private detective in fiction effectively dates from Sam Spade of 1930, although there are certainly earlier examples: done not so much in the hope of instigating new trends, as a kind of protest by the individual author against the basically artificial form of detection practised by the dilettante intellectuals.'

The characters invented by Dashiell Hammett, especially the Continental Op and Sam Spade of *The Maltese Falcon*, were based on his own experiences. Hammett had worked as a Pinkerton private eye and had had more than a few rough-house experiences, which had left him with knife scars on his leg and an indentation in his head. The mechanics of piecing together clues, surveillance and the atmosphere of a working detective agency, with its rich mix of characters, were all drawn upon in his books and translated to film. The realism, however, comes forward not so much in the trench-coat and dangling cigarette or the dramatic situations, but in the outlook of his characters towards the job and the world in general.

In a 1925 story, *The Gutting of Couffignal*, the Continental Op – the unnamed operative from the Continental Investigation Agency – reflected on his situation: 'Now I'm a detective because I happen to like the work. It pays me a fair salary, but I could find other jobs that could pay more. Even a hundred dollars more a month would be twelve hundred a year. Say twenty-five or thirty thousand dollars in the years between now and my sixtieth birthday.

'Now I pass up about twenty-five or thirty thousand of honest gain because I like being a detective, like the work. And liking the work makes you want to do it as well as you can. Otherwise there'd be no sense to it. That's the fix I am in. I don't know anything else, don't want to know or enjoy anything else. You can't weigh that against any sum of money. Money is good stuff. I haven't anything against it. But in the past eighteen years I've been getting my fun out of chasing crooks and tackling puzzles, my satisfaction out of catching crooks and solving riddles. It's the only kind of sport I know anything about, and I can't imagine a pleasanter future than twenty-some more years of it.'

Hammett was perhaps the only example of a former private eye drawing convincingly on his experience for fiction. Many of those who tried the much simpler task of relating their lifestyle accurately as fact could not even manage to avoid distortion. Any investigator who steps into the public arena finds it hard to shake off the mantle of myth; even unsung gumshoes find themselves having to sell their efficiency to new clients. Some appear to seek mystique, while others have it thrust upon them.

In Los Angeles, birthplace of the screen investigator, one private detective with a first-class reputation has turned this curious wheel full circle. Logan Clarke manages to operate in a way which even the most inventive movie writer would dismiss as fantasy. Remarkably, it happens to be true ...

4 THE KING OF STING

Life and Death in the Hollywood Hills

Los Angeles, a town of tough deals and casual meetings, has its own kind of Sunday charm. From high on a rooftop it drifts, not in a clamour of bells but in the roar of a police chopper drowning the chatter of a poolside cocktail party. Way below, the streets lie bleached and empty. Quill-shaped cypresses sway among moth-eaten palms on the slopes above Sunset Boulevard. Beyond, wooden homes climb the hillside on frail stilts – huddled in the haze like some biblical citadel. There is a distinct ebb of energy before eight million generators wind up to face Monday morning.

Two women slide beneath the dazzling mirror of the pool to surface lazily like sleek brown water creatures. The helicopter circles for a closer look, then disappears towards the grey soup downtown. At Hollywood and Cahuenga Boulevards it passes over the Bryson Building, where Philip Marlowe had his office: a twenties structure, now laced with fire escapes and fraying at the edges like an old actor's collar.

The hard-nosed, staccato-talking detectives of Chandler and Hammett were a turning-point in the Hollywood image of the private eye. Before them, the characters churned out by the studio machine bore little resemblance to their real-life counterparts. One of the first was William Powell's dapper Philo Vance, created in *The Kennel Murder Case* in 1933. He launched a generation of suave, gentlemanly PIs who swanned through their cases wearing spats and using cigarette holders.

Despite the grittiness of Marlowes and Sam Spades, or TV misfits like Rockford and Magnum, real life is never like art – in most places, anyway. But Hollywood has always been a little different. In Tinseltown the two have a habit of overlaying each other until the edges blur, and the world resembles a 3-D movie without the giveaway cardboard glasses. Hollywood is a *tromp-l'oeil* kind of town where nothing is quite what it seems. A strange place for a private eye to operate – or perhaps in some ways the ideal one.

High in the hills of Hollywoodland, the original stars' community built in 1923, private eye Logan Clarke leans on the wall of his patio and takes in the Sunday scene. It has been a hell of a week, working cases for nineteen hours a day in addition to playing second lead in a movie. Clarke plays an Egyptian hitman who has returned to take over the mind and body of the chief of US National Security in a B-movie called *The Ancient Assassin* written by Brent Mosely. In thirteen movies and a dozen TV crime series, from *Hawaii Five O* to *Hill Street Blues*, he has always been cast as the bad guy.

He has dark, hooded eyes, a Clark Gable moustache and the look of a classic movie tough guy. Acting keeps him sharp for his own special brand of detective work, the reverse sting.

'But that's where the similarity ends,' he says. 'In my business there's no take two. You have to get it right first time, or the chances are someone will blow you away.'

In his fifteen-year career Logan has been stabbed, shot at, had four partners killed and a car boot slammed on his head. Anyone familiar with his methods, on either side of the law, knows that he never gives up. Successful cases include the investigation of a DC-10 air crash, murder-for-hire in Mississippi, an acid rain controversy, countless homicide inquiries and the rescue of more than two hundred kidnapped children.

Logan Clarke is unique in that he combines the two careers of movie acting and private investigation and, somewhere along the way, the screen image of the Hollywood PI and the real investigator have become oddly intertwined. His cases are also consistently bizarre; even Hollywood screenwriters would reject them as improbable.

His friend Alan Cardoza, a successful PI from Laguna Beach, explains: 'When investigators have a case that is too crazy, or dangerous, or something they can't handle, they pick up the phone and call Logan.'

'I call it creative detection,' the man says, hitching his one-year-old daughter onto the patio wall beside him. Darnell, named after Logan's aunt, Hollywood leading lady of the forties Linda Darnell, went on her first undercover operation at the age of four months. 'Most agencies work at arm's length. We prefer to get in close. We go in there and rub shoulders with the best con-men and criminals, deep undercover, and pull the sweetest reverse stings. I tell you:

there is no feeling on earth like knowing that they were really good, but you were just that little bit better.'

Behind him, high on a ridge near the HOLLYWOOD sign, a solitary buzzard soars and circles above the gothic turrets of Valentino's former home. To the right of the house, the lone figure of a woman stands beneath a towering tree. She looks up as the buzzard lifts on an air current, dark against the sun. For an instant, the wings form a sinister cape, as though the shadow of Valentino himself is passing over the landscape.

Planning a reverse sting may take weeks until cover stories and disguise are faultless to the last detail, Logan explained. Agents then try to break each other's cover down to find weaknesses. Some stings, however, have to be improvised on the last minute, 'tap-dancing', as it is known in the business.

A typical Clarke International case involved a businessman client who was approached by a highly professional con team and persuaded to invest $100,000 in a counterfeit money operation, for a return of $150,000. The fake money turned out to be little more than photographic paper, from which the image had disappeared by the time he reached home. The trick was executed by sleight of hand, using identical briefcases. The businessman, chastened but desperate to recover his money, could not go to the police, so he picked up the phone and called Logan.

The counterfeiters were tailed to a hotel, where Logan's team arrived just too late to discover at which floor the elevator had halted. Agents were quickly deployed as guests, but roaming corridors under the watchful eye of hotel security proved almost impossible.

Alan Cardoza, the PI friend of the Clarkes, tried 'tap-dancing'. He approached some decorators in the lobby and said: 'Listen, this may sound crazy, but I'm here on a convention. When I get home I have to wallpaper the house. The problem is, I don't know how to do it. If I worked for you guys for free, would you show me?'

One of the decorators shrugged and asked: 'Do you have any overalls?'

Alan happened to have a pair in the boot of his car (along with an assortment of clothes and uniforms he always carries for such emergencies) plus a paint-spattered baseball cap. With the aid of a wallpaper steamer provided by the workmen, he was able to wander around all the floors, sniffing doors for the telltale smell of counterfeiting chemicals. At one point the hotel owner walked by and commented: 'Nice work, son.'

When the right room was located a specialist was called in. Posing as a businessman, he allowed the con men to sting him, then double-switched the briefcases, leaving with a considerable amount of their money.

'We left fast, when the sting was pulled,' Logan said. 'I walked out of the hotel, calling off the team one by one. Alan dropped the wallpaper steamer, someone else threw a magazine down. We all split. It was like *Mission Impossible*.

'Then, half-way across the carpark, we saw this grey-haired guy, the leader, walking slowly towards us. He had his hand in his pocket and was looking me right in the eye. He knew. And he knew that we knew, too.

'I whispered: "This is it. He's going to blow us away." One of my men was packing, but there wasn't a thing we could do. He pulled his hand out of his pocket and everything went into slow motion. He stood in front of us, then reached out and shook my wife's hand.

'"I don't know who you people are," he said, "but you're damn good. I hope I never see you again."

'He climbed into his car – just left everything right there in the hotel – and took off. For me that was the kick. We had come up against the best and knew that we were just that little bit better.'

A creative detective needs to gather his thoughts. From Monday to Friday Logan retires to his bedroom between twelve and one to watch re-runs of *Bonanza*, the western soap opera screened between 1959 and 1973. Helping Lorne Greene, Mike Landon, Dan Blocker and Pernell Roberts to sort out problems on the Ponderosa Ranch clears his mind for the cases in hand. Saturdays and Sundays, Darnell has a similar effect.

A cool breeze floating through the afternoon heat gently lifted the tablecloth and let it fall. Logan's wife Dona, also an investigator, ruffled her hair, as though it helped to clear her mind of the cases they were working on.

On their first date, when she had left the New York Ballet and was working as a Hollywood choreographer, Logan picked her up in his car. She had just settled into the back when a man built like Mount Rushmore suddenly opened the front passenger door and got in beside Logan. The PI knew he had already killed several people and was looking for him. He had a split second in which to toss his gun into Dona's lap and tell her to keep it pressed against the back of the front passenger seat, right in line with the man's spine.

'If he moves a muscle,' Logan hissed, 'squeeze the goddam trigger.'

He laughed at the memory. 'Dona was shaking so much, I prayed he didn't smoke. If he had reached for a pack of cigarettes, it would have been the St Valentine's Day Massacre.'

The Clarkes lived and worked in a rambling Spanish villa originally built for a silent movie star. It was later the home of Bryce Taylor, the black baseball star turned preacher, who used the living room for Sunday services. Chandler, Sherman & Woodruff, the developers, built the community for the rich and famous who wanted to escape the tepid air of Los Angeles.

'In 1923 the first steam shovel moved its way along the beautiful slopes of the Hollywood Hills,' their sales brochure burbled. 'Skeptics laughed. Who would be so foolish as to hope to wrest from nature a home-place above the march and turmoil of the restless city? ... Today Hollywoodland is an outstanding home community, bringing health and happiness to hundreds who live here, bringing joy to thousands who see its beauty ... '

Nearly seventy years on the HOLLYWOODLAND sign erected by the builders has lost its last four giant letters, but the area remains essentially unchanged. Shaded roads wind round the hillsides among pink and white stucco houses which run an alphabet of styles. A brief tour is like flipping the pages of the *Encyclopaedia of World Architecture* from *adobe* to *ziggurat*. All around, the only sounds are the hissing of lawn sprays and sparrows squabbling in sentinel palms. Celebrities keep a low profile, but their homes are still recognizable – the welcome mats have been replaced by signs warning: 'Armed Response'.

Back in 1956 the Clarkes' street was used as a location for *Invasion of the Body Snatchers*, generally considered a classic of the genre. As a chiller it rated somewhere on the level of *Bambi*, but the irony of it was interesting. Body snatchers turned out to be one of Logan's specialities. And, like the horror movies, the bad guys rarely look like monsters, more like the folks next door.

Child kidnapping is one of the most disturbing and fast-growing problems in the United States. Each month more than 100,000 children are reported missing across the country and many never return. A large proportion are snatched by husbands and wives who have split up with their partners, but do not have legal custody of the children. The police term such cases 'friendly abduction' and are often reluctant to intervene. Parents have little option but to enlist the services of a private eye, which can often be a costly business.

Logan Clarke is one of an élite handful of private eyes who specialize in child abduction cases. He feels so strongly about the plight of kidnapped children that he donates his spare time free to Find the Children and church tracing organizations. The term 'friendly abduction' makes him visibly angry.

'Take it from me,' he says, 'there is nothing friendly about the people responsible for screwing up small lives. I have known kids to have had their hair dyed, their name changed – anything to avoid detection. I have found some of them drugged, or hysterical, and others bound and gagged. Parents who do these things are not motivated by love, as they like to claim.

'"Friendly abduction" makes as much sense as "reasonable homicide". Just how friendly was the father who snatched his baby son from his ex-wife, and then for three years took the kid to lay flowers on a grave every week? The boy completely believed his mother was dead. Any man who is prepared to go to such lengths deserves anything he gets.

'Kidnapped children can be very emotionally disturbed. Anything can happen when you track them down and snatch them back. They sob uncontrollably, scream, freak out. When I plan a case, every move is choreographed for the safety and security of the child. Mom – or whoever the legal parent might be – always comes along.'

A typical example was an ex-California Highway Patrol officer who kidnapped his young daughter from his former wife, and constantly moved her around to avoid detection. Undercover work among friends and relatives revealed that, as an ex-policeman, he had an arrogant belief that no private eye could ever catch him.

Logan and his agents located the man and kept him under

surveillance until the moment was right. The father took the girl to a burger restaurant and sat her down at a table while he crossed the room to place his order at the counter. Within the space of a few seconds, Logan walked through the restaurant, picked up the child from her seat and carried her out.

It was over in the blink of an eye, and probably no one in the restaurant noticed. But anyone re-running the scene in slow motion would have seen three distinct stages. As the private eye lifted the girl from her seat, he simultaneously turned her towards the window. At the same instant, the door of a van parked outside slid back. Sitting inside, directly in the child's line of vision, was her mother. As for the father, the team were two blocks away before he returned from the counter.

Child abduction had taken Logan on many bizarre journeys to the dark side of the human psyche. In the hothouse of the obsessive mind, fantasy, desperation and sexual violence can grow like a cancer, eating steadily at the strands of balance and restraint which hold most people together. When children become the objects of compulsive need, whether sex, money or an image parents feel they must live up to, the detective has always had a difficult case on his hands. Logan had raided adoption rings running baby farms, rescued children from paedophiles and tried to reconcile runaways with their parents. He was successful at what he was hired to do, but once a file was closed, only time and love could heal the wounds.

'At times some decisions are hard to take. As a detective I have to check out my clients and satisfy myself that they have a legal right to the child. But, even when the papers are in order and the law is on their side, it still does not mean that when I get the kid back it is going to be the best solution for everyone.

'I remember tracking down a kid who had been wrongfully abducted by her father. I kept watch on the house, planned the right moment and took my client, the mother, along. As soon as I grabbed the girl and she saw her mom, she started screaming that she didn't want to go back with her. I was sweating because I knew that, at any moment, the guy was going to walk out of the house – and he could be armed.

'The mother froze because, in her dreams, it was the last thing she had expected. I told her: "You've got ten seconds to make a decision. It's going to affect your life. I can't make it for you. Take her, or let her go. Either way, we have to do it now."

'The father made it for her by walking out of the house at that very moment. There was shouting and screaming and I calmed everyone down while we listened to the girl. More than anything she wanted to stay with her daddy. The woman sensed it deep down, even though she had every legal right to take her. It took all of her courage to make that decision and let her stay.

'On the way back in the car, the mother was heartbroken. It just brought her to the floor. But in the end it was the right thing. Before we left she talked to the girl, who was seven, and explained how she felt. Maybe it was the first real time they had talked. The kid promised to write to her, and she did, regularly. The mother and daughter built the relationship they should have had, by being apart. When the girl was old enough, in her teens, she left home and moved in with her. They still keep in touch with me.'

With the exception of such unforeseen events, much of Logan's case planning is carried out in the poolroom adjoining his office. Here, surrounded by showcases of old Hollywood memorabilia and framed photographs of showbusiness friends, the balls spin to the click of cue sticks and crash noisily into pockets. As detectives stalk the table, waiting for their shot, schemes are laid and strategies developed. Sometimes the game is abandoned completely and everyone leans over the table as balls are used to plan the position of cars being followed or houses being watched.

'When I first started retrieving abducted children,' Logan recalled, 'the laws were against anything a private investigator could do. We actually had to re-kidnap the children from the people who had kidnapped them in the first place. This made an already painful situation even worse. If we got caught in a state other than the one we were hired in, we all got thrown into jail. No matter how legal our papers were, they were never recognized in another zone.

'That was all changed by California Assemblyman Gray Davis, who introduced revisions in the law and formulated the Parental Abduction Bill AB2791 in 1986. It was a big breakthrough because it recognized the rights of parents in California to reclaim their missing children.'

Gray Davis approached Logan Clarke in 1986 and asked him to gather evidence for his reforms and to address the State Assembly, a move which is thought to have greatly eased the passage of the Bill. The problem itself, however, has worsened. The Kevin Collins Foundation for Missing Children, based in Los Angeles, took studies from two California towns of 40 children under seventeen who were kidnapped in 1983. Most of them were girls and most were sexually molested and released alive after just a few hours. The majority were dumped from cars before a search could be carried out or 'missing' posters printed.

'I remember when I was a young man working for a newspaper in Chicago,' Tom DeVries of *California* magazine wrote in 1989, 'the assistant city editor looked at me and said flatly: "Any restaurant fire is presumed arson, and any missing teenage girl is presumed shacked up until there is evidence to the contrary." Back then this was useful wisdom. It isn't any more. It is more dangerous to be a kid now than it was then.'

Every child case Logan handles is traumatic but, kids being as delightfully unpredictable as they are, he has learned to expect the unexpected. He once snatched the same set of children three times in all during a prolonged parental dispute. On the last occasion, when he pulled over at the kerb, they waved and shouted: 'Hi, Mr Logan,' and jumped into the back of his car.

Logan still recalls his first child case when he was hired to retrieve a brother and sister from Wilcox, Arizona, a town where the pick-up trucks bristled with shotguns like porcupines.

'The two children I was there to rescue had been traced to separate schools. After keeping them under surveillance, we worked out that each child crossed the playground at exactly the same time, for a period of just two minutes. The problem was that the schools were several blocks apart, so timing was crucial.

'We broke every speed limit and managed to get them in the back of the van. The little boy was OK, but his sister couldn't stop sobbing. I was trying to drive and console her at the same time. I told her everything was OK ... We were on our way to see mommy ... but she still kept crying buckets.

'"Do you know what's wrong?" I asked her brother desperately over my shoulder.

'He gave me a look as though he couldn't believe I was so stupid.

'"She wants her dog," he said.

'By this time the whole town must have been out looking for us, and we knew they had a good description of the vehicle. It didn't mean a thing to the kid. She was still crying like the Niagara Falls. I reckoned another five minutes and we'd be pumping the van out. Eventually, it kind of got to me. I can't stand to hear kids upset, so we made a detour and checked them both into a motel.

'I told my partner: "I'm going back for the dog. If I'm not here in half an hour, take off."

'"Are you crazy?" he said. "We just risked our lives back there, and you're going back for a goddam dog?"

'I sat the girl in a chair and explained what I was going to do.

'"Now what's your dog's name, honey?"

'"Shep," she said. There was a film of tears on her eyes. Every now and then a sob shook her from head to toe.

'"Right. Now, I want you to give me your coat. When I find old Shep, he'll know it's your scent, and he'll come running, OK?"

'"OK," she repeated and gave me a watery smile.

'My partner was standing by the door, banging his head against the wall.

'As she peeled off the coat I patted her brother on the knee and gave him a wink.

'"You're nuts," he said disgustedly.'

Logan rented a car to avoid being recognized and drove back to the ranch where the children had been taken by their father. The front door was open a few inches and he pushed it further. He could see the dog, lying on the floor in a distant room, but when he whispered its name it ignored him.

'That was the moment I discovered I couldn't whistle,' he says. 'I puckered my lips and blew, but nothing came out.'

Ranch hands, curious about the car, were making their way back from the fields towards the house. Logan dived for the dog, grabbed it, and ran headlong for the rental. He threw the animal in the back just as the shout went up. As he accelerated down the drive, trailing a cloud of dust, he saw ranchers running for Jeeps and pick-up trucks in the rear-view mirror. After a hectic chase, the PI managed to shake off his pursuers and return to the motel to reunite the girl with her bewildered pet.

Even then the drama had not ended. Two hundred and forty miles into the Arizona desert, with a fleet of pick-up trucks somewhere behind, the van ran out of petrol. It was the one item in weeks of meticulous planning that Logan and his partner had overlooked.

They found a can in the car boot and trekked miles to an Indian reservation. As they explained their plight the Indians held a whispered conference and decided it was an ideal opportunity to take revenge for the white man's invasion of their lands. The price, they announced, was ten dollars a gallon. When Logan protested, the cost rose until his partner warned: 'Keep your mouth shut before they charge a hundred.'

However, such moments are occasional; there is rarely a lighter side to child abduction. As Tom DeVries reported: 'Many of the children in the Department of Justice files seem simply to have vanished. There are no witnesses, no ransom notes, no abandoned clothing, no body. Nothing for the police to work on, or the families to hold on to. They are just gone, leaving behind wrecked homes and inexpressible anguish.'

At any given time, about half-a-dozen files on Logan's caseload involve missing children. That Sunday, as the afternoon sun shimmered on his Hollywood patio, he took stock of some of them and planned his moves for the week ahead. Circumstances varied, but the underlying grief was the same. A US marine on duty overseas had been told that his daughter had been kidnapped during his absence, probably by his former wife. There was a rumour that she was somewhere in New Mexico. A distraught San Diego mother had walked into her yard and found that her four-year-old son had vanished. Statements indicated that the estranged father, with a history of sex offences, had failed to turn up at court for sentencing on a rape charge and had snatched the boy from over the fence. The County Sheriff's Office was extremely concerned for the child's welfare. An Australian living on a boat at the marina had retained Logan to fly to Brazil to recover his daughter from a remote village where she had been taken by his former wife. He had sold his house and most of his belongings to raise money to get the child back.

Any private eye who has handled cases of this type will confirm that parents will go to any lengths to recover stolen children. The moment of truth for the investigator, who has perhaps hired aircraft and dozens of agents to accomplish the mission, is when the reunion is over, life returns to normal and he sends in his bill.

'It's a tough business,' Logan reflected. 'I have had wealthy clients who have instructed me that money was no object. When the child is safe, they query the bill item by item and often refuse to pay. They forget very quickly that we are the guys who have put our lives on the line. Detectives always smile when they hear the expression "money is no object". What it usually means is they object to paying it. I took some sound advice from an old PI many years ago about child cases. "Son," he said, "always bill them while the tears are wet."'

On the other side of the coin, there are occasions when no amount of personal wealth can repair the deep rifts in parent-child relationships and the private investigator asks himself why he took on the case in the first place. Logan was once hired to take legal custody of a headstrong teenage girl who had disappeared from Los Angeles' Cedars of Sinai Hospital in the middle of a drug rehabilitation programme. Her wealthy parents simply provided him with the necessary papers and instructed him to bring her back.

Logan knew she was violent and elusive before he followed her, late at night, into an LA park. He was ready for anything. Well, almost …

'There was no way she was going to come with me quietly. I grabbed and she fought back. We were rolling around in the bushes. She pulled a knife and stabbed me in the leg and started hollering: "Help. They're kidnapping me. They're gonna take me to Iran and sell me into prostitution." I could see lights going on here and there and managed to get the knife away and put some handcuffs on her.

'She kept fighting and screaming until a van pulled up. These guys who were in a college football team jumped out and decided to be heroes. In the middle of all this, while I was trying to hang onto her, getting the shit kicked out of me, an L.A.P.D. patrol car arrived.

'These officers knew who I was, but they were playing very cool, like, "What's the trouble here, ma'am?" I told them: "Look, I'm a licensed PI. This girl has escaped from Cedars of Sinai and I have all the legal papers to take her back."

'"So you're a PI?" they said, straightfaced. "Then we're sure you'll have the ID to prove that."

'I was getting mad with these guys, but I thought, if that's the way they want to play it, then I'll go along. I patted my pockets and realized that I had changed coats without bringing my ID along. It was the first time it had ever happened.

'"I don't have it with me," I said. "But just ring my wife, she'll come right here with it, now."

'The officers exchanged looks and one said to the other: "He doesn't have it with him ... " Then they turned to me and said: "Well sir, this is what we'll do. We'll take these cuffs off of this lady here, and we'll put them right on you."

'And that's just what they did. I couldn't believe it. The girl took off into the bushes and they drove me downtown. They thought it was some kind of joke. When they took me into the precinct – and I looked a real mess by this time – all the guys were grinning and saying: "Hey, here comes Rockford again."'

Logan's work has taken him around the world in search of missing children, following leads in South Africa, Australia, England and the Far East. Once a child crosses an international border, enormous problems can arise in bringing it out of the country again. Foreign states who are signatories to the Hague Convention, established before World War One as an attempt to arbitrate in international disputes, tend to make the task easier. Less enlightened nations which have sidestepped the rights of parents to be lawfully reunited with their children – Britain is one of them – place enormous and unnecessary pressures on all sides.

Mexico is a notorious haven for child snatchers, who take advantage of cumbersome bureaucracy which makes the repatriation of abducted youngsters a nightmare. Years ago, Logan learned much of this specialized aspect of his craft from a veteran private eye called Walt Zwonitzer.

'He had a big name and no one could pronounce it, so everybody just called him the Big Z,' he explained. 'There were two PIs we sometimes came across – they're still around – who could never get it right. They loved car chases, helicopter chases and left wrecks everywhere. We call them Happy and Peewee. One time they got themselves into a real mess on a child case down in Mexicali and called the Big Z and me to bail them out.'

Logan peeled off his T-shirt as the afternoon sun slanted through the windows of his tiny office. The long shadows gave it the appearance of a Mike Hammer PI movie set. There was room for a shredder, a desk covered with case files, two chairs and little else. Towering over it all was a bentwood hat stand hung with a trenchcoat and fedora, the Hollywood symbol of the private eye. The walls, bamboo blind and well-worn filing cabinet were covered with handbills about missing children. On a bookshelf radios crackled, filling the room with bursts of static as agents called in from surveillance operations. In a wooden frame, behind glass, a cutting from the *LA Times* carried the heading: 'If Bogey were alive today he would be playing Logan Clarke.'

'Retrieving a stolen child from Mexico is never without problems,' he said. 'Going in is a piece of cake – there are never any *Federales* waiting at the arrival gate – it's the getting out that's pure hell. The laws are not just grey in this area of detective work, officials have a palette to paint them any colour they choose.'

Happy and Peewee had been hired by an American military attaché and his wife when a maid absconded with their baby. They had tracked the woman down to a block of flats on the outskirts of Mexicali where she ran a babies-for-sale racket, in an area patrolled by gangs armed with shotguns. Happy had succeeded in dating her but had forgotten to slip a quantity of sleeping draught into her bedtime milk. When she went to the kitchen, he panicked, jerked his hand and poured in a whole phial. The woman became delirious, singing and dancing round the room, before sliding into a deep sleep.

'In desperation, he called Cal, a girl PI who was also a registered nurse,' Logan went on. 'Cal took one look at her and said: "If you don't get her to hospital in the next twelve hours, you're going to spend time in a Mexican jail." That's when Happy and Peewee called us. There was no way they could get the woman and the baby past those guards.

'We flew out with no client, no file and, worst of all, no retainer. But what we did have was Cal. As the Big Z used to say: "If she was a man, her balls would outweigh her brains."'

Logan and the Big Z calculated that the only way to avoid suspicion was to use an ambulance. From a bar half a mile away they made a hoax call and, when the two-man ambulance crew arrived, offered them a wad of dollars to borrow their uniforms and vehicle for half an hour. The ambulancemen readily agreed and settled down at the counter with a round of drinks. Logan, lean and tall, and Zwonitzer, big and stocky, had trouble squeezing into the jackets and trousers.

'By the time we arrived, Cal had bought packs of beer for all these organized crime figures. She was playing the tourist, trying to do a Mexican dance on the grass outside the apartment, with her shirt tied up round her stomach. These guys couldn't take their eyes off her, so we just slipped in with the stretcher.

'With Happy and Peewee's help we got the woman and baby out to the ambulance, but people started gathering round, asking us in Spanish what was going on.'

The PIs shouldered them away and, as Cal made a last-minute dive for the rear doors, roared off. At the bar they left the woman in the ambulance and told the crew to take her to hospital, providing the happy men both with money and a genuine call. Unfortunately, some of the baby farm guards were in pursuit. Happy and Peewee's getaway vehicle turned out to be a VW Beetle. There was a problem shoehorning the Big Z inside as several shots were fired, but eventually they out-manoeuvred their pursuers and returned the baby safely.

The caper is one which has undoubtedly improved with the telling, but the facts are indisputably on the case file. It serves in some way to illustrate the layers of Logan's character. Despite the meticulous planning which has to go into an operation to ensure personal survival, he still gets a charge of adrenalin from the action and, above all, creative satisfaction in outwitting criminals who have planned with equal care. Which is why he has a reputation, above child cases and any other type of specialized work, for the reverse sting.

The talk turned to the subject of dangerous stings. Logan, drawing on a long-necked Corona beer, recalled one of his several encounters with Southern California's tough Hell's Angels gangs.

The case was that of a Hollywood attorney whose son was charged with stabbing to death two Hell's Angels. Despite his plea of self-defence, there were fourteen Hell's Angels witnesses who claimed otherwise. When the outcome looked bleak, the lawyer sent for Logan.

The PI walked into the bar where the deaths had occurred, wearing a baseball cap and a T-shirt bearing the slogan 'Stunts

Left: Vidocq, the convict turned detective who founded the French Sûreté and later became the world's first private detective

Below: William Anthony, last of the 'Charlies', the eighteenth-century watchmen engaged to guard property in London

Allan Pinkerton
(motto: 'We Never Sleep'),
the USA's pioneer
private eye

(Chicago Historical Society)

Photographs from
Pinkerton's own files
used to identify
safebreakers

American police methods of identifying
criminals were inspired by Pinkerton's
private 'rogues' gallery'

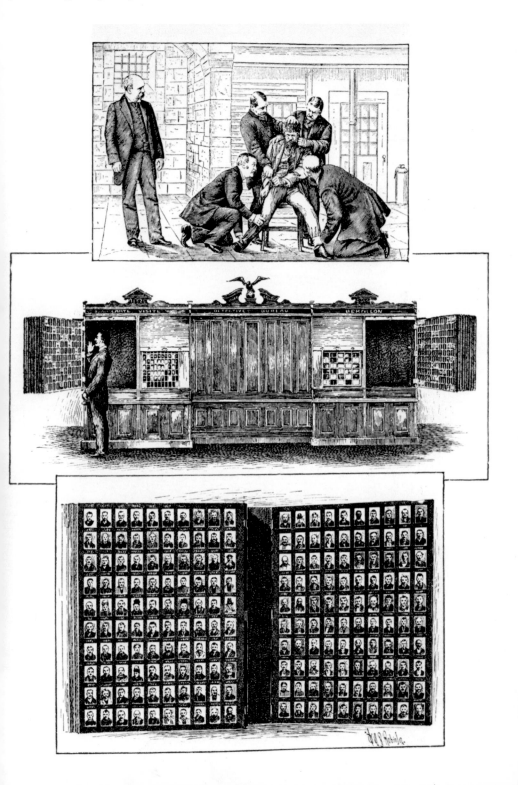

The James Gang, who left a trail of train robberies across the Midwest, were high on Pinkerton's target list

Left: William Burns, arguably
the USA's greatest private
investigator, with one of his
agency cars

(Burns International Security Services)

Below: Burns, pioneer of private
forensic studies, in his laboratory

(Burns International Security Services)

Right: A Burns agent guards the
platform at the 1988 Presidential
inauguration of George Bush

(Burns International Security Services)

Left: Annette Kerner, veteran British detective of the 1940s and 1950s, used a wardrobe of disguises

Below left: Charlie Chrystall in his seedy Piccadilly offices, *circa* 1955. Chrystall's love affair with publicity led to his eventual downfall

Oscar Heinrich, 'the Wizard of Berkeley', the American investigator who developed many of the forensic techniques later used by the FBI

Left: The boat detective: Peter Clark's secret operations take him as far as Rio and the Caribbean

Right: 'I cover the waterfront' – private eye Hector Pyas (centre) at work in Gibraltar

Left: Oldham P.I. Jim Lyness, now retired, who took on the daunting task of tracking the Yorkshire Ripper

(*Lancashire Evening Post*)

Above: The Tytell family in their laboratory off New York's Wall Street. Martin, Pearl and Peter are among the USA's foremost document experts

Clockwise from right:
Murder investigator Bill Dear in his Dallas office – the guns are all loaded

Dear's fortified headquarters in the Dallas suburb of DeSoto

Veteran P.I. Dick Riddle on a case with Bill Dear. The black Corvette is their mobile communications centre

Dear (left) tries to reconstruct the death of businessman Glenn Courson behind the generator truck

Right: Jay J. Armes in the well-guarded
grounds of his Texas home, with son
Jay and Siberian tiger Gemini

Below: Armes in his hi-tech
El Paso office, reminiscent of a
James Bond movie set

Right: Italian police evaluate a haul of counterfeit goods after a raid in Milan organized by Carratu

(*Carratu International*)

Vincent Carratu, the former Scotland Yard officer who became the world's leading expert on anti-counterfeiting

(*Carratu International*)

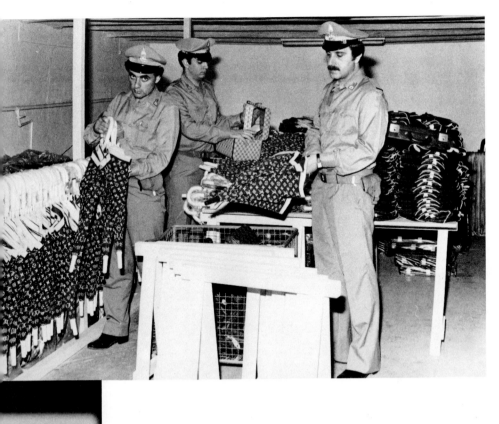

Below: Fake watches impounded
during a raid by Carratu International
on premises in Germany

(*Carratu International*)

The King of Sting – Hollywood actor and
licensed P.I. Logan Clarke, with beard to
disguise his appearance

Unlimited'. The bar was owned by the Angels, their girlfriends were the waitresses, and few outsiders had ever dared to venture in.

Logan drank there for a week, threatened by stares. On one occasion, an Angel kicked a hole in the cement floor with the steel toecap of his boot, and said: 'Imagine what that would do to your chest.' Logan agreed that it would hurt very much, but doggedly continued to patronize the place.

Finally, as he hoped, the Angels gathered round and asked what he was doing. There was an obvious consensus that he must be out of his mind. Logan explained that he had to arrange a movie fight scene, and was looking for the right location. (His attention to detail was so great that he actually wrote a complete movie script to cover his story.)

To focus their interest, he offered the Angels $100 a bike to leave their Harleys outside for 'atmosphere'. The proposal was received with approving murmurs and they soon began to ask him about the fight scene.

'Just come in here any Saturday night,' one of them volunteered. 'You'll see plenty.'

'I can't,' Logan explained. 'See, it has to be done this certain way.' And he described a fight not dissimilar to the one in which his client had been involved. The Angels took the bait.

One of them, quite drunk, commented: 'Hey, that's like the guy who came in here the other week and stabbed two of the Chapter.'

Heads nodded in agreement.

'What happened?' Logan asked.

'Oh, some cowboy walked in for a drink, so we broke a pool cue over his head.'

'Jeez. I bet that put him down.'

'Naw, it didn't. So we broke another over his head. It was then that he pulled a knife.'

The case was clearly one of self-defence, despite the Angels' distortion of the facts to the District Attorney. Logan's problem was obtaining a witness statement to prove it.

'You know, that's fantastic,' the PI said, visibly impressed. 'Much better than the stuff I've got here in the script. In fact, it's terrific. Look, could you write that down for me, just as it happened?'

The Angel shrugged and obliged, laboriously scrawling the details of the pool cues and the attack.

When he had finished, Logan read it and beckoned him closer, in confidence. 'You know, this is so good,' he said, 'I want to make sure you get a consultant's fee. Trouble is, you can't trust nobody in movies. If they saw an idea like this, they'd just rip it off.'

'Oh, yeah?'

'Yeah, believe me. It's your idea and I want them to know it's yours. Look, put your name on the bottom here, and there'll be no mistake where it came from.'

The Angel scratched his name and, after another drink, the detective left. Back at the DA's office, the staff could barely believe that he had obtained a witness statement from a Hell's Angels gang member.

'Well,' Logan explained. 'He doesn't *exactly* know it's a statement. See, he thinks it's a movie script.'

His client was released without trial.

Clarke International is one of the few agencies which has a twice-weekly case conference to monitor progress on each file. Agents assemble in a basement bunker, known as the War Room, to report on how their individual work is moving, and what needs to be done. The room, which has only one tiny window, is cooled by a twenty-four-inch fan and dominated by a blackboard and full-length photographs of James Dean, Clark Gable and Humphrey Bogart. Detectives run through their caseload, while Logan interrupts to issue orders or give advice. It may be that a detective has obtained a subject's phone number, but is unsure how to make the best approach to gather the right information. More often than not, Logan will ask for the number and make a 'gag call' there and then.

'I have no idea what I am going to say until I start dialling the number,' he explained. 'I may be representing a credit card company, offering them a year, charge-free, if they answer a few questions, or a phone company, or a travel bureau. Using the name of a real company can get you into trouble – I always invent them, and people never question it.'

He sees the calls as a kind of art form, created completely off the cuff but within a framework of tested rules.

'If your cover is good, there is nothing you cannot uncover,' he went on. 'The key to the whole thing is picking the right cover, the right con. But once you have picked the right one, you must always leave yourself a back door to get out of. For example, we do a lot of cons where we make up a credit card, say the Citywide Visa Corporation, which is going to appeal to a middle or lower class income group.

'Now if you call and offer them a free credit card and they say they've already got one, your call's over. You need a backup to keep the con going. You have to say: "Yes, we know you already have a credit card, but this is a new one specially for travel. If you answer a few simple questions you don't have to make your first payment for six months."

'You also have to be able to put them on and take them off again, so they are never aware of what you are doing. If I call a bank, for example, to check a multi-million account there is a chance that, the next time he talks to his client, the guy will say: "So and so called to check you out – they said you had applied for a loan."

'So you have to get all your information out of them, wait five minutes and call them back. You say: "Remember I called about Lew Rogers? Is that Lew *R*. Rogers?" And they say: "No, Lew *A*. Rogers."

'"Was he born in '47?" ... You know he was born in '51.

'"No."

'"Man, I really screwed up. I got the wrong branch, the wrong guy, even the wrong birthday."

'You apologize and take them off completely. So when they do talk to their client, they're not about to mention it to him, because it was all a complete mistake. You put them on and you take them off. If you don't take them off, as we say in the business, it's going to piss backwards on you.'

At the time Logan was working on 49 cases, each of them worthy of a TV movie. Uppermost in his mind is the executive who creamed off eight million dollars in kick-backs from company contracts and successfully moved the money offshore. When he was sacked, he served his former employers with a multi-million-dollar lawsuit for wrongful dismissal. Unfortunately, he was fired with insufficient evidence. Unless Logan can save them, the company stands to pay dearly for its oversight.

The detective has already put a plan into action. 'Everyone has a weakness,' he says. 'Most people need something, whether it's money, sex, drugs, whatever – in his case it's money. He has bought a company which imports statues to funnel his cash back into the country. We plan to place an order so big he won't be able to resist it.'

A letter of credit for $3 million had already been placed in a bank account opened by two women agents. They intended to call at the suspect's business, admire the statues, and place an order for them bigger than he could ever hope to fulfil. As days went by there would be angry faxes from their overseas clients asking for the suspect's credentials. The women would accuse him of being unable to meet the deal and suggest that he was a man of no substance. A combination of skill, luck and the right kind of pressure might force him to reveal assets he would not normally admit to, rather than lose the sale. It was a simple, direct appeal to greed. The executive, of course, would have no idea that the two attractive women had papers granting them authority to seize his assets.

However, events had taken an unusual turn. The suspect had suddenly offered to go to his former employer's attorneys and make a voluntary deposition. Logan was extremely suspicious, particularly as he had discovered that the man was going in alone and unrepresented. At the back of his mind lurked the uneasy thought that the screw had turned too tightly and, in desperation, he might be planning to shoot up the attorney's office.

After the briefing, Logan deputized Steve, a young detective, to sit with a gun under his coat at the law offices which he feared might be shot up by the corrupt executive. In the event, nothing happened and the meeting went without incident.

There were other matters to attend to. A con man who had absconded with $260,000 had been traced to Phoenix, Arizona, and detectives there were waiting for Logan to fly out and interview him. The Phoenix case file read like the plot of a TV movie: Joe, the client, started life with one ambition – to become a movie producer. The only way he could raise capital was to invest in pornographic films. He had some success in this and eventually made $3 million. Joe then invested one million in a legitimate movie and lost it all in an elaborate con.

Then he invested another million in a movie, which was actually made. Ironically it was about a private eye. Unfortunately, Joe was ripped off on the distribution and lost his second million. The only way back to the top was to invest in porn again, this time discreetly: after all, one day he hoped to have a reputation and he was not anxious to ruin it.

Joe then meets Rick and Brett who are planning to make a porn movie. It seems a good idea. So Joe, still chasing his star, hands them $260,000 in cash. The front door has no sooner closed behind him, than Rick's parole officer arrives and insists that he takes a drug test. Rick, who had smoked a little pot that morning, declines. He is arrested on the spot and taken away.

Brett, a con man with a weakness for other people's money, finds himself alone in the house with a briefcase containing $260,000. He follows his instincts and runs. Joe hires Logan to recover the money, it isn't easy. The signs are that Brett is burning through it at the rate of $10,000 a day. He already has a speed boat, a new car and several other luxuries.

But there is hope. Logan has traced him to Phoenix where his mother lives. Brett also has to report there weekly to his parole officer. Unfortunately, as Logan is closing in, Brett's parole officer goes on holiday, telling the con man that he has no obligation to turn in and report. Logan plans to fly to Arizona with a karate black belt and tell Brett that there is no way the money is going to last him the rest of his life. Because that is at least how long it will take for him to hide. Hopefully Brett will concede defeat and hand it over. This particular case turned into such a miasma of accusation and counter-accusation between the parties that Logan disconnected himself and left them to it.

Surveillance work has become increasingly complex in recent years. A vast selection of microphones, lenses and remote eavesdropping devices are available through trade magazines. 'Many of them are not as efficient as they look,' says British sound recordist Simon Bishop. 'They all claim to be highly effective state-of-the-art stuff, but technically many are less than perfect. There is now such a variety of them on offer that the market is clearly enormous.'

While the age of information moves inexorably towards more sophisticated hardware, Logan Clarke prefers to observe, not through a telescopic lens, or with the aid of a parabolic mike, but at close quarters, relying on the old-fashioned yardstick of intuition and experience. He places great emphasis on a subject's body language, eye contact and voice tone, which transmit tiny signals electronic equipment is incapable of receiving.

In many ways he has reverted to the technique of the traditional Hollywood PI who rubbed shoulders with his target. In the office, computer tracing still occupies a large percentage of each case. It is fast, efficient and saves hundreds of man hours. The Clarkes view high technology as tools rather than toys. Staff attend computer seminars to keep abreast of new developments, but in the field they always prefer to make personal contact.

The qualifications to hold a California Private Investigator's Licence are stringent. Each applicant must have 3000 hours on-the-job training, logged and verified. Then he or she has to study for a ninety-minute written examination, followed by oral questions. The selection process is purposely difficult and the failure rate high. Emphasis is placed on practical training because, despite a plethora of textbooks and manuals, some aspects of detection come only with experience.

Logan sees close undercover work as a skill which is acquired only gradually. He regards the con as a creative art form and, within the industry, there is a high regard for his type of expertise. Detectives can buy instruction books on how to con records from telephone companies. The techniques are fairly simple, widely used, but highly illegal.

A *Study of Telephone Records* by Ralph D. Thomas carries the careful disclaimer: 'The information found in this report is for illustration only. Certain activities and devices, if actually used, would be a violation of certain federal, state and local laws ... This report deals with a highly sensitive subject. It should be kept out of the hands of children and criminals.'

But apparently not private detectives. The first print run sold out almost immediately, and a second edition is currently on sale. The book, tongue in cheek, is 'dedicated to the proposition that all men have an equal right to quest for knowledge'. Whether that knowledge happens to be someone else's business is not explored.

The ploys explained would enable anyone to obtain unlisted numbers, records of long-distance phone calls, copies of telephone bills, or addresses for phone numbers. The only qualifications required appear to be a cool nerve and a confident manner. According to the author, telephone company staff can be persuaded to read out, or post, confidential information, if the enquirer is plausible enough.

Methods include posing as someone who needs a bill because they are straightening out their financial affairs in preparation for a divorce; pretending to be a subscriber who is going away for a long time and wants to pay his bill up to date; or a resident requesting proof that his flatmates have been making long-distance calls and have not paid for them. The permutations are endless and ingenious.

Here is a brief example, quoted in Mr Thomas's spirit of the equal right to quest for knowledge:

'Telephone company sales: Thank you for calling. May I help you?

'Customer: Yes, this is Joy Trackemdown. I had my mother staying with me last month. She made all these long distance phone calls and I gave them to her to pay. She lost the bill and now doesn't remember making them. Could you give them to me again so I can refresh her memory?'

Some detectives, of course, prefer to do it the easy way and have a contact inside the company who will run checks for $50 a time. Multiply that by several PIs, each with a heavy caseload, and the answer is a lucrative second income.

Failing that, there is always the desperate method inspired by Al Pacino, who played a lawyer in Norman Jewison's 1979 movie ... *And Justice For All*. It was the night before an important court case and he was unable to locate a vital witness. After spending weary hours ringing everyone with a similar name in the telephone book, the postman walked into his office with his phone bill. Pacino, in a flash of inspiration, realised that his contact's bill would also be delivered that morning. Somewhere on it would be a list of calls made to the witness. The lawyer raced round to the contact's apartment and plucked the bill from the letterbox.

In the movie, the case was saved. In real life the technique guarantees a heavy fine or jail sentence for tampering with the mail. Instead, as Ralph D. Thomas points out, many PIs take a leaf from the security services' little black book and purchase a spray which makes an envelope transparent, before the moisture evaporates without leaving a trace.

Such dirty tricks are unlawful, unconstitutional and infringe the right to privacy. However, it remains an unpalatable fact that pressures on private eyes from people determined to obtain information on other people are at an all-time high, and show every sign of rising. Clients are not necessarily multinationals, insurance companies contesting claims, or defence lawyers, but ordinary people seeking information, for a variety of reasons, on neighbours, partners and friends. Private eyes argue that, far from getting out of hand, the investigation industry is doing what, historically, it has always done – trying to keep pace with the demands of a rapidly changing society.

In Britain, where there is a climate of greater secrecy regarding the exchange of information, the Association of British Investigators insists that its members work within the law. Nevertheless, a handful of companies who are not registered members make exceptionally high earnings sidestepping legalities. One company, which rarely advertises, produced bank statements, standing order payment slips and telephone records within 24 hours at a client's request. As Jay J. Armes the El Paso PI once boasted: 'They don't call bank staff tellers for nothing.'

Logan Clarke's preferred method of personal contact, based on an unusual acting gift, means that evidence is invariably proffered directly by the subject himself. San Diego marina proved to be a classic example.

Cam and Logan drove to San Diego on a hot Sunday afternoon in July, joining the thundering herd of weekenders heading south on the freeway in the quest for a cool sea breeze and cold beer. High overhead, a long thin cloud trailed landwards from the Pacific like a flock of lazy white gulls. No rain had fallen on Southern California for more than six months. The sunshine, like the PI's seven-day week, was unrelenting.

Their client was a woman company president whose long marriage had broken up acrimoniously. Her husband was claiming maintenance from her on the grounds that he was unemployed and disabled, and his former wife had the means to provide for him. The woman had heard that he had a girlfriend and was living on a $200,000 seagoing cruiser, moored in San Diego dock. She also suspected that, far from having the back injury he claimed, he was fit and healthy. The court hearing was scheduled for one week's time, and the agency had promised to produce results.

Cam, a movie actor in addition to working as a PI, was tall with sun-bleached hair and a sandpaper voice that sounded like a rock singer after a three-month road tour. He looked every inch the yacht bum his role demanded. Logan, dressed like a Hawaiian holiday-maker with his beach-shirt collar turned over a white linen jacket, was a film producer. He had supposedly hired Cam to help him find a boat to charter for a promotional video he was making for a British boat haulage firm. The company, Sealand, was real and a director had been talked into sending a fax on headed paper to confirm the story. They knew, even as they drove south, overtaking lumbering campers and Beetles laden with surfboards, that the subject would not be there. He had been invited to a family wedding, and his absence suited them perfectly.

At the boat dock, they slipped through the mesh gates behind a yachtsman who had a security pass and worked their way down a long line of moored boats, well away from the cruiser they were interested in. The PIs took in the sea air, gossiped with boat buffs and generally spread the word that they were hoping to hire a 40-foot seagoing cruiser.

'You could try the guy moored at the end there,' an old-timer said, emptying a slop bucket over the side, 'but I think he's away at a wedding. Maybe I could give him a message.'

'Better than that,' Logan replied. 'I'll leave you my card and maybe you could get him to call me.'

They left the old man studying a card which featured a roll of movie film with the words *Hollywood Capers Inc.* across one of the frames. From a psychological viewpoint, the approach was ideal. The story would come, not from two strangers, but the subject's own neighbour who would enthusiastically pass on the word that there was money to be made. Logan was always happier if the subject could be manoeuvred into taking the initiative, rather than working cold to sell him a line.

Cam and Logan returned to LA confident that the man would ring the next day. The business card carried the number of a special gag line reserved for such enterprises. In that way, no detective who happened to be passing a desk would pick up the phone and accidentally announce, 'Clarke International Investigations'.

In the afternoon of the following day the gag line rang, a signal for general conversation to drop to a whisper and incoming calls to be diverted to other rooms. As they had guessed, it was the subject, asking if someone was looking to hire a boat.

Logan, who always appears most relaxed when playing a role, slipped into world-weary producer mode, cleverly slackening the line before reeling him in.

'That's right,' he said, 'but I'll tell you upfront there isn't too much money in it. Maybe around $500 a day for two-and-a-half weeks. Peanuts, I know … '

From the silence at the other end, it was more akin to giant coconuts.

'Sounds interesting,' the subject said, trying not to sound interested. The voice filling the room from the speaker box possibly came from deep beneath a designer sports shirt and gold medallion.

'Well, the problem is I'm looking for something kinda special. I don't think your boat's quite right. What I really had in mind was a forty-foot seacruiser.'

'That's me,' the voice said. 'I've got a forty-foot seacruiser. That's what I've got.'

Logan sounded doubtful. 'Yeah, but what I need is something with an awning on the back. You know, you can get a lot of bad reflection off the water … '

'I got an awning.' The ratchet of desperation wound up a notch.

'You have? Yeah, that's right,' Logan said. 'I remember now. But I don't think we can use it. See, the film crew's got to have something that projects about three feet over the water … '

The voice rose an octave. 'Mine does. My awning goes out at least three or four feet. That's exactly what it does.'

Logan paused, lost in thought. 'Then there's the drinks problem,' he said.

'Drinks?'

'Hey, you know what film crews are like. Between takes they're looking for a floating bar.'

'I got drinks on board,' the voice said. 'Name a drink, I've got it.'

'No, no,' Logan said with gravity. 'We are talking wine coolers here.'

'No problem. There must be, what, two, three wine coolers here.'

'Mmnn.' Logan sounded unimpressed. 'OK,' he said doubtfully, 'I'll come down and see you. Do you work, or can I come tomorrow?'

'No, I don't work. I'm getting a divorce, you know? I've got a heap of problems.'

The man was now talking so much about his divorce, the PI had a problem shutting him up.

Logan arrived at the dockside on a baking afternoon which made the wide blue horizon shimmer in a heat haze. Even the golden girls usually sunning themselves on boat decks had retreated to the air conditioning below. Cam, in shorts and T-shirt, was in his role as yacht bum. Alan Cardoza, a PI friend from Laguna Beach, played production executive, with a video camera tucked under his arm.

Logan had a brief problem when he discovered that one of his detectives had helpfully taped a list of his most-used numbers to his new mobile phone. They included L.A.P.D. vice squad and homicide department. He hurriedly peeled them off to find that they had been printed on the back of a Clarke International business card. Logan caught up with the others to greet the subject who was waiting for them.

Aboard the cruiser a welcome breeze rose from the water and the conversation was relaxed and informal. When Logan asked the owner if he could move the boat up to the dock a little, he was anxious to oblige. He jumped ashore, unwound the rope from a bollard and physically hauled the craft to the required position.

'Jeez,' said Logan in admiration. 'What does it weigh, a boat like this?'

'About ten tons maybe,' the man replied breathlessly.

'How do you get to be so fit?'

'Oh, working out,' he said modestly. 'I go down to the gym most days.'

Back on board and under way, down the narrow channel which connects the marina to the open sea, the owner sat at the wheel and talked about his divorce. The camera under Alan's arm was running to capture evidence to use in court.

'Don't talk to me about women,' Logan said sympathetically at one point.

'You know,' the man said, grinning, 'she even tried to put a PI on my tail. She must think I'm stupid, or something.'

'Wow,' said the detective slack-jawed. 'I never saw a private eye for real. What do those guys look like?'

Logan's client, who won her case, was delighted with the results, particularly a section of tape in which her former husband claimed that his attorney had advised him to fake a back injury to strengthen his case. Later, behind the wheel of his Chrysler Le Baron, climbing home up Beachwood, past Bette Davis's old home and the village coffee shop Barry Manilow wrote a song about, 'Beachwood Café', Logan wound down and reflected on the job.

'It gives me a rush when something goes well like that,' he said. 'I see people's lives like a circle. Whenever there's a break in it and it's not complete, they call me. Some of them are desperate, but I always quote some lines to them:

> He drew a circle that shut me out:
> Oh, what a tremendous thing to flout.
> But wit and I had the will to win,
> We drew a circle and took him in.'

Not all stings have the good fortune to work so smoothly. One of the most dangerous operations to emerge at the briefing had gone hopelessly wrong and might have endangered the lives of Logan's wife Dona and another woman agent, Brenda.

The Clarkes had never met their client. They had been hired by his family and dealt only through his attorneys, who knew him as a wealthy Jewish businessman. At the family's insistence, strict ground rules were laid at the first meeting – they were never to make any attempt to contact him and his name was never to be mentioned outside the office.

He was serving an eighteen-month sentence at Lompoc Prison, a grim fortress of coiled wire and watchtowers on a peninsula 300 miles north of Los Angeles. The businessman, imprisoned for selling helicopters to the North Koreans, was held in an area of relaxed security known as Club Fed. In contrast to the high-security wing, which housed Cubans who had burned down a prison in Miami, Club Fed had a gym, jogging track and tennis court and was regarded as a jail for white-collar crime. Some of the Watergate people had been held there, along with the Wall Street share dealer Ivan Boesky and an assortment of fraudsters and financial racketeers. But Club Fed was far from being the penal paradise it appeared.

The pecking order established by hardened criminals in high security dominated every section of the prison. Lompoc was run by four organized gangs whose members were recognized by a secret code of tattoos. Everyone was obliged to swear allegiance to one of them, and those who declined faced unthinkable consequences.

The gangs, whose activities were known throughout the US penal system, were particularly influential on the West Coast. The most disruptive, according to the *Georgia Criminal Activity Bulletin*, a restricted-circulation publication issued to prison staff, were the Mexican Mafia, the Nuestra Famila – formed for protection against the Mexican Mafia – the Black Guerrilla Famila and the white supremacist Aryan Brotherhood.

Logan's client, as a Jew, had been singled out for racist persecution by the powerful Aryan Brotherhood and feared for his life. Two prison friends had already been kicked down a flight of steel stairs for reasons explained as 'attitude adjustment'. What terrified him above everything was that there was no hope of reporting the nightmare he was forced to suffer, as certain members of the prison staff were also suspected of belonging to the Aryan Brotherhood.

As the first year of his eighteen-month sentence drew to a close, the client looked forward to transfer to a half-way house, away from the violence and intimidation. Under normal circumstances, it would have been a fairly automatic procedure, rubber-stamped by a committee of six guards, or 'line hacks', who had immediate control over him. Despite five of them offering no objections to rehabilitation, the move was blocked without reason by their immediate superior, who was thought to be an Aryan Brotherhood member. With no hope of relief, the client was living each day in desperation.

The *Georgia Criminal Activity Bulletin* carried a footnote on the organization: 'Formed at San Quentin in 1967 and evolved from the Diamond Tooth Group whose membership is closely controlled and represents the motor-cycle gang type inmate, who is against the prison system because of a violent dislike of authority of any kind. Members, primarily racists with drug contacts, formed an

alliance with the Mexican Mafia based on mutual hatred of blacks
and a common desire to control drug traffic. An alliance also exists
with the Charles Manson gang over drug matters. Fierce rivalry
exists between members of opposing groups.'

For a mild-mannered Jewish businessman, it was as though all of
his worst dreams had come true.

The main thrust of Logan's case was somehow to prove that the
staff officer was racist in order to get the half-way house opportunity upheld and his client out of Club Fed. Dona and Brenda drove
to the town of Lompoc (pronounced Lom-poke, as in cow-poke), a
thriving community deriving its income from the penitentiary,
nearby Vandenburg Air Base and the NASA-funded Air Force
Space Shuttle Project.

The local library had material about the history of the prison,
since its foundation in 1959 on the site of an army disciplinary
barracks, and numerous magazine articles on the penal system.
Oddly, the library's catalogued files on racism and white supremacy
had all been removed. The women decided to infiltrate Club Fed and
the penitentiary as students working on a master's thesis on penal
reform.

The plan worked well, despite the unthinkable consequences of
being caught, or anyone in the prison knowing the true purpose of
their regular visits. But one day the unthinkable did happen, and
only by remarkable good fortune did it occur on a day when the
women were not at Lompoc but writing reports in the office.

Someone at the prison had checked the registration number of
their car and linked it to the agency. For around three dollars
anyone in America can run a trace on an automobile licence plate,
but the authorities, sensitive to civil rights, always notify the owner
about the enquiry. Private detectives, after lengthy lobbying, are
allowed to check tag numbers without the knowledge of the registered owner.

Soon afterwards, Lompoc's warden, R. H. Rison, called Logan
and told him he had reason to believe that two detectives were
working undercover in the prison. If no satisfactory explanation
was given, he warned, the matter would be reported to the FBI.

The two women were shocked by the thought that their cover
might have been exposed while they were inside the prison perimeter. Brenda was particularly jittery. The previous day, after

leaving Lompoc, she had stopped for petrol and was propositioned by two huge, Nordic-looking biker-types in a pick-up truck, whose arms were tattooed with Aryan Brotherhood symbols. The PI made an excuse and drove away, but the incident left her suspicious and nervous.

Logan managed to talk his way out of the problem with the warden, but it was now clearly too dangerous to try to obtain information directly from the prison. Instead, they discussed an alternative route which involved tracing the suspect prison guard's former wife, who might be persuaded to make a statement about his political affiliations.

Dona and Brenda, meanwhile, had made contact with a prison officer who continued to feed them information to help with their 'master's thesis' in criminology. The guard, referred to in their reports as Mr S., presented a grim picture of the influence of the Aryan Brotherhood inside the penitentiary.

'Just about all inmates, both in prison and camp, are a member of a gang, whether they had gang involvement on the outside or not,' Dona explained. 'If they don't join they are singled out as being weak, or scared, and are easily antagonized. It is not unusual for someone who is weak to be singled out and severely assaulted or even killed. It usually takes about two to four months for a hit to be planned and go down. The guards can often tell what group is responsible for a hit by the flow in the dining room, and which groups are talking to each other.

'Three weeks ago an inmate approached a rookie guard manning the gate between one unit and another. The inmate said he had a book to return to another inmate. Luckily, the guard did not open the gate. However, an eight-year veteran took the book and, on opening it, a bomb blew up in his face. He did not die, but his injuries were serious. That hit was planned by the Aryan Brotherhood.'

Mr S. invited the two women agents for a drink at a bar near the prison after his shift. In the lounge the entertainment was provided by a skinhead comedian with Aryan Brotherhood tattoos who told racist jokes.

When their cover was exposed, for reasons which were not entirely clear, the Clarke International women continued to carry out investigations into the background of the prison guard suspected of white supremacist connections who had blocked their client's parole. Then, without warning, their fees from the go-between attorney issuing them dried up. The problem, it turned out, had been two days spent cooped up in a Lompoc hotel awaiting the attorney's instructions. Clarke International had included the holding period on their bill and the prisoner's family had stepped in to challenge it.

Such occasions are not uncommon between private eyes and clients. Unlike the police, their skills are a matter of commercial transaction. Clients, as any PI will shake his head wonderingly and say, often fail to settle accounts when a case has been successfully resolved, or even stop inquiries in the middle to argue money aspects.

Good investigators, like Clarke International, will give an honest assessment of the costs involved at the first interview, with a proviso that, if events take an unexpected turn, costs could rise but would be monitored carefully. At last report, Clarke International were still awaiting further instructions from the lawyer. The client himself, meanwhile, had little idea if he would survive the remainder of his sentence.

5 SPECIAL SERVICES

The Dangerous World of the Specialized PI

'Data! Data! Data!' Sherlock Holmes cried, in Conan Doyle's story 'The Copper Beeches' (1892). 'I can't make bricks without clay.'

Gathering clay in the course of private detection in Britain has always been a problem and investigators have been jailed for succumbing to temptation by cutting legal corners, such as unauthorized use of the National Police Computer. American private eyes have a wealth of legitimate access to data through broader disclosure of information laws, but they had to earn the high level of public esteem they currently enjoy. Pinkerton, Burns and others helped by forging new frontiers in crime detection, employing forensic methods and compiling criminal records which were later adopted by the police on a national level.

In the nineteenth century, apart from divorce and the shady area of anti-trade-union work, the American private eye concerned himself almost wholly with the detection of crime. In the twentieth century the emphasis shifted to security, which spread many new ripples across the investigative pond. There are now specialist corporate investigators, agencies running CIA-style courses, kidnap and ransom experts, celebrity protectors, gumshoes specializing in aircraft theft, boat fraud, the de-programming of teenagers freed from religious cults – the list is endless, and highly lucrative.

So just how special was a special investigator? One of the pathfinders of specialized detection was Edward Oscar Heinrich, whose principal weapon against America's rising crime in the 1920s and 1930s was not a snub-nose detective special, but an antiquated brass microscope. In the inter-war years there were few law enforcement agencies on America's West Coast which had not been grateful for his services, including the FBI.

In 1938, British consultant criminologist Louis Mansfield interviewed Heinrich for the London *Evening News* and looked back on his career. One incident he recalled typified the detective's laboratory skills. In August 1933 an FBI field supervisor sent Heinrich a

note left by the kidnappers of Marylou Will, the daughter of a
well-known Californian industrialist. The supervisor told Heinrich
that the bureau suspected one man and promised a sample of his
handwriting as verification.

Heinrich took only a brief look at the note and told him: 'Don't
bother. This was written by a woman – a middle-aged one. I think
you'll find she's a domestic. She was educated at a Californian
school, learning to write between 1895 and 1900. She only had an
elementary school education. Incidentally, she shows such an
extraordinary knowledge of her victim's home that I would say she
had worked there as a domestic.'

The same day the FBI broke the case by arresting Jennie Barret,
a 48-year-old maid working in the Will household, who immediately confessed. There was an air of Holmesian mystery to his
deductions.

On another occasion the police handed him a human ear which
someone had found in the street. At first a rag day stunt by medical
students was suspected, but Heinrich thought otherwise. The next
day, according to the *Evening News*, he telephoned police headquarters. 'This is no rag,' he said. 'It's a case of murder. That ear
came from a young woman who was already dead when it was cut
off. The congestion of blood and lack of oxygen in it prove that she
was suffocated – perhaps with a gas of some sort. You'll find her
body lying somewhere in the marshes in the East Bay section of San
Francisco. There are some grains of silt on the ear. And that silt
comes only from those marshes. Her body has been there for about
four days.'

'Is it any wonder, with clues like this,' wrote Louis Mansfield,
'that the police found a murder victim and arrested her killer within
forty-eight hours?'

Heinrich was the son of poor German immigrant parents. He
started life as a newsboy in California, earning money to study
pharmacy at college. From there he turned to chemistry, which
became his greatest love, and went on to study physics, electrical
engineering, anatomy, medicine, biology and psychology. Such
was the breadth of his experience that he was regarded as a
qualified court expert witness on handwriting, fingerprints, blood,
hair dust and dirt fragments, explosives, fabrics, fibres, ballistics,
arson, poisons, microscopy, photography, X-rays, ultra-violet rays

and infra-red rays. He also gave expert testimony in several other specialities without having his competence challenged by the defence.

'As if Heinrich does not already know enough,' Mansfield wrote, 'he does not hesitate to take sufficient time off to master any subject which may have the slightest bearing on a case which he has to handle.'

An interesting illustration was a conspiracy case in World War One which hinged on letters being passed between India and Berlin. Unfortunately, despite extensive research, no one could be found to understand the language they were written in. Fascinated, Heinrich put all his other work on the back burner and began to live in public libraries, reading forgotten textbooks on Indian folklore and anthropology. He discovered, and went on to master, three dialects from the eastern coast of India which had been extinct for almost a century.

Using a combination of the three language structures, he was able to translate the letters and bring the conspirators to court. Heinrich's advantage as a specialist freelance investigator was not only his encyclopaedic knowledge, but the speed at which he worked. On many occasions he was referred to as 'America's Sherlock Holmes', a description justified by his reputation for never having fallen down on a case.

Every private detective has one file on which he looks back with particular satisfaction. For Heinrich, a small, quietly-spoken man with receding hair and an intense, piercing gaze, it was probably the Pacific Express robbery of 11 October 1923, a hold-up which made headlines across America. The Southern Pacific Express, carrying a large consignment of mail, had slowed on a steep gradient near the Siskiyou tunnel in southern Oregon. As it reached almost walking pace, three masked gunmen wearing overalls emerged from behind a rock at the side of the track and swung aboard. Two of them immediately overpowered the footplate crew, while the third held up the guard at gunpoint.

The engine driver, fireman and guard were ordered onto the track and covered by one of the robbers, while the others tried to break into the mail van. The postal clerk, who had seen what was happening, locked the reinforced steel doors of the mail van and refused to come out.

One of the robbers shouted: 'If you don't come out in one piece, we'll blow you out in a million.'

When the terrified clerk refused, the two robbers placed dynamite on the track beneath the van floor, and lit the fuse. The resulting explosion wrecked the mail van, which completely collapsed on its chassis, killing the clerk in the process.

The two bandits clambered into the wreckage and stuffed the singed mail into bags, while the third sprayed the carriages with bullets whenever curious passengers stuck their heads from the window. Then, having filled as many mail sacks as they could carry, one who appeared to be the leader ordered his associates to kill the three-man train crew. The driver, fireman and guard died immediately at the side of the track from a ferocious round of revolver fire.

Federal agents made a thorough search of the Siskiyou tunnel and found several items of evidence – a recently-fired revolver with the identifying numbers filed off, two sticks of dynamite and a pair of overalls dropped by one of the killers. Later that evening agents arrested a motor mechanic who worked near the Oregon tunnel and had been identified by some of the passengers. There was insufficient evidence for a conviction, so the overalls were sent by messenger to Heinrich's laboratory, at the University of California at Berkeley, together with a description of the man in custody.

Heinrich immediately set to work among his microscopes and test tubes and made a careful examination of the items. The first thing he noticed was that the overalls were smeared with sticky sap from fir trees. Among the dust in the pockets he found fragments of fir needles, some carefully-snipped nail clippings and a quantity of minute wood chips. The wood chips actually accounted for about three-quarters of the dust in the right-hand pockets and only about six per cent in the left ones. He also discovered a single hair twisted round one of the buttons. It was smooth and round and light brown in colour. When the minute examination was complete, Heinrich noted on his pad that the overalls had been originally designed for a six-foot man, and had been rolled up at the bottom.

Two days later he sent a wire to the Federal agent in charge of the investigation: YOU ARE HOLDING THE WRONG MAN. THE OVER-ALLS SENT WERE WORN BY A LEFT-HANDED LUMBERJACK WHILE WORKING FIR TREES. HE IS A WHITE MAN, BETWEEN 21 AND 25

YEARS OF AGE, NOT OVER 5FT 10 INS TALL, AND WEIGHS ABOUT 160 LBS. HE HAS MEDIUM LIGHT BROWN HAIR, LIGHT BROWN EYEBROWS, NOTICEABLY SMALL HANDS AND FEET AND IS RATHER FASTIDIOUS IN HIS PERSONAL APPEARANCE. APPARENTLY HE HAS LIVED IN THE PACIFIC NORTH WEST. LOOK FOR SUCH A MAN. THE MAN YOU HOLD IS INNOCENT.

The personal description differed so much from that of the man held in custody that three Federal agents were despatched to interview Heinrich at his laboratory. The detective explained in the *Evening News* how he reached his conclusions:

'The fact that the overalls were covered with fir-tree gum ruled out the motor mechanic immediately,' he told the agents. 'I knew that the killer must be a lumberjack from the woodchips in his pockets. These, and the Douglas fir tree needles, showed that he must have lived and worked around the Pacific North West. And I knew he must be left-handed from the concentration of wood chips in the right-hand pockets.'

'You see,' he told the Federal agents, 'when a right-handed man is swinging an axe he always stands with his left foot forward in order to balance his body. That brings the left of his body nearer to the tree from which the chips are flying. If his pockets are open ones, as in the overalls, the left-hand pockets will naturally catch more of the flying chips than the right-hand ones.

'With these overalls, however, the position is reversed. The right-hand pockets held more chips than the left. That showed he must have stood with the right side of his body to the trees and swung the axe with his left hand.

'It was the careful way the fingernails had been cut that told me he was fastidious,' Heinrich went on. 'And their small size showed me that he must have small hands, and, therefore, small feet. But the length of the trouser leg proved he must be somewhere about five feet nine, or ten at the most. And on a fairly tall man like that, small hands would be noticeable.'

'Okay,' said one of the Federal agents, 'but how do you know he's a white man?'

'And how do you know his age?' another asked.

Heinrich gave a shy smile. 'That part was easy,' he said. 'The hair was round and smooth. It could only have come from a white man because a negro's hair is elliptical and an Indian's is coarse and straight. By photographing the pith, or the medulla, of the hair I was able to deduce his approximate age. Incidentally, the colour of the hair told me, also, the colour of his eyebrows. His weight I deduced from the overalls themselves.'

Those were not the only clues Heinrich was able to supply the agents with. Ripping open the seams of the pockets, he found a tiny scrap of paper on which the number 236L was printed. On further examination it proved to be part of a receipt for a money order.

The Federal agents took it back to headquarters and began to run traces on it. Eventually, they found an order which had been issued, for fifty dollars, by a Roy de Autremont to his brother Ray. The point of dispatch happened to be a lumber camp in the Pacific North West.

Louis Mansfield took up the story. 'In the United States mail robbery is a Federal offence. So the whole of the Department of Justice swung into action against the three brothers Ray, Roy and Hugh de Autremont, who, it was ascertained, had disappeared from the town of Eugene the day before the train robbery.

'However, the killers were not brought to justice for nearly four years – four years during which Heinrich's test tubes and microscopes directed the hunt, gradually heading off every move the bandits made.

'Hugh was eventually arrested in Manila in the Philippines, where he tried to enlist in the army, while Ray and Roy were picked up in Steubenville, Ohio. When Heinrich brought his overwhelming evidence into court, an Ohio judge sentenced the three killers to life sentences in the Oregon State Penitentiary.'

Edward Oscar Heinrich was ahead of his field in forensic science. A small stride had been made in 1902, when a French biochemist, Bordet, had his tests on the biochemical analysis of blood accepted as evidence in a British court. Other significant advances were made around the turn of the century, but generally the police were slow to see the possibilities opening up before them. By the time Heinrich had wrapped up the Pacific Express murders, a modest forensic science training school had been opened in Lausanne, Switzerland. American police continued to rely on the work of private individuals while their own resources developed. Britain lagged further behind; the first forensic science laboratory, estab-

lished by Captain Athelstan Popkess, Chief Constable of Notting-
ham, did not open until 1932.

Today, there are still private forensic laboratories tucked away in
odd corners of the investigation industry. One of the most specialized and unusual is a family business almost hidden among the
bustle of New York's Wall Street district. The Tytell Typewriter
Company and Questioned Document Laboratory are run by three
private detectives, Martin Tytell, his wife Pearl and son Peter. Their
skill at repairing typewriters and photocopying machines opened a
new field of investigation. Martin Tytell, 76, began repairing typewriters at the age of fifteen. As a soldier in World War Two he
converted typewriter keyboards to foreign languages for the US
Army, which was supplying them to the Allies. When government
investigators required minute examination of typewritten documents, they turned to Martin for his experience. After the war, in
civilian life, he opened two parallel businesses in New York, specializing in typewriter repairs and document analysis. The Tytell family
have appeared as technical witnesses in many court cases and are
regarded as the foremost experts in their field.

The company will clean and service typewriters for a modest
charge, or even build custom-made typewriters for clients, but the
other side of the business is in constant demand. The Tytells
specialize in the analysis of documents – both typed and hand-
written – finding telltale clues in legal contracts, wills, photocopies,
even poison pen letters.

They played a part in helping to break an Internal Revenue case
in 1982 against Unification Church leader, the Rev. Sun Myung
Moon, whose followers are known as the 'Moonies'. Moon had not
paid taxes on funds in certain bank accounts because it was
claimed they were the property of the church.

'The question boiled down to who used those bank accounts: the
church or Moon,' Pearl Tytell told journalists.

'Moon's defence,' according to *Celebrity* magazine in 1986, 'was
that he had not written the cheques that had been cashed against
the church's accounts in the early 1970s. He claimed that when the
cheques were written, he did not know how to write English.'

However, the Internal Revenue prosecutor obtained sample
copies of personal cheques drawn on Moon's personal account from
1973. They were enough to enable the Tytells to get to work.

'I checked that handwriting sample against his at the time of the trial and found them to be the same,' Pearl explained. 'At the time he said he didn't know how to make out a cheque in English, he had written personal cheques to a department store.'

Another aspect of the trial centred on money in certain accounts which the Moonie leader claimed came from loans and was, therefore, not taxable.

'He typed up phoney loan agreements and backdated them,' Pearl said. 'But I could just tell by holding the paper up to the light that the paper had not even been manufactured until after the dates on the loan agreements. Of course, I later proved my hunch through the use of watermarks and the original records at the papermill.'

'You can't type on a piece of paper that does not exist,' Martin Tytell added. 'In many cases of backdated documents, people would have to come back from their graves to sign them. Some time ago, Peter was examining some stock certificates suspected of being phoney – and he found that the type was not designed until a year after the date on the certificate.'

Like Edward Oscar Heinrich, the Tytell Typewriter Company has made pioneering progress in areas which police often have neither the funds nor the manpower to develop. They are acknowledged experts in the minute examination of photocopy paper which is known to carry its own distinctive 'fingerprints'. A typical case which the investigators were called in to solve occurred in 1983, when IRA sympathizer Bernard McKeon was charged with conspiring to smuggle weapons out of the United States.

'One of the key pieces of evidence against him was a photocopy of a letter,' Peter Tytell explained. 'Copy machines leave trash marks – tiny black specks on each copy they make. By analysing trash marks on the photocopy we were able to show that the copy was made on a machine in the office of McKeon's wife.'

Pearl Tytell is also an expert in handwriting analysis, a field now used extensively by police around the world. In difficult cases, especially where the writer may be anonymous, Pearl's experience is highly regarded. One celebrated case involved two comic strip creators Al Capp and Ham Fisher, now both deceased.

Capp was pressing hard to obtain a broadcasting licence in the late 1950s, but his efforts were constantly thwarted by anonymous letters to the Federal Communications Commission alleging that lewd and pornographic themes were concealed in his famous Li'l Abner drawings. The letters claimed that if the cartoons, syndicated across the world, were held at a certain angle, an obscene effect was produced. The contention was absurd, but it was giving Capp serious problems. By a combination of hunch and elimination, Capp suspected that Ham Fisher, who once employed him, was behind the poison pen letters.

'We got a copy of Fisher's marriage licence and the handwriting matched perfectly,' Pearl told reporters. 'Apparently, Fisher was just plain jealous of Capp. He was embarrassed, but he was never charged.'

In contrast to having a field almost to themselves, some private investigators have chosen to specialize in crime areas already amply covered by police. Despite close co-operation, the official arm of law enforcement has data and intelligence files which no private agency could hope to compete with. However, there are always exceptions. It should be remembered that the private eye is a resourceful entrepreneur as well as a detective. If there is an opening in the market he will undoubtedly plug it to his own advantage.

This, incidentally, is one reason why some investigation agencies are wary of employing former policemen. 'After years on the force, they simply lack the basic commercial drive to crack cases,' one British investigator contends. 'If no headway is made on a police case, the tendency is to shelve it, because so many others require urgent attention. The private investigator has to stick with it, or he does not earn his fee. We may not be as big but, like Avis car rentals, we try harder.' His is one opinion. In the inter-war years many British agencies were founded by retired police officers and operated successfully. In America, too, ex-cops who go freelance are generally highly regarded by fellow professionals.

It is rare for freelance investigators to create an area of highly-specialized expertise by building intelligence files which cannot be acquired through normal channels. There are dubious ways in which police records can be obtained, but it is a brave and adventurous operator who sets out to compile his own. One such case is Peter Clark, Europe's foremost boat detective, who now has data probably superior to that of the police. He is also one of the best examples of how the police and a private investigator can pool their resources and work together to each other's mutual benefit.

Like many good private investigators, it is difficult for outsiders to guess what Peter Clark does for a living. The whereabouts of the headquarters of his company, C-Claims, is a well-kept secret. He operates through a postal box number, and few people, even the marine insurance companies who employ him, visit his secluded offices. Finding him involves negotiating roads which are not signposted and, at times, wishing you had chosen to travel in a four-wheel-drive vehicle.

Around the final bend of a long and rutted cart track, a magnificent Victorian farmhouse unexpectedly swung into view. It nestled in a fold of Essex hills and woodland, protected by a walled courtyard and high iron gates. Beneath the clock tower, in a coach house off the cobbled yard, Britain's most sought-after marine private investigator was at work.

Peter Clark hung upside down by his ankles on a back-sufferer's suspension frame, mulling over a case. Dozens of hours driving around marinas each week had compressed his spinal discs, a condition for which hanging bat-like provided the only relief.

Clark dictated a letter and swung upright in a space between the desks where his mother and sister sat punching marine crime data into computers. His company is a family affair, with a friendly atmosphere far removed from the deadly serious matter of tracing luxury yachts spirited away by drug smugglers or recovering expensive stolen power boats. Outside, his children played on swings in the summer sun, and an old bay mare plodded leisurely past the window. A mile away, an elderly lady who is a friend of the family sat in a garden outhouse typing interrogation reports.

Clark, who is in his thirties and has a beautiful Swedish wife, needs the rural calm and support of his family to keep a clear head. He handles a daunting number of cases simultaneously, covering an area which may reach from Britain, across Europe and as far as the Gambia on the west coast of Africa and Rio de Janeiro. His quarry is a mixture only the lure of boats can draw together – sea dreamers, opportunists, lone con-men, organized gangs and drug barons with records of violence.

Like many private investigators, he is not quite what he seems. In ten years of interviewing criminal suspects he has acquired a mask of control which would unnerve a poker player. At work, Peter Clark's eyes adopt a formal expression of frozen stone. When he relaxes, an engaging lopsided grin breaks through. He has a rapid, encyclopaedic memory and paces the room with restrained energy when working out the moves in a case.

He is bright and articulate and sees his job as an intellectual battle with criminals, particularly in cases of deception. 'I approach fraud as a three-dimensional object,' he explains. 'The way to tackle it is to turn it around and around to try to discover the chink. Once you find it, the art is to drive in a wedge and smash it open. If it sounds brutal, I'm sorry, but it really is. Some of these people are almost predictable in their pattern. There is a distinct chemistry in the way they respond to your questions. It is almost like a litmus test.'

In the boot of his car he carries a full set of what could be mistaken for burglar's tools – keys, crowbars, cordless drills, bolt cutters – for breaking into stolen boats and recovering them before thieves can spirit them away again. A textbook Clark operation involved a Princess 45 motor cruiser, 'a big, luxury gin-palace of a job', which was stolen from Britain and moored temporarily in Cherbourg in northern France, probably en route to Spain. Clark received a tip-off and hurried across the Channel. After breaking into the boat and immobilizing it, he placed a tread alarm under the cabin rug, linked by radio to an agent's car at the harbourside. When the thieves returned with provisions, they triggered the alarm and police moved in.

'It's like a pyramid,' he says, 'They start off by doing a job like that. Then they move to the next stage and buy, perhaps, a big drug consignment in Morocco and ship it up to Rotterdam. They go up the ladder, becoming all the time more powerful and more confident. It is a very predictable pattern. My job, as I see it, is to find their weak spot and wallop it hard.'

The strength of C-Claims' operation lies both in Clark's astute deductive powers and the formidable data bank he has built up over the years. Many private eyes have been heavily fined or jailed for obtaining police records. Clark, who is a legitimate investigator careful not to overstep regulations, keeps his own data. At present it is the only way in which he feels he can lawfully operate under what he sees as absurd restrictions. The boat detective has passionate views on Britain's idiosyncratic information laws and wants to lobby hard to change them. He argues that access to certain facts is essential in fighting rising crime.

'Criminal records are not a state secret,' he says. 'They are a statement of public fact. The records are available in newspapers in any public library if you care to go and find them. If you want to collate that information there is no law to prevent you doing so.

'We at C-Claims cannot possibly do it thoroughly and that is the problem we face. Policemen should not be put in the invidious position of not being able to divulge a simple question of fact – whether or not a man has a criminal record. To me it is an absurdity and a complete conflict. Either a man has a criminal record, or he does not. Likewise, it is either disclosable or it is not. We already have protection within the law which says that when a certain number of years have elapsed a criminal record should not be disclosed. All that remains is the question of changing the rules of access to the police computer.

'In America, Sweden and Germany there are Freedom of Information Acts. With licensed access, my agents in Florida and California can go to their local police station and obtain someone's criminal record. They are not breaking any law, and that person has no right of complaint because it is a matter of public record. If someone has a criminal record it should not be a secret. They have committed an offence against society and, until it is expunged from the record under the 1974 Rehabilitation of Offenders Act, they have to face the consequences. That is part of the penalty.

'It does not make our job easier, so we have another way of cracking the nut. It is not one we use very often, but if we really suspect that someone has a criminal record but cannot prove it, we tell him that he has the right under the Data Protection Act to apply for it, or an extract of it, from the police computer. If someone insists that they do not have a record, and we think otherwise, it balances the equation. It clears him, or it damns him, and I think that is fair. I say this in the light of the high number of fraudulent insurance claims we have to contend with.

'The people we deal with are very astute. If you go back ten years, the volume of fraud was much less for a number of reasons. There has been a general moral decline, which is a fact of life proved by statistics of all kinds. There is also a greater understanding of how the system works as people who have benefited from an improved education become older. A lot of people who grew up through the war had their education interrupted and they never really got to grips with the system we live under. The picture today is very different – and it does not make our job easier.'

It is also possible to obtain details of a conviction from the courts, providing the right information is available. On occasions Clark has used police contacts, not to obtain records but to provide him informally with the crucial date of a hearing which enables him to make the right approach to the keeper of court records. What makes the whole question of licensed access impossible in Britain, of course, is that, after three-quarters of a century of lobbying, investigators have failed to receive official recognition.

Peter Clark drifted into his line of work almost by accident. He began his working life at Lloyd's of London because his father had always been in insurance. After obtaining the appropriate qualifications, he happened to be talking to a yacht insurer about what happened to written-off boats. Clark enjoyed working with his hands and thought he might be able to purchase one or two to restore. For a time he caught boat fever and found himself working evenings and weekends. It soon became a choice of which career to pursue but, as marriage was looming, the security of insurance seemed wiser. It was about this time that he ran into a marine loss adjuster who offered him a job out of the blue.

'My old boss and I are still good friends,' he said. 'I worked for him and a naval architect for four or five years. We built up a network of agents around the country and a good reputation with insurers. I never really thought much about the investigation side, it was something I learned as time went on. The field was wide open. The yacht insurance market was totally unserved in that area.'

Peter Clark was brimming with ideas. He set up a central theft index and persuaded the company to buy a rudimentary computer. On the reputation he built up, he was offered a partnership in Florida. Clark went over for a trial period, decided against it, and returned with six months' savings and no work. He rang around a few insurers to ask if they would care to hire him and was amazed at the response. He was overwhelmed with cases before he even had time to print his business notepaper. Today, he handles any kind of marine theft, from a sailboard to a million-pound yacht.

It is an unpredictable business in which the simplest cases can turn into crimes of great complexity. The trail of two water sport jet skis, bought on deposit and never paid for, led him into a tangled web of interrelated offences totalling, to date, one million pounds. The purchase of a boat on a stolen building society cheque led to a ring of organized fraud which involved shipping boats to the Mediterranean, using the proceeds to purchase drugs and smuggling the narcotics back to the UK. Even then, Clark felt that he had uncovered only the tip of an underworld iceberg.

The cases illustrate a major problem of rising marine crime against a background of police undermanning and lack of communication between forces.

'The Achilles heel of marine police work is that it is very much defined by boundaries,' Clark explained. 'Some counties do not even have marine police sections. There is one in Devon and Cornwall, and the section in Dorset has one boat. Four officers have one boat to cover Hampshire, and that is the entire unit. Sussex abandoned their marine police section ten years ago. Kent, Essex and Suffolk have very good sections, but Norfolk has none.

'There is no central marine index apart from my own. Most of the marine police sections work from card indexes, or computer systems which cannot talk to each other. Every four or five years I have the honour of being invited to address the Marine Police Conference. On the last occasion I offered them our computer program, which we devised ourselves, but nothing happened.

'Through experience, you learn that thieves are not quite as complete in their approach as you might think. For the most part, big yacht thieves are not that professional. They are either dreamers, they just have an illusion they are going to make a lot of money, or they are running away from something.

'However, there are professionals. We had an operation which started in 1987 and is still going on. We have recovered sixteen or seventeen very big boats, some from as far as Rio. A lot were not reported as stolen, but were claimed to have been sunk off Spain or Portugal.'

The key to Clark's success is intelligence. Unlike many investigators who walk into a case cold, he is able to analyse crime patterns, boat movements and records of similar crimes.

'All intelligence is good intelligence,' he explained. 'That is a very firm maxim. I am an avid collector of anything I think may be useful at a later stage. I still miss more than I actually collate but, nevertheless, that is the principle of the operation.

'With a card index and a computer you can assimilate a lot as an operation goes on. The odd name or alias will crop up, a passport number, a registration number – everything goes into the jigsaw. Once you establish a pattern, the computer enables you to piece things together swiftly.'

A case he has been trying to break for two years, like so many others, involves expatriate Londoners holed up in Spain. Clark hitched himself onto his desk and leaned over to punch a computer key. Pages of data scrolled up until he found the one he was searching for.

'The problem here,' he said, indicating the screen, 'is that there is such an influx of villains from every country down there now. Spain is like a big university of crime. It is getting dangerous and I am wary of sticking my neck out. It is not like England where I could ring 999 and get help from the police if I found myself in a corner.'

Peter Clark used undercover agents to report on two south Londoners whom he was convinced were behind a £1 million insurance swindle in the mid-1980s. Both took out heavy life insurance, bought a luxury boat, and disappeared when it mysteriously sank.

'The so-called widows bludgeoned the insurers for several hundred thousand pounds. But we know for sure that these two guys are alive and well, and living in luxury behind the Marbella hills. I even have one witness who was almost knocked down by one of them in his Range Rover the other week.

'The problem is to break the case and then get the Fraud Squad involved, but I have to go in well-prepared. I have to have all the evidence, the surveillance, and no doubt in my mind what names they are using, what passports they are carrying. If I had an open chequebook I could do it tomorrow. As it is, I have to do it in my own way, which is slowly, biding my time.'

Peter Clark effectively pulled out of Spain in 1984 because he was becoming too well recognized in an area populated by heavyweight criminals from all over Europe. Then he teamed up with Hector Payas, Gibraltar's only private eye, and found a way of working from behind the comparative safety of the border. C-Claims is now regarded as being back in force on the Costa del Crime.

Payas is a quiet, dignified ex-Gibraltar police superintendent with an impressive number of contacts on both sides of the law. His office is situated in Irish Town, a narrow street teeming with bars with loud juke-boxes and louder beer-swilling British squaddies. Notices demanding 'No T-shirts and jeans after 5 p.m.' go ignored.

'Gib' is a cramped, claustrophobic barracks community, which has never known the luxury of space and gardens, squeezed into the toe of Spain like an irritating speck of granite in the toe of a shoe. The Rock dominates everything – thrusting skywards like a fist in defiant salute, bristling with the antennae of listening stations and shrouded in cloud.

Hector Payas's office is a suite of three tiny rooms in its shadow, an Aladdin's cave of domestic junk, repossessed for hire purchase companies, all carefully labelled for sale. There are twenty-two staff on the payroll, but room only for seven, at a squash, in the office. Members of the public drift in, squeezing past a motorbike between the door and the reception desk, to browse among cameras, sun lamps and broken photocopiers for bargains. Gib has such an acute space problem that Payas cannot find room for all the cars he repossesses. Staff periodically leave the office to switch them round the town when parking periods expire.

In the midst of this eccentric confusion, Payas mans his office phone, a heavy wooden police truncheon within easy reach. He is probably the fastest, most efficient and honest investigator on the southern Iberian peninsula, and definitely the busiest.

Over the border lies Clark and Payas's hunting ground. The Spanish coastal highway, known locally as the 'Road of Death' because of its high mortality rate, is an endless ribbon of construction. Cranes and earthmovers litter the landscape. Giant billboards advertise the merits of half-completed apartments. On the hillsides, the abandoned concrete shells of developments which ran out of money rise like rows of rotten teeth, a stark reminder that anything under the sun can befall the speculator in a hurry.

The area has become a place of pilgrimage for organized thieves involved in drug running. Thefts of upmarket vehicles from London, which are then driven to Spain for personal use, are common. Payas stopped a Londoner in a Range Rover who had foolishly hopped over to Gibraltar on business. The vehicle had been reported missing for more than a year. 'I tapped him on the shoulder as he was locking it up and showed him the papers,' Hector Payas smiled. 'He simply handed me the keys and strolled away. He had had twelve months' use out of it and would probably arrange to get another one.'

The same week he successfully recovered a £10,000 boat on Peter Clark's behalf and returned it to its rightful owner in Britain. The yacht had turned up in Puerto Banus, the millionaires' marina four miles along the coast from Marbella. Thieves had sailed the boat into port, moored it and asked the local yacht broker to put it up for sale.

'Fortunately, it was recognized from one of our circulars,' Clark said. 'The police sealed it, and the owner was on his way to collect it. Then, at five o'clock on a Friday afternoon, I received a phone call – why do I always get them at five o'clock on Fridays? – the two thieves had sold the boat.'

Clark knew he had to act quickly. When the broker showed them the police seal, the villains produced papers to prove the yacht was theirs. 'If those clowns had got hold of the boat, we would have lost the whole thing over again. I phoned Gibraltar, and Hector asked the Spanish police to arrest them. Unfortunately, they couldn't because the British police had not got around to placing an extradition warrant on them. Eventually we managed to recover the boat in time, and the villains lived to fight another day.' He shrugged philosophically. 'That's the way it goes, sometimes.'

Clark makes no secret of the fact that he represents insurers; this, combined with his fearlessness in meeting big-league criminals, has made him a figure of local interest. Gangsters who periodically liquidate their assets have approached him to negotiate the buy-back of art treasures walled up in the basement of a villa, and gold bullion in one-ton consignments. Clark is prepared to talk about anything that furthers his quest for intelligence.

In 1989 he was summoned to Gibraltar by an urgent message from Hector Payas to recover the *Charade of Hamble*, a yacht stolen

more than two years earlier from the Isle of Wight. He flew over
with a Ryde banker, Peter Piper, who had owned the yacht with a
sailing partner. Piper, who had been compensated by the insurers,
was needed on site to make a positive identification of the former
love of his life. It turned out to be a nostalgic journey for him, and a
nightmare for Mr and Mrs Walters, the couple who had bought the
boat in good faith from the thief.

The Walterses had sailed into Gibraltar for a few hours to enquire
about repairs to their sails, when the boat was spotted by one of
Hector Payas's network of waterfront agents. Payas impounded the
vessel and placed a security man on 24-hour watch, but allowed
the Walterses to stay on board until Clark arrived, because he felt
sorry for them. Mr Clive Walters, an ex-policeman, and his Swiss
wife had sold their home on Jersey and given their furniture to their
children so as to embark on a wandering retirement on the
£33,000 yacht. When the news was broken to them, they were
deeply shaken, homeless and virtually without savings.

As a grey drizzle swept over Gibraltar harbour, Peter Piper
identified the *Charade*, despite its repainting. In the cabin, Clark sat
with the Walterses and quietly explained the legal position. Their
yacht belonged to the insurers and the papers they had acquired
with it were false. In the course of the next two hours he gently tried
to obtain all the information he could about the man called Carson
who had sold them the boat.

When he emerged, with statements taken and papers duly
signed, C-Claims' responsibilities were officially over. Clark had
some other jobs to attend to – a boat whisked away by a con man in
the space of ten minutes; another stolen craft beached by drug
runners over the border in Spain. But he was essentially an investigator, and the thought of Carson leaving a trail of personal misery
privately appalled him. He allowed the Walters to remain on the
yacht for a few days to sort out their affairs before crossing the
border on the trail of the man who stole the *Charade of Hamble*.

His main threads in the case were the yacht surveyor and broker
who handled the sale; boats, like houses, are surveyed and sold by
brokers who act as estate agents. At the border he was met by the
surveyor who was standing on the Spanish side of the checkpoint in
white slacks, white loafers and a designer sports shirt. A Porsche
928 was parked at the kerbside. The surveyor had a flat, tanned

face with receding hair and a voice like a London gravel pit. On the journey to the broker's office in Estepora, Clark was able to learn a little more about Carson, who had been seen around the marina on several occasions. The broker, a blond North Yorkshireman, had an office on the waterfront, overlooking the neat white harbour designed by Franco's former Minister of Labour, an eminent Madrid lawyer. The broker was engaged to be married to his daughter.

Armed with a description of Carson and approximate dates of when he was seen, Clark visited the harbourmaster in the hope that his passport might have been routinely photocopied. When that failed, he knocked on doors at every broker and ship's chandler boat supplier in the harbour. They appeared to be manned almost exclusively by Britons who had a habit of calling everyone John. By the time Clark made his last call at the waterfront, the subjects of his previous visits had leapt into cars and on motorbikes to race there before him. The men packed into the crowded office were deeply suspicious of him and at times heated arguments broke out about why he was asking questions. Clark left with a little information, but without his man.

A few weeks later he traced Carson to an address in Essex and kept watch on it. Enquiries revealed that the bird had flown – to the Caribbean, it was rumoured, by yacht. Clark suspected otherwise and arranged for agents to watch an autumn gathering of boats in the Canaries, where they congregate to cross the Atlantic to the West Indies together each year.

In December 1989, Carson slipped back to his home and word of his whereabouts soon reached Clark. Police from Essex and Southampton were informed and the possibility of a raid discussed. Before any action could be taken, Carson received a visit from a caller who wished to interview him about the *Charade of Hamble*. He disappeared from his home and has not been seen since. The visitor, it was said, was a private investigator hired by the Walterses' lawyers.

Peter Clark received the ironic news with a philosophical shrug. 'I have a feeling that Carson is on his way to Tunisia,' he said. 'He may have flown, but we have something he doesn't. We have the boat – and we have all the time in the world.'

As crime has become more specialized, private investigation has adjusted in turn, diversifying into fields in which many police forces do not have the expertise to cope. Organized crime which crosses and re-crosses international frontiers can hamper police operations and – as in the case of Peter Clark – demonstrates the flexible quick response of the private investigator.

The activities of these highly specialized agents dispel the myth of the lone gumshoe immersed in divorce and writ-serving. Unfortunately, they do not seek publicity like their American counterparts, and little is generally known of the high esteem in which they are held. The business is not an easy one to examine objectively, but an overall impression is that top British investigators working on an international level are more efficient and better respected than their high-profile American competitors. One indication of this is the number of American clients who select British first division agencies for international work, rather than opt for similar specialists on their own doorstep. Price is not a consideration when millions of dollars are at stake. The yardstick is always results.

Carratu International, who have offices in Cheam, Surrey, and London's Trafalgar Square, are highly regarded in their particular field. As a measure of their status, it is perhaps significant that the vast majority of their clients are based overseas. They specialize in the rarefied world of commercial fakes which can result in enormous losses for record companies, perfumiers or jeans manufacturers when piracy goes unchecked.

The company, run by former Scotland Yard Fraud Squad officer Vincent Carratu and his son Paul, has saved drinks and chemical manufacturers millions of pounds by tracking down counterfeiters. At one point Carratu International was storing 750,000 bottles of fake perfume, six miles of cloth used for making imitation designer fashion bags, 80,000 handbags, 5000 pairs of shoes, 2000 shirts and 750 forged perfume boxes. All the confiscated goods bore the name of international fashion and perfume houses and had a street value of up to £1 million. None of the manufacturers were aware that their products were to be used for illegal purposes.

Counterfeiting can go undetected for long periods because there is often little to arouse suspicion among company auditors. Receipts and invoices match and the only explanation for falling sales is that the perfumier or fashion house is having an inexplicably bad year.

'The real money is in fashion accessories, particularly designer watches such as Rolex and Cartier,' said Paul Carratu. 'Commercial counterfeiting is on the increase, but it is very hard to quantify because much of it goes undetected or unreported.'

Many counterfeit goods are almost undetectable from the originals and can even fool cursory tests by experts. Vincent Carratu was hired by Chanel in 1984 to investigate evidence of 'beautifully camouflaged' bogus Chanel No. 5 and No. 19 perfume, as well as Aramis Derin aftershave. The products turned up in alarming quantities in airport duty-free shops, on planes and ships, and in boutiques and department stores. Wholesalers bought the perfumes at discount prices believing them to be what are known as parallel sales – bulk consignments of genuine goods bought in France to escape import duties and taxes.

In fact, as Carratu discovered, they were being manufactured in secret locations in Mexico, Spain, and the back streets of east London in a massive operation thought to be funded by the Mafia. The difference in aroma between the fake and the real thing was almost imperceptible because the gang bought authentic perfume essence and diluted it. Raw materials for their smallest bottle cost about £1 and retailed for the enormous mark-up of £36. However, they made two basic miscalculations which eventually gave them away. The bogus perfume wore off much more quickly than the real thing, and plastic stoppers were used in the bottles rather than the cut glass of the originals.

Carratu International worked closely with detectives from Thames Valley Police to uncover the racketeers, who planned to flood the world market with their products. Carratu's hunt for clues led him to Acapulco, on Mexico's Pacific coast, where one faction of the gang had opened a £1 million manufacturing plant equipped with new machinery which in some cases was more up-to-date than Chanel's own. The base was chosen because trade description and copyright infringement laws were only loosely enforced in Mexico.

Carratu had a team of investigators keeping watch on the Acapulco operation and monitored a meeting between gang members on the fourth floor of a beach hotel. To obtain the evidence he wanted, the investigator used a ploy which might have been taken straight from a James Bond movie. An agent, wearing a parachute and towed by a boat, went parasailing outside the hotel. As the boat accelerated, he ascended to the height of the fourth floor where the meeting was taking place, and took pictures through the hotel windows.

The scale of the operation was so vast that a Carratu agent flying to the Middle East bought a bottle of Chanel No. 5 duty free on Kuwait Airlines and found that it was a fake. While Mafia backing money was suspected, allegedly arranged through a lawyer based in Jersey, some of the proceeds were thought to have been channelled into arms for the Palestine Liberation Organization. A high-ranking official of the movement was named in the court case, but never arrested.

The fake operation was organized on an international level, with authentic Chanel bottles purchased from the Vicasa company in Madrid, stoppers from the Trezzano company in Milan and packaging from Germany and Holland. The gang also recruited a production manager who was fluent in Spanish and English to run a manufacturing plant in Barcelona. Carratu agents back in Acapulco discovered that, after operating for some time, Mafia bosses began demanding a bigger return on their investment. The gang pulled out of Mexico to London and continued production in King's Cross and Hackney.

Chanel were disturbed at the way in which fake versions of their products were now flooding the market. In Cambridge, two women were dining with their husbands at a restaurant when one of them commented on the 'sickly' smell of the other's perfume. 'It's Chanel No. 5,' she was told acidly. The women discovered that they were both wearing the same brand. Next day experts analysed the bottles and found one of them to be a fake. Stories like this began to trickle back to the company, who by now were extremely concerned at the extent of the piracy.

Vincent Carratu, meanwhile, was closing in on the gang. The trail had taken three months and led his agents across six countries. The investigator, who dresses expensively and has a well-groomed, cosmopolitan air, made contact with the gang after posing as an exporter and arranged a meeting at an address in west London. Carratu, wired for sound, drove his Rolls to the meeting and was offered 40,000 bottles of fake Chanel at £6 each.

From the information he gathered, Carratu was able to work closely with police planning a raid on the hidden manufacturing centres in London. The premises had been rented in false names and paid for in cash. Police had already followed one of the gang's financial organizers from a bottle-buying trip to Madrid to his home near Chesham in Buckinghamshire. He was later seen in two London hotels, the Hilton and the Curzon, handing over containers of concentrated perfume essence to another man.

When the gang set to work fulfilling Carratu's order in 1985, the police moved in. The factories contained bottling machinery, packaging and huge vats of base essence, bought for as little as £3000 for 50 litres in Geneva. Even Carratu, an old hand at the game, was staggered when he saw the extent of the illegal operation.

The investigator, who has handled many similar cases and is as experienced in the field as any private detective worldwide, is an enigmatic figure. 'Carratu himself,' said Peter Martin in the *Mail-on-Sunday* in January 1987, 'is such a jolly and gregarious type – his parents were of Italian origin – it's hard to imagine he was ever a policeman. His chief asset is his plausibility. He has never gone in for elaborate disguises but, with his plummy voice, five languages and stylish Continental manners, he could be anyone from Herbert Lom playing a glossy diplomat to Ronald Fraser going slightly over the top as a spiv of the fallen rich variety. "Will the real Vincent Carratu please stand up?" has been a running office joke for years.'

Counterfeiting is now thought to be the biggest and fastest-growing type of theft, estimated to cream off at least five per cent of international trade. Carratu International has built up extensive records of 900,000 known counterfeiters throughout the world on its computers, each carefully indexed and cross-referenced by names, aliases, working methods and fields of operation.

'Some of the names on that massive list would surprise you,' Paul Carratu said. 'They are outwardly respectable. The work can be dangerous. We have had agents beaten up but, thank heavens, no more than that.'

Manufacturing fakes is a multi-million-pound business which causes serious damage to the reputation of established companies. Emperor Hirohito once posed for an official portrait wearing a pin-striped suit and Hermès tie. The tie had been purchased by an aide at a Tokyo department store which was not licensed to sell Hermès products in Japan. Discreet inquiries revealed that the Emperor's tie was a counterfeit with a fake label. Similarly, in 1980, when a wealthy Parisienne had problems with her Cartier watch, which carried a lifetime guarantee, she returned it to the factory for repairs. The company found that it was a fake and confiscated it. According to the *New York Times*, Cartier claims to receive two or three watches a week in this manner.

There are more dangerous effects of the fake business. In 1979, Kenya's coffee crop was wiped out by a bogus fungicide, bought by growers in good faith. Counterfeit brake pads of inferior quality have been found fitted to British buses, and fake parts were almost used on a 1976 NASA space shuttle but discovered at the last minute.

One of the world's most lucrative counterfeit fashion companies grossed $24 million before being raided by Vincent Carratu in 1980. 'Its mastermind, Gianfranco Chih, owned a large country house outside Milan, luxuriously furnished, a city apartment, a restaurant, a Range Rover with telephone, an expensive motorcycle and a girlfriend with jewels on every finger,' the investigator said. 'The phone rang non-stop with orders from all over the world. They were not worried – they had paid for police protection.'

Italian police from a neighbouring town had to be drafted in for the raid. Thirty officers and eleven vehicles were used to storm the premises and arrest Gianfranco Chih. He was eventually imprisoned and the factory closed down; it took five days to list the fake goods which were taken away in a convoy of eight lorries. The evidence included 8483 handbags, 44 suitcases, 10,500 belt buckles, 362 wallets, two miles of designer fabric, plus moulds and dies for making bogus trademarks. The company exported fake Cartiers, Guccis, Diors and Valentinos all over Europe and had orders destined for Miami, South Africa, Nigeria, Zambia and the Middle East.

Counterfeiting is almost as old as civilization. For centuries coins were forged on a wide scale, making currency unreliable, but the industrialized twentieth century with its established brand names gave international piracy its real impetus. After World War Two there was a huge trade in fake watches, bearing reputable Swiss and French names but manufactured in workshops in Italy and Hong Kong. After the fashion boom of the sixties, off-the-peg designer clothes and accessories became the main targets. A routine customs check on the Swiss–French border in 1979 revealed 363 fake items of luggage, supposedly made by the hundred-year-old manufacturers Louis Vuitton, packed in the baggage of two sleeping-car passengers. They were arrested and later imprisoned. Police later discovered 37,600 metres of fake Vuitton fabric, carrying the distinctive trade mark, at a mill near Lecco, Italy. The pirates had 220 orders from clients all over the world.

A party of British MPs touring a textile mill in Taiwan in the late 1970s were astonished to find rolls of cloth labelled 'Made in Huddersfield' and '100% British Worsted'. Door locks, batteries, car parts, cassettes and countless other items fill the display cabinets of Carratu International's black museum at their Cheam head-quarters in Surrey.

'The discovery that one's products are being copied is traumatic,' Vincent Carratu said. 'The effect on a company's sales and repu-tation can be disastrous. But the trouble is that a hasty investi-gation invariably results in injunctions, writs and possibly orders to search premises – all excellent measures to let the world know that something is being done – but they do not identify the source of the problem. In my experience, if you act precipitately, the trail goes cold and the operation is driven underground until it is safe to start again.'

'Counterfeiters are becoming better organized,' he told the *Finan-cial Times* in 1979. 'Their operations are often financed by the proceeds of crime. The money from a bank raid, for example, may be used to set up a counterfeiting business. The investment can be large and the rewards even bigger. In one case a gang put up £30,000 to forge the products of a well-known perfumier, and the expected return was £20 million over five years. An awful lot of these operations in America are backed by the Mafia and, in the Far East, the Triads are very big in counterfeiting. Make no mistake, we are up against villains, rogues and fraudsmen who are milking the public.'

By developing its own intelligence networks and data banks and by co-operating closely with the police, Carratu International has elevated private detection above the unfortunate image it acquired in the past and pointed the way to interesting future possibilities. The industry, however, continues to be dogged by bad publicity, fringe operators and lack of professional status. British operators like C-Claims and Carratu International have earned their own recognition as highly respected international operators. There are others like them who have proved that integrity and example can succeed where eighty years of lobbying have failed.

The scope of Carratu's operations goes beyond intellectual property protection to cover white-collar crime, insurance fraud, money laundering and risk management services. Directors of the company have backgrounds in the legal profession, Ministry of Defence counter-intelligence, the Customs and Excise Investigations Branch, the Rotterdam Fraud Squad and Scotland Yard.

It is the spread of counterfeiting, however, which continues to occupy the bulk of their activities. Vincent Carratu himself sometimes spends up to eight months of the year travelling on international investigations or undercover operations. In combating fakes the agency fights a criminal determination rarely encountered elsewhere. Every known loophole in the law has been breached by organized gangs.

'A Taiwanese watch counterfeiter who had his stock checked by US Customs escaped because his Omegas and Seikos carried the names "Homegas" and "Aseikon",' Carratu explained. 'The officers had not realized that a drop of spirit removed the first and last letters at the retail end. A counterfeiter in Italy was offering quantities of fake Chanel eau de toilette delivered inside nondescript outer cartons. They could be safely held in stock until required, then removed from their cheap covers as and when needed.

'The United Kingdom is an importer of counterfeits from the Far East, continental Europe and South America. We also produce our own copies. We have the dubious reputation of manufacturing excellent copy perfumes and in the area of tobacco we lead the world. Bulk tobacco is imported from Belgium and Holland and then packed in identical wallets to those used by Old Holborn and other well-known brands. It is a massive and lucrative trade.

'Some private investigation agencies offer an anti-counterfeiting service but unless they have direct experience they can do more harm than good and may drive the counterfeiters underground. One method of operation, for example, is for an agency to invite a company to pay a fixed amount for each copy found. The company concerned may think this an excellent idea until they realize there is no incentive for the investigator to find the source.

'Not every country recognizes counterfeiting as a crime. Indeed, in some it is regarded as an excellent method of generating hard currency and often has full government support. In Thailand the government publication *Nation Review* does a hard sell to tourists for the country's copy products and gives the best places to find them. For many years the Taiwan government refused to acknowledge that counterfeiting was a problem, although their copies were exported throughout the world. It was only when the US and European governments threatened economic sanctions that Taiwanese laws were made more effective and in general are being enforced.

'In Europe, the governments of Italy, Spain and Greece have been slow to deal with the problems of their countries. As a consequence, fakes are to be seen everywhere. Copy Gucci, Dior and Louis Vuitton bags are sold in every street market and even in some of the better quality stores. The US is one of the rare countries that clearly defines counterfeiting as a criminal offence, and its Trademark Counterfeiting Act 1984 has proved effective. Under this legislation, a person convicted of intentionally trafficking in goods or services they know to bear a counterfeit mark can be sentenced to five years' imprisonment and fined $250,000. Proportional sentences apply to corporations. The law provides a virtually mandatory award of treble damages if the suit is successful.

'Within the EC, committees have been set up to draft new legislation and in the United Kingdom the Department of Trade has expressed a willingness to consider the problem. Much of the impetus for this progress is due to the efforts of the Anti-Counterfeiting Group, whose members are drawn from the major companies susceptible to having their merchandise copied. Until the authorities take determined action to stamp out this crime, the problem will not go away.'

Private detection in general has become a form of service industry, constantly diversifying and moulding itself to shifts of public requirement and commercial demand. Across Europe, and particularly in America, countless small agencies exist, some only one-man operations, who will mail anyone's garbage to you within 24 hours, find an old flame, locate lost dogs or teach wives how to check on errant husbands. Specialization has been the key to the industry's survival and there appear to be no limits to how far agencies will go to find a market.

One highly successful niche, which has done much to promote investigators as 'user friendly', is the Cheap Detective Agency, established in Los Angeles in the early eighties. At the time, hiring the services of an American private eye cost around $36 (£24) an hour, and nobody ever had a problem which could be cracked in so short a time. Deanna Short, a former policewoman, saw that many ordinary people never considered using an investigator because they were afraid of fees running beyond their means.

The Cheap Detective Agency paid off. Within a short time Deanna was employing twenty-two men and women investigators and had more than a thousand happy clients. The main reason was that she charged only £7.50 an hour. She has since opened a second branch in San Bernardino, California, and has other expansion plans lined up for the future. Some of the run-of-the-mill cases successfully handled by her unusual agency included tracing runaway teenagers and shadowing suspected unfaithful husbands and wives. Lost relatives and infidelity formed the bulk of the work, but there were also bigger fish to fry. A Los Angeles store hired the agency to uncover an internal theft conspiracy, often a risky business if drug addiction motivates the thefts. A Cheap Detective was taken on to the store payroll as an employee to watch and listen. Within a short time the ring was broken and thirty-five arrests followed.

On the shifting sands of the British employment front, there have been examples of former policemen obtaining grants from the government's Business Enterprise Allowance Scheme to set up investigation agencies. Phillippa Lloyd had no detective experience, but she had a shrewd eye for a hole in the market. She lived at home in Walworth, south-east London, and owned a dog. Finding lost dogs is the one task almost every agency in the world is guaranteed to turn down. Yet people parted from their pets suffer genuine heartbreak and are prepared to pay for professional help.

Phillippa knew how they felt because her own mongrel Boots disappeared one morning in 1987. She pestered the police, called incessantly at local dogs' homes, searched the streets and discovered that the problem was widespread and no one could really help. After ten days of detective work the pair were reunited, and the experience gave Phillippa the inspiration to launch the first detective agency specializing exclusively in dogs from her home in 1988.

'I suddenly realized that searching for a lost dog can be a full-time job,' she told journalist Sharon Bexley of *Chat* magazine in September 1988. 'And a lot of people whose dogs go missing are at their wits' end. They can't always think clearly about the best way to find them, but I can. I still get terribly involved, although I try not to.'

Phillippa worked out a scale of fees – £25 for a two-week hunt, £40 for a month and £50 for three months, with a £40 reward fee if the dog was found. Her methods were as logical as those of any working detective agency. She interviewed the owner and took details of the dog's distinguishing marks, together with a photograph and a reconstruction of how the dog disappeared. Then she walked the dog's favourite haunts, placing advertisements in shops, vets' surgeries and police stations. At two-day intervals she checked lists of new entries of strays at Battersea Dogs' Home, where her own Boots turned up. If the dog had settled in a new home, tug-of-love battles were not uncommon. The agency, not unexpectedly, was called Doggone.

Finding old flames is not an entirely dissimilar business, and is a facet of small-agency investigation which is rapidly gaining momentum. It is an operation no one will get rich on, but one in which demand always outstrips supply. Ron Crisp, in Los Angeles, is one of the fastest and most experienced private eyes at the art of rekindling old flames. Not exactly rekindling, perhaps, because most of his clients, surprisingly, have no desire to pick up the threads of old love affairs. The irresistible urge to revisit the past extends only to nostalgic curiosity. Married men and women simply want to know what kind of lifestyle their 'ex' is living, and if life has generally been kind to them.

'Fewer people than you would imagine actually want to arrange a meeting,' Crisp says. 'I find that what they really want is just to find out how their high-school sweethearts are doing now. Perhaps the fantasy of going back to another place and time in our lives is born of the hardships common to us all – fortunes are gained and lost, contented marriages end in nasty divorce suits, dreams are not fulfilled. A little light goes on in our head and we say: "I wonder

whatever happened to him … I wonder what her life is like."
Suddenly we are overcome by a desire to meet or talk to that
person; we feel the need to recapture our innocence. Just for a day,
an evening, ten minutes, we can verify our past and gain perspective for the future. And, who knows … ?'

Attempts at turning back the clock and meeting face to face can
spell disaster, but occasionally there is a happy ending. Crisp told
one interviewer the story of a wealthy businessman who asked the
detective to find out how his first love was faring. He found that she
had fallen on hard times and was dying of cancer in reduced
circumstances.

'The man was happily married, but he desperately wanted to do
something, and financially he was in a position to act. He visited
her regularly, bringing her a videotape recorder and other things to
make her last months more comfortable. He really cared for her –
and he was so pleased that he had found out in time that she was in
need of a friend.'

Lloyd Shulman, who runs an agency similar to Crisp's Old Flame
Finders, also in Los Angeles, also loves a happy ending. One of his
favourites, he told the London *Sunday Times*, concerned a retired
marine who had met a girl in Hawaii, just before the Japanese
attack on Pearl Harbor in 1941. 'He had only seen her twice while
he was cutting the lawn at the military base. He never exchanged
more than ten words with her. Forty years later, the marine
telephoned her. An hour later he was on a flight to Miami and met
her at a Holiday Inn in Fort Lauderdale. They are now living
together. My business is to reunite people that life has separated.
When people get old, when they divorce, they wonder what life
would have been like if they had stayed with their first love. So they
come to me.'

By the time a yearning for the past arrives, however, many
marriages have become a pressure cooker of suspicion and deceit.
Predictably, there are even agencies to cope with that, too. Most
investigators undertake what they call 'peace of mind' inquiries,
reporting to spouses on whether husbands or wives are having
illicit affairs. The Wives Infidelity Service was a little different. Like
many small agencies inspired by a bright idea, it vanished swiftly
from the face of the industry. But, for the twelve months it lasted in

1984, the service offered by Ron and Gigi Moers from a small office in the Chicago suburb of Schaumburg attracted a regular flow of clients.

For $75 for a five-week course – or a one-day crash course for really urgent cases – suspicious wives learned how to use telescopic cameras and surveillance equipment, and how to persuade motel receptionists to open their registers to check who had been sleeping with whom. Students were encouraged to rummage through their husbands' wallets, car glove compartments and desk drawers for unfamiliar telephone numbers and restaurant receipts for dinners for two.

'What's a little embarrassment when your marriage is at risk?' Gigi believed. 'Most women who come to us say they just have that feeling that there is someone else. If an affair is brought into the open quickly enough and a husband is forced to face the options, the whole situation can be saved. Faced with the divorce courts, alimony payments, the whole sordid cost of a fling on the side can be a very sobering experience.'

Spurred on by the Moers' counselling, one wife dressed up as a male brush salesman and knocked on the door of 'the other woman'. The lover invited 'him' in, and, over coffee, poured out the whole story. The disguised wife captured all the details on a concealed tape recorder.

Wigs and changes of clothing were advised for tailing operations. Students were instructed to carry a dog lead if they walked through strange neighbourhoods, so as to blend with the scenery. Once husband and lover checked into a motel, confrontation was not recommended. 'Be cool-headed and safety conscious,' Gigi advised. 'Wait until they walk out of the motel room and then get the picture using a telescopic lens and high-speed film.'

America was built on ingenuity and inventiveness, and private investigation has proved no exception. Most US agencies in general practice have one speciality for which they are noted. In Vincent Parco's case it is an unusual flair for tracking down tenants who sub-let apartments. Thousands of Manhattan residents live in rent-regulated apartments which they re-let for up to six times what they are paying for them. In the detection business it is known as primary-residence investigation, but Parco's agency has become known as the Lease Police. When the investigator himself is featured in the New York press, he is usually referred to as the Sherlock of Homes.

Parco stumbled on this lucrative market by accident in 1980. A doctor client in the Murray Hill area of New York wanted to enlarge his practice by expanding into an apartment next door. The resident, an attractive young woman who seldom seemed to be there, refused the doctor's offer of $25,000 to move out. When he asked Parco for help, the detective followed the woman from New York to Florida and discovered that she was the lover of the president of an international perfume company. The executive had bought an expensive apartment for her in New York's Beckman Place and the girl happily moved in, sub-letting her own fixed-rent apartment in New York to a travel writer for five times her normal payment. When confronted with Parco's dossier, the perfume president readily agreed to the doctor's offer.

'These were high-profile people who did not want to end up in court,' Parco said. 'I had names, dates, pictures – all the evidence. As soon as they saw it they decided to settle. From that day on we were swamped with landlord-tenant cases.'

Vincent Parco Associates now handles 15,000 such cases a year with a staff of fifteen full-time investigators. Together with his other investigative work, he grosses $10 million a year, an income he confidently projects for the next five years. Parco is a fast-talking detective who takes a pride in his appearance. His daily routine is a whirlwind of cases, all of which he tries to wrap up in record time. New York journalist Nancy Marx Better, associate editor of *Manhattan* magazine, caught him in mid-flow at his dilapidated brownstone headquarters on 35th Street, near Third Avenue, preparing for a regular staff meeting in 1988:

'He's wearing a tan seersucker blazer, beige shirt and taupe tie. Tucked into his breast pocket is a khaki handkerchief; tucked into the waistband of his brown pants is an impressive piece of hardware, the Walther PPK revolver preferred by James Bond. Parco struts around the office, genially barking orders at his secretaries. The investigators who are filtering up his back staircase are mostly in their mid-thirties and seem to share a predilection for sunglasses, even indoors. The men wear ties, the women spike heels. They crack jokes and smoke cigarettes until Parco calls them to order.

Sitting on the corner of his desk with his arms folded, grasping a thick computer print-out, Parco begins reciting a litany of wrong-doing: "Now, this one's a mess. I found out last night that this guy's dealing in narcotics and people are after him, and he's after people, and everybody owes everybody money, and all this other crap ... This guy doesn't care, cause he's a real wiseguy; he lives on the edge anyway ... Dolly, this is for you. It's a loft and they're running an agency for models and actresses and things like that ... So go up there and use your imagination. Make up a bullshit résumé. Say you went to the American Academy of Dramatic Arts, and the Lee Strasberg School and the Robert De Niro School of Impressionism, and whatever else you like." His employees find this hysterical and Parco grins broadly, pleased with his audience's reaction. "Okay, okay, this one's the Bulgarian spy, the one who thinks he's James Bond ... How are we doing on that California case? How did the sweep go on in St Mark's Place? How many did we nail?"'

Ninety per cent of the time, Parco's investigators never leave the office on lease cases. They check computer data bases, such as Motor Vehicle Department files, electoral registers and records of home ownership. Parco estimates that as much as twenty per cent of Manhattan's rent-regulated apartments have illegal tenants. 'These apartments can add up to hundreds of thousands of dollars for an owner, especially if he is planning to convert the building,' Parco observed. His company never advertises and welcomes cases which are a little out of the ordinary. Poisoned racehorses, headless corpses, or the sexual proclivities of college professors are not unusual investigations on the books.

However, after nine years as the biggest agency in the lease police business, the sub-letting trend is showing signs of decline. Renting in Manhattan is slowly being overtaken by co-ops and condominiums owned by individuals or groups of former tenants seeking a life free from landlords. Tenants, too, act more cautiously because of Parco's efficiency. He has already expanded into corporate areas, such as asset-searching and the screening of potential employees. Vincent Parco is a businessman as well as a detective and, in America, that may mean the sky's the limit.

The frontier energy Americans harness to work and commerce has diversified the investigation business more widely than in Europe. The pleasure of using peculiar skills to create wealth has carved strange backwaters of detection. Tom Reddin, for example, Los Angeles' former police chief, is a PI specializing in reconstructing scenes which lead to police officers facing prosecution for breaches of regulations. Mike Pascal, also of Los Angeles, has built a reputation for rescuing teenagers from religious cults. Al Zaretz of New York is hired by foreign governments to conduct political intelligence operations, and was retained by both sides in the Iran–Iraq War. Jack Hennerby of Pacific Investigations probes rigged boxing matches; John Eppick traces stolen aircraft.

In Britain detective life is more mundane. But the trend towards specialization, which grew out of the shift of emphasis from investigation to security, has produced some esoteric companies. Kroll Associates, an international agency dealing in corporate investigations, is well known in London boardrooms. Its investigators, who look more like executives or currency dealers than detectives, work from a building in Curzon Street, Mayfair, once used, appropriately, by the counter-intelligence agency MI5. The company, founded by former American district attorney Jules Kroll, grosses $40 million annually for examining dirty dealings in the City.

Hostile bidders create desperate anxieties, and worried directors have turned increasingly to the services of private eyes, though they invariably deny it. The ferocity of modern takeover bids and mergers has bred an atmosphere of paranoia in which companies snoop on each other at the slightest whiff of predators. In 1986 it was widely alleged in City columns that the Distillers Company hired a private eye known as Nicholas 'the Greek' Vafiadis to search for dirt on the Argyll Group which was attempting to take it over. 'The City,' warned the *Daily Telegraph*, 'is seeing shadowy figures on every street corner.'

Private detective Keith Walker fanned the embers of suspicion by claiming in the *Daily Telegraph* at the height of the takeover rumours that 'there isn't a board room or an office in the City where you can be sure of talking privately'. Walker added: 'What is perhaps more frightening is the fact that many of the listening devices planted in the City today – and there are literally thousands of them – may not be activated for years.' It was the kind of unsubstantiated assertion which, if true, served only to illustrate how far the cowboy element in British private investigation had proliferated. The bugging of telephones is a highly questionable and usually illegal exercise, unless the client also happens to be the subscriber.

The suggestion that private eyes were employed in the Distillers–Argyll bid was raised with the Department of Trade and Industry by Labour's terrier-like MP, Tam Dalyell, who was concerned by reports that the private eye Vafiadis had been gathering information on the personal background of Argyll boss Jimmy Gulliver. Fragments of the story were leaked to national newspapers, giving the whole affair a patina of seediness.

According to Stephen Leather in the *Daily Mail* in March 1986: 'The investigator began his campaign to smear Mr Gulliver by interviewing a former employee at a London hotel shortly after the launch of the takeover bid. At the Cavendish Hotel was Mr Vafiadis with the former mistress of a top Argyll executive, and Mr Harry Singer, former managing director of another Gulliver firm, Alpine Double Glazing. "Vafiadis wanted to know about Mr Gulliver's history with women, and any dirt concerning him," said Mr Singer.'

In contrast to such cloak-and-dagger dabbling in detection, Kroll Associates have built a reputation in the corporate investigation field, using methods honed over seventeen years of high-level commercial inquiries. 'Investigation techniques vary with each case,' Jules Kroll told *Business* magazine in November 1988. 'If the firm is acting for a company that is the target of a hostile takeover, for example, operatives will try to identify and interview former disgruntled employees of the predator corporation. They will also search court records to try to establish whether a corporation or its officers have been convicted of criminal offences. Tax rolls and other official records are also fruitful sources of information.

'Kroll,' according to *Business*, 'says that his employees usually identify themselves and the purpose of their enquiries. But he adds that there are circumstances in which operatives will work undercover or use subterfuge. To obtain information about a company, he volunteered, Kroll agents have been known to use the pretext of applying for a job to give them the opportunity to ask questions. When a company suspects its employees are stealing or committing fraud, a Kroll agent may go to work at the company under an assumed name. But, he says, "pretexts are used in less than five per cent of our cases".'

Pretext and subterfuge, on the other hand, are very much the stock-in-trade of the burgeoning K & R (kidnap and ransom) business. While this book has tried to confine the story of private detection strictly to investigation, the private eye's family tree has split into many branches. Although K & R is more concerned with the safe release of a kidnap victim, rather than the tracking down of the kidnappers in an investigative sense, it is interesting to note that the ploys of the business have evolved from a marriage of private detection and military intelligence techniques.

Private and company insurance in the UK against kidnap runs at around £40 million a year in premiums, a yardstick of the anxiety the possibilities evoke. As part of the intense security surrounding the subject, premiums never appear on company financial statements and even the policies themselves are referred to in code to discourage kidnap attempts. Rates are high to deter insurance fraudsters – around £40,000 for £1 million worth of K & R cover – and adjusted monthly in accordance with the travel itinerary of the insured. The rates include the cost of K & R specialists being flown on site in the event of kidnap and subsequent negotiations with the kidnappers.

The skills of the K & R experts centre on psychology and intelligence. Search and rescue, or indeed anything which may place the life of the victim at risk, is not part of their brief. The success of K & R experts, such as Control Risks, who employ thirty counter-insurgency experts, lies in educating policy holders to reduce the chances of kidnap in the first place. Their bargaining methods in dealing with kidnappers are said to have reduced total ransom demands worldwide from £582 million to £94 million in a ten-year period up to 1985.

The special talents of former SAS and military intelligence experts are put to a curious variety of uses in the investigation and security industry. In the summer of 1989, Country Guard, based in Mayfair, offered its services in the wilds of Scotland against deer gangs who were wiping out the stag population in some parts of the Highlands.

The company, established by SAS founder Colonel David Stirling, turned its attention to deer after widespread success against salmon poachers. The ripples from the annual illicit slaughter in the heather were far-reaching; police teams discovered that poaching profits were used to finance international drug deals.

'The company will assess the resources available, liaise with the police and talk to estate workers and local residents to make an appreciation of the problem,' Country Guard announced. 'We are also investigating the marketing of illegal game to make distribution more difficult. These poachers belong to criminal syndicates and are much more professional than the old one-for-the-pot man. They are likely to be involved in salmon poaching and cattle rustling, and will be highly organised.'

An indication of the gangs' determination and lawlessness in 1989 was the discovery of eleven pounds of Semtex explosive tied beneath a police informant's car, in the Highlands, and the sinking of Sheikh Mahommed el Rashid bin Maktoum's £250,000 yacht in the Kyle of Lochalsh when he stepped up security against poachers on his Scottish estate at Inverinate.

Specialization has become the flagship of the investigation industry, enabling it to survive and grow as society becomes more complex. In Pinkerton's day, chasing bank robbers seemed a simpler and more romantic business than sifting company records or scanning data banks for trademark infringements. Fiction latched on to the private eye as the loner with the gun or, in Britain, the intellectual unraveller of knots. Today's hi-tech specialists are unlikely to spawn a genre of novels and movies, but they are perhaps more ruthlessly professional – and cost effective – than a whole army of Lew Archers or Sam Spades.

Oddly, one of the oldest branches of the industry has changed little in formula, apart from cranking up its methods. Celebrity protection was one of the first new avenues of the business, after the drift to property protection. In the ensuing years it was elevated to something of a muscular art form and finally adapted to the electronic age by its outstanding exponent, Gavin de Becker of Los Angeles. De Becker's refinements in a field not usually noted for them concentrate on state-of-the-art computers and psychological profiling to protect clients who will happily part with $475,000 a year for peace of mind.

De Becker recoils at the suggestion that he and his staff are bodyguards, dismissing them as 'rent-a-hulks' and 'overweight one-time rock 'n' roll roadies'. He sees celebrities and high-profile public figures as potential targets for a crazed assortment of lovesick fans indulging in fantasy and, more disturbingly, for psychopathic killers. De Becker's studies of those who pose the greatest risk and his extensive data files on them are highly praised by experts. Dr Park Dietz, prosecution psychiatrist at the trial of John Hinckley, who tried to assassinate President Reagan in March 1981, acknowledges them as the best centralized records of their type in America. The FBI's Behavioral Sciences Unit also regards them as invaluable in filling a void which the government has neither the time nor the resources to cope with.

Working from letters in de Becker's files, Dr Dietz found that most cranks sent a photograph of themselves; verse, photographs of other people and a wide variety of nasties, including a dead coyote, blood, hair, teeth and bullets, also featured.

The investigator spent years researching reasons for fans' bizarre behaviour. According to the *Los Angeles Times* in August 1989, 'De Becker theorised that the frenzy accompanying Frank Sinatra's rise became socially acceptable behaviour and "our relationship to well-known people changed forever. If, in 1850, someone had stood up in an audience and screamed at the top of their lungs and pulled out their hair, they'd have gone off to an asylum."

'The magic of modern sound systems has created more problems, he noted, by making it possible for performers to communicate with audiences in so "intimate" a way that even fans in the third balcony believe that the message is just for them. "Idolatry in America is normal," but "what's a mild drug for most people is a poison for some people," de Becker said. He argued that the 80's are a time in which there has been an "explosion in degrees of famousness", with celebrities subject to obsessive interest by fans and the media. "There's bound to be someone out there who thinks you're representing the devil" or who is convinced "that little wink you gave before you left the stage was for him," he said.

'Further, the globally ubiquitous presence of television gives fans "a presumed intimacy" with their idols, and the medium gives schizophrenics "an excuse to be all alone," to fantasize about what they will do with or to a chosen celebrity, he said. TV airs a drama about a person who gets blown up while turning on the lights; a client soon receives a similar threat.'

The great fictional detectives of the forties picked a living on the underbelly of the American dream; real-life specialists of the eighties, like de Becker, inhabit a world in which the electronic age has turned into a nightmare. Fundamental changes in moral values and the nature of society forced the investigation industry to adapt and improve its effectiveness. Private eyes who have moved with the times currently enjoy a success and demand their predecessors could never have imagined. Like Allan Pinkerton, they have become corporate figures, close in commercial style and outlook to the clients who hire them. Information has become a sought-after commodity and the investigator, who has historically specialized in collecting it, now finds himself on the brink of a new era if he can respond to the challenge.

6   FAREWELL MY LOVELY

Women Investigators

The story of women private eyes can be traced back to a specific afternoon in 1856 when Allan Pinkerton's secretary announced that a young woman was in the outer office enquiring about a job. The detective recalled his first impression of Kate Warne when she walked into the room: she was a slim, brown-haired widow, 'graceful in her movements and self-possessed. Her features, although not what could be called handsome, were decidedly of an intellectual cast ... her face was honest, which would cause one in distress instinctly to select her as a confidant.'

Kate Warne sat down and wasted no time telling the bear-like Pinkerton that she wanted to become an undercover detective. Despite the huge success of his agency, he had never previously considered employing a woman, possibly because he did not imagine anyone would express interest in such a tough profession.

One of the first questions he asked Kate Warne was why she thought she qualified for the job. When she pointed out that she could 'worm out secrets in many places to which it was impossible for male detectives to gain access', the possibilities intrigued him.

The lone private eye may have become a cult figure of modern times, but his female counterpart has yet to find a convincing niche in the collective unconscious. Television series such as *Charlie's Angels* have done poor service to the image of the woman investigator. Female agents are as efficient and hard-working as their male counterparts – many more so – but there remain certain areas of detective work in which a woman attracts unwanted attention.

A male PI, for example, may spend an evening propped against a bar keeping observation, or maintain watch on a subject's house from his car for twelve hours. A woman in such circumstances might raise suspicions. The advantages of hiring women investigators, however, outweigh such disadvantages. Few people would suspect a woman of being a private eye, particularly as most of them take care to dress well and adopt a sociable, low-key approach.

Writ-serving is one area where one would least expect to encounter a woman. Subjects who doggedly avoid process servers relax when the knock at the door is only a pizza delivery girl. Few suspect that, when she hands over the food, there is a court order beneath it. Similarly, most men do not object to being approached in the street by an attractive market researcher with a clip board requesting personal information.

Pinkerton foresaw some of these possibilities. His biographer, James D. Horan, says that the detective stayed up most of that night mulling over the novel idea, and 'the more he thought about it, the more he liked it'. When Pinkerton worked a case, he took a delight in delivering the unexpected and outwitting criminals with a combination of planning and surprise. The notion of a woman agent opened up new opportunities, particularly in cases which demanded great secrecy or a delicate touch.

Kate Warne stayed with Pinkertons for many years, rising through the ranks to become a branch superintendent. Pinkerton increasingly saw situations in which Warne, and other women he later took on, could be a major asset.

During the American Civil War the investigator was summoned to Washington by President Lincoln and his cabinet for discussions on how Southern sympathizers in the capital could be kept under surveillance. He was later asked by General George McClellan to travel secretly to his Cincinnati headquarters to set up a secret service for the army. Kate Warne and another woman agent, Hattie Lawton, were among the first he gathered round him for the task.

Earlier, in 1861, Warne had played a vital role in heading off an attempt to assassinate Lincoln in what became known as the Baltimore Plot. She was instructed to book two private sleeping cars on a train out of town for 'a sick friend and party'. She then smuggled the president elect out of danger in Baltimore and travelled with him as personal protector.

Pinkerton regarded her so highly that he left special instructions in his will that the grave of Kate Warne, in Chicago's Graceland Cemetery, should always be maintained to perpetuate her memory.

Kate's modern equivalent at first appears to be a world apart, with her well-cut dress and golden hair styled in a cascade of curls. But Nancy McGuire, who runs Pinkerton's busiest bureau on Los Angeles' fashionable Wilshire Boulevard, shares the same cool-headedness and stiletto-sharp intellect. Nancy has a master's degree in criminology and directs an office bustling with ringing telephones, humming faxes and computers, and an endless ebb and flow of agents and clients. She often works a seven-day week and can be found writing reports at her desk after 8 p.m.

Most of Pinkerton's LA casework is corporate, which requires a high level of efficiency and diplomacy. Nancy juggles the cases of twenty undercover agents while monitoring sixty more on rota protection work at a foreign consulate. She was previously a research analyst in the savings and loan industry before playing a key role in the Rand organization problem-solving think-tank in Santa Monica. 'I had research in my blood,' she said. 'And investigation is just another form of research. Once you know how to find something you can find people and solutions to problems.'

Nancy put her theory into practice when she joined Pinkerton's as an agent. She still recalls her first case: 'I had to locate an adopted person by going through probate records. I was searching for a name, but everyone said I would never find it. When I turned to the last page of a family will it was there. I knocked on the man's door and said: "I'm Nancy from Pinkerton's and I've been looking for you for three months." When I told him his grandmother was looking for him, he began to cry and I cried, too.

'The job is exhausting but exhilarating. I was in the field for a number of years before I went into management; it's a different kind of high, but it's still a high.'

As she spoke, the telephone rang and an agent on surveillance checked in for instructions. The client was a major corporation which had an employee with a drink problem. After an argument at work, he stormed out and bought a rifle and made threats against his employer. Pinkerton's placed the worker under 24-hour surveillance, following him from bar to bar and documenting his movements. A restraining order had been served on him not to molest the client, and the agency had to ensure discreetly that he adhered to it. The client, meanwhile, had been placed under armed protection. Nancy listened to the agent's report, nodded several times, and ordered him to stick at it.

'Drugs are another area on the increase,' she explained. 'They are more pervasive everywhere, especially in the workplace. The drug and theft problems go hand in hand. In order to support a drug problem you might need to steal, and company product is readily available. Employers who think they just have a drug problem are often dismayed to find they have a theft problem, too.

'What we at Pinkerton's offer that's a little different from other agencies is an internal survey. I train my agents to go in and do a fly-on-the-wall. They look at everything and report on everything, so that we end up with a very good picture of what employee morale is really like, and what degree of supervision there is. We then make recommendations to beef up certain areas they might have problems in. In addition to this we go in and interrogate the bad guys to get them out of the situation, or prosecuted, whatever the client wants. The prosecution route is generally time-consuming and costly, so we may try to move them away from that – unless the problems are so ugly that there is no other way to get around it.

'Everyone benefits. Employers just want to get the bad apples removed and put some morale back. The people who are most unhappy about having druggies on the workforce are their fellow workers, because they really feel the abuse of the system it causes. We often leave an undercover operative in there, just to see how everything improves and to hear the good comments. Then we'll pull him out, so the client can actually see that things are improving.'

The corporate field plays an important part in Pinkerton's business. Nancy McGuire's Los Angeles office carries out background investigations for employers, from new applicants to executives seeking promotion. Banks request asset searches, creditors require 'judgement and means': 'I've got a $1600 judgement; should I collect?' 'No, it's going to cost you $900 to get the information, so let's think about this.'

There are integrity tests, where agents go into shops, bars, restaurants and hotels to find out how courteous and trustworthy employees are; skip-tracings, surveillances and, indigenous to LA, celebrity protection. Pinkerton has long-term contracts with studios to protect stars on location from obsessive fans. The agency often traces the writers of crank letters, in several cases to mental hospitals, and persuades them not to continue. The work is varied and unrelenting.

'I'm looking at sixty cases now,' Nancy said, surveying her desk, 'and I've got thirty-six more just come in. Some of it is mundane stuff, verifying information, but I find everything interesting. We spend a lot of time in court going through records, researching files, trying to glean pieces of information. The very last line of the last page in the last volume is often where you find it. I don't know how interesting that is to other people, but if you are an investigator and you have just spent the last nine hours in the archive of the county courthouse, it's pretty damned exciting. The case opens up again and you move forward into all kinds of things.

'Investigation is now getting much more computerized than it has ever been – and is becoming more so. It is convenient but it doesn't replace getting up and pounding the pavement, and never will. It will never replace the good pretext phone call, but it helps us to run a bunch of stuff quickly, and it's still exciting when you get a hit.'

Outside, six hopefuls wait to be interviewed for jobs as Pinkerton agents. Nancy's office is rapidly becoming Pinkerton's training base for agents from all over the country. Some of the applicants are policewomen.

'I have to retrain them,' Nancy said, preparing to leave. 'The police are used to getting their own way. Private work and public work are very different. We have to be a little more suave and convincing. Pretext is the name of the game. We can't knock on a door with the butt of a gun and get answers.'

Pioneer women private eyes did not court publicity to the degree of some of their male counterparts. They quietly got on with the job which, in Britain, was largely involved with obtaining evidence for divorce judgements. Occasionally, a feature writer in search of an unusual story would track one of them down. Before World War Two it was not uncommon to find women working for agencies, but interviews with them were quite rare.

Tit-Bits spent much of the inter-war period digging out sensational stories – a trend which began with a bizarre exclusive after the Armistice ending World War One: 'How We Lost The War, by the Kaiser'. In 1939 it turned its gimlet attention to women detectives and profiled a Mrs May Greenhalgh, who worked from home in Walthamstow, north-east London: 'Tall, handsome, stately, you would take her perhaps for an operatic prima donna –

but never for a detective. That is one of the secrets of her success … '

Mrs Greenhalgh, a middle-aged mother of six, had been sleuthing for twenty years by the time *Tit-Bits* discovered her. She was the daughter of a Lancashire schoolmaster and spent most of her girlhood reading detective fiction. After leaving school she trained as an artist, a fitting occupation for a young Edwardian girl, and later became a telephone operator and an insurance clerk. She appears to have been alert and self-possessed, and when a friend asked her to make some enquiries on her behalf she quickly produced the information. Up to this point she had never considered detection as a career. The favour for her friend spurred her to join an agency run by a former Scotland Yard officer. After changing employers several times, Mrs Greenhalgh decided to open her own business.

Her bread-and-butter work was gleaning evidence for divorce, with a few commercial clients on the side. It was all perhaps a little too routine for *Tit-Bits*, which felt it time to inject some colour: 'Some of these activities take her into questionable quarters where she has to prowl at dead of night. On these occasions she tells the local police what she is up to, and carries a police whistle.'

One curious facet of Mrs Greenhalgh's story was her fascination with disguise, a trait of almost all the women detectives who reminisced in print up to the 1950s. They sported wardrobes of blond wigs, old ladies' shawls, reversible coats and collections of spectacles. Most of them actually put these to good use on surveillance, though the fashion has almost died out today.

Like her counterparts, the homely Mrs Greenhalgh, who sounded more comfortable at home baking scones than hiding in bedrooms, had a disguise wardrobe which would have done justice to a music-hall entertainer. 'A little acting ability – a relic of my schooldays when amateur theatricals interested me – and a little imagination, are needed,' she advised *Tit-Bits* readers. 'I've been a bent old woman; a primly dressed, spectacled welfare worker; a door-to-door canvasser; an "accident case" swathed in bandages; housekeeper, tramp, wealthy widow, political agitator, and a hundred and one other things.

'People are wary of talking to you if they think you're a 'tec. A charwoman or a welfare worker is a useful sort of character to assume if you want to put likely informers off the scent. It's a grand job is sleuthing. I wouldn't give it up for worlds.'

The queen of disguise was probably Annette Kerner, born into a family of wealthy property owners, who trained as a mezzo-soprano before opening the Mayfair Detective Agency in the early 1920s.

'Who can keep up with this woman with a hundred faces?' *Leader* magazine demanded in 1948. 'At one moment she is a neat, matronly children's nurse pushing a pram in Hyde Park – to confront a gentleman blackmailer who enjoys feeding the birds by the Serpentine. Then – in a flash – she's an untidy waitress in a dingy backstreet restaurant where fences feed, or a cheerful char whose clumsiness with the wastepaper baskets is far from acci-dental. Take your eyes off her for a moment, and up bobs the Society woman vamp or the modest widow. And this collection by no means exhausts the repertoire of herself and her women col-leagues.'

Mrs Kerner was photographed in a variety of disguises to illus-trate the article. Indeed, it became such a prerequisite for an interview with any woman detective that one wonders if some of the outfits were kept in waiting for the press rather than for investigatory purposes. The last of this magnificent breed of theatri-cal lady detectives was Zena Scott-Archer, who recently retired from agency work but is still an active official of the World Associ-ation of Detectives, an international body of PIs who can call upon each other for help.

In 1983, when Mrs Scott-Archer was sixty-one, the *News of the World* was still following the reliable old trail laid down by *Tit-Bits* half a century earlier:

'You wouldn't give Zena Scott-Archer a second glance – she looks just like any other middle-aged housewife. But underneath the ordinary exterior is one of the world's top gumshoe girls, and a master of disguise.

'Zena, from Liverpool, has a wardrobe of wigs and special outfits for work. And she has a talent for imitating accents. She said: "I had to check on how honestly a bingo hall was being run, so I dressed up as a little old lady in a grey wig, flat shoes, thick stockings and a mac.

'"Flat shoes are helpful in disguise because they change your height and walk ... two dead giveaways. Posture identifies people more than their faces."'

The grand old ladies of British detection reeled off tips for disguise like recipes for Victoria sponge. Behind the performance put on for the press, however, there were some skilful investigators among their ranks. Few of them were specialists and, in keeping with other private eyes in general practice, they had to take whatever cases came along. Inevitably there was the usual unprofitable crop of cranks among them. Mrs Greenhalgh, Walthamstow's celebrated mother of six, related a typical example:

'A telephone call summoned me urgently to a London suburb. I didn't know what was expected of me. My caller didn't explain much, but emphasized the need for haste.

'Arriving at my destination I found a deserted road. It was pitch black night. There were only a few street lamps. The house to which I had been called was a large old place, standing back from the road behind a rambling garden. I walked up the path. My footsteps echoed loudly. I stood in the shadowy porch before a big, grim-looking front door. All was silent as a graveyard. I began to think of my police whistle, for I could feel there was something in the air, but I was outside the area of the police patrol.

'I lifted the knocker. It creaked. Bang. Bang. Two knocks rang through the house. Then there was silence again. Bang. Bang. Bang. Again I thudded on the door. Still mysterious silence.

'Then, slowly, the door began to open. First a few inches, then a foot, two feet, three feet. Inside was black as a cave. I could see nothing. My heart beat faster. A cold finger seemed to be running down my spine.

'I controlled myself with an effort, set my teeth, and stepped in. The door closed with a click. I turned sharply and, horror of horrors, standing by my side was a ghostly figure, clothed from head to foot in white.

'"Ah, you have come," said the apparition in a whisper. "Follow me." It led the way slowly upstairs. Gingerly, I followed.

'When we got into the light of one of the bedrooms I found that the alarming figure was none other than my client, the elderly woman who had rung me up. She was completely enveloped in white rubber sheeting, with white rubber helmet and top boots to match.

'It turned out that she was suffering under a delusion that her neighbours were plotting to electrocute her by pushing live electric wires through the walls and floors.

'"Take off your clothes and get into the bed next to mine," she said. "You must sleep with me and guard me."

'I didn't undress, but lay on the bed, remaining very much awake. The woman climbed into her bed, still dressed in her shroud. Soon, she dropped into a fitful sleep. Then, suddenly, I had another shock. She threw off the clothes, jumped out of bed and cried: "Listen."

'I heard nothing, but she declared there were movements under the floor. It was her neighbours busy with high power cables, she insisted. And so, in the middle of the night, I had to tear up lino and prise up floorboards to show that there were no hidden murderers.

'I had four days of this nightmare, and eventually had to call in the local electricity officials to prove that the insulation was in order and that there was nothing in her fantastic beliefs.'

Mrs Greenhalgh might have profited from sub-contracting her services to someone like Nella Jones who, though not a private investigator in the accepted sense, employs her talents to help police track down criminals.

Mrs Jones, a London housewife turned full-time medium and writer, works on major police cases on which it has been felt necessary to consult a psychic. The police are normally reticent about discussing help from paranormal agencies, but one senior detective in the Metropolitan Police Art Squad, who has worked with Mrs Jones and other psychics, went on record with his views in *Psychic News* in 1982: 'There are two problems with using psychics,' he said. 'Firstly, the police have to establish a psychic's genuineness. Secondly, clues from psychics can be frustrating because they cannot just produce the whole answer to order.

'I, and other colleagues, have always been impressed by the fact Nella is genuine. She is not a fraud. The official police view of psychics is that, though we are always happy to have help, so far their record is that they have not been able materially to assist the police. But Nella has proved her paranormal ability. Her premonitions have startled and impressed me.'

Mrs Jones stresses that she is not really interested in catching criminals, but occasionally, if a serious crime is about to happen, she receives a picture of it. And, because of her reputation, the police take her seriously.

'I told the police about an armed robbery on a Saturday afternoon in Lewisham High Street in the late 1970s. They staked out the road but nothing happened. Then the following Saturday, the robbery took place just as I had described. Sometimes things go wrong because the clues are misinterpreted – but the clues are right.'

Her first success was the recovery of a valuable painting, 'The Guitar Player', by Vermeer, which was stolen in a £2 million art robbery from Kenwood House, Hampstead, in February 1974. Unfortunately, her advice was so accurate that she was twice almost arrested as an accomplice to the theft.

'I had a vision of a lake and a field near Kenwood House where a clue was hidden,' Mrs Jones explained. 'I was so convinced I rang the police. Instead of treating me like a crank they asked me to help. I said something metal was in the field. I found an alarm system from the back of the painting at the spot. I also located the picture's frame. It turned up in a churchyard next to St Bartholomew's Hospital, in London.'

Some women private eyes were daughters of investigators, or of policemen who retired to open their own agencies. Kathleen Cummings, a working London private eye, went into detection in 1952 without any family connections. She had five years' training arresting shoplifters for the John Lewis Partnership before becoming an investigator. Her career decision, she recalls with amusement, was considered a disgrace to her family. The stigma of having a daughter who arrested people in the street was eclipsed only by the trauma of her becoming a private detective.

'Women private detectives were almost unheard of then, and certainly few ran their own agencies,' she recalled. 'My parents were shocked. "Women can't do that sort of thing," they cried.'

Kathleen has proved that there are some cases in which the feminine touch is indispensable. She was asked to investigate an allegation of malicious slander by two women schoolteachers in Kent, who suspected that unpleasant rumours about them were being spread around their village. Kathleen headed straight for the most reliable source of local gossip, the village hairdresser, and booked herself an appointment. Then, posing as a parent thinking of moving into the area and placing her children in the local school, she toured shops asking questions.

'It was true,' she said after tracing the source of the gossip. 'The village was rife with rumours. In this case a man would have stuck out like a sore thumb.'

For some well-to-do parents with daughters who had investigative aspirations, the shock was not so great. Working for a living was considered 'modern' and tolerated with amusement while a strong-willed girl waited for marriage. The stage and a modelling career, something of a middle-class closed shop in the pre-war years, were deemed acceptable, provided they were not taken too seriously and created no obstacle to a suitable engagement. It was from this unlikely background that Melodie Walsh came. In the years following World War Two she not only broke with convention and made a career out of private detection, but provided a much-needed service for members of London society who had problems which they might not have wished to entrust elsewhere. Melodie Walsh, whose father was a close friend of G. K. Chesterton and Hilaire Belloc, was accepted socially, and a wide variety of work came her way.

Like Annette Kerner, whose parents owned the freehold of most of London's Wardour Street, she spent some time in the theatre before opening her agency. One typical case illustrates the way in which many women detectives handled not only a wide range of work but also successfully managed to break away from the dreary round of divorce and writ-serving.

One of Melodie Walsh's clients was a large London store which, in the early 1950s, was losing several thousand pounds' worth of furs from its stockrooms each week. The senior director was reluctant to call in the police because he suspected an inside job and hoped to avoid a scandal. He had told no one about the missing stock, not even his junior partner, and hired Melodie Walsh as a model to keep observation.

The detective immediately spotted a weak link in the system. Furs were removed from the stockroom every day and taken by sales representatives to clients' homes for approval. They were booked out and booked back in again, but it would be quite easy to remove three furs instead of two. The most likely suspect turned out to be the junior partner, whom she described as 'Mr J.'. Melodie sat down one evening with the senior director, 'Mr C.', and went through the fur storeroom book and check slips for two years.

'During the year we were checking, there had been several changes among the representatives. Those who had left might have taught their successors the trick, but it was very unlikely. What was much more likely was that Mr J. – the only man who had been there all the time – was the thief. I did not breathe a word of my suspicion to Mr C. I had no evidence yet, and I did not want anybody getting in my way.

'Mr C. was a grand chap – a fine fatherly type and as open as the day. His face would have given him away to the junior partner every time they met if I had told him my theory. That would be red light enough for a smart operator like Mr J. I carried on working in the store as usual, but with one eye always on my suspect. Each time he took out furs to a client I had an assistant waiting outside the store to tail him.

'It took us only three days to catch him delivering a handsome chinchilla cape to the home of a young lady who was certainly no client of ours. Well, the case itself was pretty humdrum, you'd say, and so it was. But when we put Mr J. on the spot we found that every fur he had stolen had been carefully stored away, not sold. They were all eventually recovered without much trouble.

'His plan was slowly but surely to bring the business down by these thefts until it was on the edge of bankruptcy and the senior partner was ready to get out on almost any terms. Then the stolen furs could gradually be brought back. The reason the young man wanted to ruin his partner in this particular way was simply to prove to Mr C.'s daughter that he was a better man than her father. It appears he had been courting her unsuccessfully for a long time. She had refused him because she found him weak and unreliable, not a bit like the sturdy, forthright father whom she adored. Mr J. was out to show her she was wrong.'

What happened to the desperate Mr J. is not recorded.

Some of the well-to-do women who became respected investigators drifted into the business in an almost dilettante way. Francesca Woodhouse, according to the *Sun* in 1984, was in her early twenties, and unable to pursue the police career she had hoped for, when she became a private eye. 'My father is a solicitor and my parents don't approve of what I do at all,' she said. 'They think being a private detective is not at all respectable.' Zena Scott-Archer was one of several who picked up the reins from a detective father. There were also women who found themselves forced into investigation by necessity.

Anne Summer, a convent-educated girl married to a London lawyer, went through the trauma of a marriage breakdown in 1964. She was twenty-seven at the time and her health had broken under the pressures of the separation. Her three-year-old son had to be placed in a home until she recovered. Anne Summer's husband obtained right of custody over his son and removed him to the family home, where he hired a nanny to look after him. Anne had to have psychiatric treatment for a nervous breakdown, which helped to ease her back on to the path to health. She knew, however, that the only route to a complete recovery would be by seeing the divorce through to its conclusion.

In an attempt to take her mind off her problems, her solicitor asked her for a favour at short notice. A client who was leaving the country the same evening wanted to find out if his estranged wife was living with another man. The solicitor rang round several investigation agencies, but no one could cover the case. Anne Summer happened to be sitting in the office, so he asked her to help.

'It will be therapeutic,' the lawyer said. 'Shake you out of your depression. Give you something to do. Why not have a go?'

'It was probably the combination words of "something to do" and "having a go" that talked me into it so easily,' Anne wrote in her autobiography, *But I Couldn't Do That* (1968). 'I'd been feeling so monumentally frustrated and helpless about my own affairs. There was nothing I could do about anything personal. No way of having a go at anything to ease my position. Nothing legal, that is.'

The solicitor lent her his Bentley to drive to a mews address off London's Westbourne Grove to approach the woman. Anne found the address from an *A–Z*, glanced at a photograph of the woman, and knocked at the door. Without working out any kind of plan, she announced herself as a market research interviewer and was invited inside. A list of questions about washing powder and groceries quickly revealed that the woman was washing and cooking for a man she was living with. Probably she used the ploy because it felt most comfortable – Anne had worked for J. Walter Thompson, the advertising agency, some years earlier.

She could hardly have known at the time, but the same pretext is used by private detectives around the world. A favourite variation is employed in industrial compensation or insurance claims, when the subject purports to have lost his or her sense of smell. A woman investigator will knock at the door with perfume samples, 'conducting a market survey', and ask the claimant to test them.

Anne Summer went on to run her own successful detective agency, which turned out to be whimsically different from most of her competitors. Encouraged by the discovery of her own hidden talents, she employed housewives, actresses and out-of-work journalists to carry out enquiries for her. Their success did not detract from the skills needed for investigation, but indicated, perhaps, what an important part ingenuity and resourcefulness play in the pressure of casework.

There is no doubt that women investigators are equal to men on any type of case. Zena Scott-Archer, however, believes they are better. 'I'm biased, of course,' she told *Weekend*'s Tony Wilmot in 1984, before her retirement. 'But many of our cases are matrimonial and wives find it easier to talk to another woman about intimate problems. Women are more observant and more conscientious in taking statements. They are less likely to flannel. If there is nothing to report, they say so.

'A man will say of a house, "Oh, it was a bit drab." A woman will say, "The curtains were shabby, the wallpaper upstairs was peeling, the front door needed a coat of paint, there were five unwashed milk bottles on the step and a child's tricycle in the hallway."'

Mrs Scott-Archer joined her ex-Scotland Yard father's detective agency as his secretary in 1946. She soon took to investigation and discovered the advantage of being female.

'A woman can follow someone into shops more easily without attracting attention to herself. It's more natural for women to be browsing. She can also watch somebody in the mirror of her make-up compact. One of my women agents once had to follow a woman whose husband thought she was having an affair. All the wife did was go from thrift shop to thrift shop. Now a man following her would have stood out after a while.'

Women detectives have always been expected to undertake any kind of work and one male detective actually staffed his agency entirely with women because he considered them more effective. David Gregory, who ran a Bristol detective agency until 1987, employed six women who were trained in self-defence and fast driving. In the manner of *Charlie's Angels*, they could muster between them skills in skiing, horse-riding, motor-cycling, para-chuting, skin-diving and archery.

'Women make better detectives than men,' he said at the time. 'They are discreet, charming, dedicated, and they work harder than men.'

One of his agents, Karen Payne, who qualified on a combat training course, spent five weeks undercover in America watching a contracts manager whose employers suspected him of making deals on the side.

'I had to pose as a secretary, snooping as hard as I could to find out, by fair means or foul, exactly what he was up to. The kind of information I was looking for doesn't lie around on desks, so I had to chat up all his business friends and go through files whenever I got the chance. My adrenalin never stopped running and when I think now of the risks I took, my blood runs cold. Nevertheless, I managed to nail him. He was siphoning money out of the firm into a batch of private bank accounts and had been doing it for so long he got careless. That's when the good detective steps in.'

Her colleague Sue Greig shared the view that women have an edge over men: 'The advantage that a woman sleuth has over a male is that men will confide in her because they think she's a brainless, harmless bundle of fluff, and women will confide just as eagerly because we're part of a sisterhood. Charm and glamour are useful weapons when it comes to pumping information out of men, and they don't realize how easy they are to outwit.'

Sue and Karen were engaged to track down 20-stone financier Keith Hunt, when he disappeared in 1983, leaving two thousand worried investors in his troubled Warwick-based company, Exchange Security, but Hunt successfully evaded both the women and the police. In the same year, however, they located runaway jeweller Robert Chatwin of Leamington Spa, who was interviewed by Spanish police and arrested under the Theft Act when he returned to Britain.

Their work contrasted greatly with that of Annette Kerner, who was perhaps Britain's best-known woman detective in the late

1940s and early 1950s. Mrs Kerner was brought up in the sheltered ease of a middle-class home, but always showed a rebellious streak. Her first bid for freedom occurred shortly before she was sent to finishing school when she tried to catch a bus into the city for an unchaperoned sight-seeing trip. The second came at seventeen when she fooled her parents into thinking she was visiting Switzerland for a holiday with family friends, but secretly negotiated a contract to sing in a Geneva club. Annette had studied singing in London with Ivor Novello's mother Clara, and Novello himself urged her to sing professionally.

Her family strongly objected to the idea and thwarted all attempts at a stage career in Britain. Annette secretly arranged the engagement in Geneva and made the journey by crossing the Channel to France. The trip had a marked influence on her future choice of career. She began the voyage by flirting with a young English fellow passenger, who later explained that he was an intelligence officer keeping watch on a suspected foreign agent. The contents of this passenger's briefcase were vital evidence of his guilt. She coolly stole the case and so impressed the agent that he contacted his headquarters in London and urged them to engage her for special freelance work. The officer persuaded the Geneva club to release her from her contract and then secured her bookings at a Zurich nightclub which was a favourite watering hole for intelligence agents. When Annette finally returned to England, she found it almost impossible to settle to a routine existence and became a private detective. Although small in stature, she built a fearsome reputation. When a thief told his defending counsel that he had been arrested by Annette Kerner, he was told: 'Then you had better plead guilty.'

The files in her Baker Street office contained many sensational cases, including a scandal from the 1920s known as the Billie Carlton drugs case. To obtain evidence successfully, Annette had to convince a suspect that she was an opium addict. While working undercover she was taken to a London opium den, which she had arranged for the police to raid. Lice crawled on the sheet on which she lay and, to play for time and avoid having to smoke the opium, she insisted on a clean sheet. By the time it arrived there was still no sign of the police and to avoid suspicion she had to start smoking. More than half an hour passed, as she fought to overcome drowsiness, before her rescuers burst through the door. A few weeks later, Annette was held captive by the man eventually found guilty, who slashed both her wrists to prevent her from escaping. Hardly the life her parents envisaged when she was enrolled at finishing school.

Annette Kerner proved her theory that women detectives can not only be tougher than men but more understanding in cases of divorce and separation. Britain's relaxed divorce laws have taken away much of the traditional work of private investigators, forcing them to explore other fields. In Ireland, however, there is still an abundance of divorce work for detectives. Sandra Mara, President of the Association of Irish Investigators, is the only woman private eye in the country to run her own agency. K Security, based in a northern suburb of Dublin, is Ireland's biggest detective agency, founded by Sandra's father who was also Eire's first private investigator.

As a child she used to travel with him on business, but he tried to dissuade her from taking it up as a career. At the age of 19 she persuaded him to let her start at the bottom, preparing case files, studying law and learning the techniques of the trade, from surveillance to giving evidence in court. The agency has handled matrimonial cases for as long as Sandra can remember. Times change, however, even in a staunchly Catholic country. Women once may have accepted their fate, but are no longer prepared to endure a bad marriage.

'We get women married only three months asking us to find out about their husband's affairs,' Sandra told the *Guardian* in 1985. 'Amazingly, some women still blame themselves for the breakdown of their marriage, even in cases of extreme violence ... It is unfair to women to put up with this violence because of so-called Catholic morality. When, on top of this, husbands have affairs, wives are not prepared to put up with the violence they would otherwise tolerate. The cases are heard in camera, so no one knows how horrific some marriages are. Generally speaking, Irish society's attitude is more lenient towards men.'

When women clients walk into the offices of K Security, they are relieved to find a woman to talk to and generally pour out their problems. The situation, in divorce or otherwise, is common to women investigators all over the world. A few die-hard Sam Spades might disagree, but a woman's emotional make-up and observation is in many ways more suited to the discreet approach of private investigation than that of a man.

To date, most of the headline-catching investigations have been attributed to male detectives, primarily because it is a male-dominated industry. Houston, which has the dubious honour of being the murder capital of the USA, produced one notable exception. In 1985, a rookie private eye named Kim Paris surprised both the police and her employers by obtaining vital evidence from a double murder suspect. Kim, the good-looking daughter of a suburban dentist, came from a comfortable middle-class background where the world of violent crime was safely confined to TV drama.

She had worked for a detective agency for less than a year, mainly on fraud inquiries. When the bureau accepted an assignment to look into the 1982 slayings of prominent Texas lawyer James Campbell and his wife Virginia, who were shot in their sleep while two of their grandchildren slept at the foot of the bed, Kim found herself on the case and boldly approached the suspect.

Philip Finn, the *Daily Express* man in New York, takes up the story: 'For ten weeks the 23-year-old detective dated David West. But she told him she could not consider his marriage proposal until he disclosed the "dark secret" he had hinted at.

'And after West, 28, revealed his involvement in a double murder as they sat in a car, Kim asked him to drop her at a shop to buy cigarettes.

'That was the last he saw of the woman he hoped would be his bride. Moments later police officers who had been monitoring the conversation swooped and charged the dumbfounded West.

'Detectives in Houston praised Kim for her cool courage and professionalism.

'Her boss, Clyde Wilson, called in by the dead couple's family, said: "West certainly wasn't going to sit down and spill the beans to me or one of my men. It seemed logical to bring a girl in to gain his confidence."

' ... Kim simply knocked on the suspect's door one night on a pretext and later spent three hours in a bar with her target. Afterwards they were together three or four nights a week, but she made sure the relationship remained platonic.

'"I kept dancing around the subject of sex. David and I spent a lot of time discussing history, politics and religion," she said.

'Kim said when he proposed she encouraged him to tell the "awful" thing about the past which he had previously mentioned. It was then that the private agency contacted the police and Kim was given a tape recorder. The love sting went without a hitch.

'Said Kim: "This was very emotional for me. You can't get involved with someone for two and a half months without there being real ties. I have no qualms about what I did, though."'

7   SAM SPADE'S FUTURE

The Way Ahead for the Private Investigator

It was just another LA morning – sirens wailing, drivers fuming on the San Diego Freeway, and the man at the earthquake survival store rolling up his shutters to start the day. Up in Van Nuys, a northern suburb of Los Angeles, where the Valley fog mingles with the city smog, the sprinklers were already hissing on the miniature golf course near Pinkerton's long, low headquarters. A few streets away, student private eyes were pushing through the tinted swing doors of the Nick Harris Detective Academy.

As they made their way to the lecture rooms, few could resist a curious glance towards the offices where phones rang non-stop and figures in California casuals held impromptu conferences. The single-storey building on Enadia Way also houses the Nick Harris Detective Agency. The one student in ten who passes the tough qualifying course hopes one day to be offered a job there.

Nick Harris is no longer around. The original Sam Spade hung up his gun and died peacefully back in 1941, leaving one of America's oldest investigation bureaux, the Nick Harris Detective Agency, founded in 1906, and the world's first detective academy established a year later, which pre-dates even that of the FBI. Nick Harris's chair as president is occupied these days by Milo Speriglio, who oversees an agency retained by 14,000 attorneys and boasts a success rate of a million assignments in 83 years.

In the wild and restless years of the fifties, Speriglio was known as Mad Milo, a rock 'n' roll DJ who retired at twenty-one to look for a new career. Mad Milo first tried roller derby, but the pace was too slow. It was in the middle of watching the private eye series *Peter Gunn* on his thirteen-inch black and white TV that Milo knew what he wanted to be. It was not quite a vision from the Almighty, but he enrolled at the Nick Harris Detective Academy and, in the best American tradition, ended up owning the company in the mid-1960s.

All his agents are former students who completed the gruelling requirements of 6000 hours' classroom and on-the-job training, plus written and oral examinations, to carry the badge of a California licensed investigator.

As students sat down for the first lecture of the day, Chief Special Agent Marcus Joseph's car bounced over the bleached sidewalk into the Nick Harris car park. Marcus, in lumberjack shirt, trainers and faded Levis, walked stiffly to his office. He was wearing a back brace to ease the pain of a recent injury but, like all Harris agents, it would take a lot to keep him off a case.

There is no such thing as a typical day for a PI working in the urban mayhem of Los Angeles, except, perhaps, irregular hours, missing lunch and wondering if the caseload will ever end. After sorting through his mail and picking up messages, he made his first call to the home of a celebrity doctor who had lost $180,000 of art treasures and jewellery in a theft.

When the doctor reported the matter, two overworked Los Angeles Police Department detectives called round and filed a routine report which joined a mountain of others awaiting attention. The doctor, anxious to recover two Dali lithographs and his wife's heirloom collection of antique East Indian jewellery, visited a psychic whose spirit guide directed him to the Nick Harris bureau behind McDonald's parking lot on Sherman Way, where the palms are knee-high in exhaust fumes.

'The police are very co-operative,' Marcus said. 'Los Angeles has one of the smallest law enforcement agencies in the country – around 1500 officers on each shift to cover eight million inhabitants. Their attitude to us is: "Go ahead. If you get something, it's justified."'

His immediate suspects were the husband and wife domestics who may have left the door unlocked to admit the thieves. The couple had disappeared after the robbery, along with the doctor's treasures. At the office Marcus tried to get a lead on them through the Harris data bank of criminal records, property ownership and other files relating to eight million residents of greater Los Angeles. Once a likely address was obtained, the job went undercover. Marcus, shaggy-haired with bright brown eyes, leaned back in his swivel chair and worked out his next move. He had to establish whether the couple were tied in to the theft and find evidence to back up his instinct.

'There are several ways I can go about this,' he said. 'I can befriend them. Maybe get a couple of toughs to pick a fight with the guy in a bar. Then, I'll step in and save him, win his trust. The thing is to get in close. Check him out from the inside. If there is one thing in his house to link him to the theft, we have a hit.'

In the meantime, he picked up the phone and called a Los Angeles detective – one of only two in America specializing in art thefts – and asked him to run down lists of fences likely to handle Dali lithographs.

In the classroom next door, students were reading reports of work they had been set outside college hours. Each of them had been told to shadow someone without being observed, and file a formal account of the surveillance. A gangly blonde in a micro skirt had her legs jammed beneath the tiny desk as she listened to advice from instructor Mark Lincoln. To her left an overweight trucker leaned back and threatened his fragile chair with collapse. The class included an ex-fireman, a woman writer, a new bride anxious to escape the constrictions of her department store job, and a para-legal from a Wilshire Boulevard attorney's office.

'The first two weeks of the seven-week course are ninety per cent raw enthusiasm,' said Nick Harris Vice-President C. J. Mastro, step-ping between piles of reports stacked neatly on her office floor, waiting to be read. 'After that, it's cry time. They become very afraid at the sheer volume of work they have to get through and need a lot of moral support. Their ages range from eighteen through to fifty-eight. Most have not taken an exam since high school, so the pressure is heavy. They start off as twelve individuals who don't know each other. By the end of the course they are very close. Two of them we had even got married.'

Students who graduate from the Nick Harris Academy are regarded as well-trained and reliable. Offers of work are not hard to find and several have gone on to operate their own successful agencies. The seven-week master's course is claimed to be equiv-alent to knowledge acquired in four years of on-the-job training. Some of the practical subjects covered include drug analysis, elec-tronic sweeps for hidden wiretaps, insurance fraud, tracing missing persons and undercover work. It is certainly highly intensive and most students feel the strain. From the outset they are told that the pass rate is only one in ten, but the academy is nearly always successful in finding them employment.

According to the brochure, 'a graduate could expect to earn $8.50 to $12 per hour, plus expenses to start. Increases are rapid. After paying your dues, within three years you could apply for a state license. The minimum per hour charged today for just a basic assignment is $45. Working full time you could earn in excess of $93,000 a year.'

The figures are accurate for a reputable investigator. The Nick Harris Detective Agency, certainly not the most expensive of its kind, publishes a guideline to fees which gives a broad idea of the remuneration available for Californian private detectives. All figures are minimum fees:

> Major investigations – $5000
> Investigations to determine child custody – $700
>   plus expenses
> Parental kidnapping, routine trace – $1000
> Lifting fingerprints – $135
> Expert advice on questioned documents – $285
> Surveillance of spouses – $45–55 per hour, plus
>   expenses. A typical surveillance costs around
> $300 a day.
> Nationwide missing heir search – $1000
> Tracing postal forwarding addresses – $27
> Criminal records search completed in 24 hours –
> $43
> Search for court judgements, completed in one
>   hour – $38
> License plate number search – $26
> Address from phone number – $19
> Property asset trace, up to five parcels of land –
> $33
> Social Security number trace – $35
> Location of hidden or undisclosed safe deposit box
>   – $385
> Search for concealed accounts – $775

These are extracts from a long list of services provided by Harris in line with most other American detective agencies. They give an indication of the wide availability of public records, on computer and microfiche, at the private eye's disposal. In many cases, only a name is required. Some of the information can be obtained merely by punching a few keys; miracles, as they say, take a little longer.

The academy is interesting because students can learn the art of investigation alongside a working agency. Some schools offer correspondence courses, but the advantage of hands-on experience is obviously greater. One reason for the continuing prosperity of the American investigation industry is the emphasis placed on training to obtain a licence. Unofficial estimates place the proportion of unlicensed investigators working in California as high as 85 per cent. In many ways they work outside the law, but heavy restrictions are deliberately placed upon them. The system makes it clear that licences are not handed out freely – federal examiners are tough on applicants – and acquiring one opens all kinds of doors to official co-operation.

The Association of British Investigators runs its own training seminars, both for existing members and people interested in joining the industry. In the absence of external regulation, the Association applies stringent qualifications to anyone applying to register for membership. Some years ago there was a qualifying examination, but it was thought to lack the thoroughness of face-to-face vetting. Because the government has consistently refused to introduce any form of regulation for the 3000 private eyes working in Britain, the Association, with its 500 members, does its best to screen applicants itself. Potential members are grilled by a four-man panel of investigators to establish their honesty and skill. In addition, credit checks are run against them to ensure they are capable of running an agency efficiently.

The Association also tries to run checks to discover if applicants have criminal convictions, but this is almost impossible within the limits of the law. Many members of the ABI feel, like boat detective Peter Clark, that criminal records should be a matter of public knowledge. 'Britain is hidebound by secrecy,' says ABI member George Rivers. 'American colleagues cannot believe that even a simple matter of tracing car numbers cannot be done legally. The situation is, in fact, worsening. Some London Boroughs now refuse to have electoral registers on display in public libraries. If you wish to find an address, the librarian goes away to see if it is listed. If it isn't, there is no way of running further checks on the register. It is quite common for solicitors to offer us work which we have to turn down because it is impossible to obtain the information without breaking the law.'

In January 1989 five private investigators were prosecuted at Winchester for collaborating with policemen to obtain criminal records and names of vehicle owners from the Police National Computer. It is ironic that these offences, and others like them, would perhaps never have existed if Britain's laws governing access to information were in line with those of many other countries. Secrecy breeds secrecy, and the cloak and dagger approach of some investigators, which those who value civil liberties find unacceptable, would be largely unnecessary in a more liberal environment. To compound the inconsistency of the system, there have been many allegations that government intelligence agencies themselves have retained fringe investigators for work of questionable legality. If this is true, it would seem paradoxical that one hand of the Establishment encourages cowboy operators, while the other denies reputable investigators the means to regulate their own industry.

The final ignominy, say private eyes, is that they are not allowed to promote their services on TV or radio because, they say, they are regarded, along with sex shops and other dubious services, as undesirable advertisers. They point out that solicitors, who advertise widely on local radio, would not be able to conclude many of their cases without the help of private detectives. With the Home Office effectively closing the door on countless pleas for recognition, the answer may lie in European legislation. Associations of investigators from all the EC countries are preparing for a further campaign when European trade barriers are removed in 1992.

Michael Gough, president of the Association of British Investigators, is optimistic about the future. 'In Europe there is a licensing system,' he said, 'and by 1992 something will be done here. There are too many cowboys and no regulation to say that someone cannot open up in business and call themselves a private investigator. There is nothing to stop anyone, for example, coming out of prison and calling themselves a private investigator. We get such confidential information from clients that if someone was inclined, we could blackmail them. The aim of the Association is to make sure there is statutory control to stop it.'

There have never been regulations in Britain to prevent anyone from calling themselves a private eye. In 1956, Richard Herd of the London *Evening News* tested the shortcomings of the system by setting himself up in business as an investigator. Together with a colleague, he obtained a form at the office of the Registrar of Business Names in Bush House and answered ten basic questions on it, ranging from the name of the business to the date Herd proposed to commence trading. The *Evening News* office boy was then dispatched with the form and five shillings and the reporter was informed in due course that he owned a registered private detective agency.

'No one made any inquiry about our background,' Herd wrote. 'We could have been ex-prisoners or bankrupts, we could have been potential blackmailers or thieves.'

The situation remains exactly the same as it was more than thirty years ago, with standards maintained only through self-regulation and training. In Ireland, opportunities to improve investigative skills were offered at a course in private detection by University College, Dublin, when the September term of 1986 opened. The first course was made up of twenty two-hour lectures given by experts on law, insurance fraud, forensic science and electronics. Students, who came from investigation agencies, banks and insurance companies, also carried out field studies and watched court cases re-enacted on video. The final series of lectures covered anti-terrorist techniques, counter-industrial espionage and VIP protection.

America has always been a little more bizarre. For £1800 anyone can enrol for a seventeen-day course at the Academy of Corporate Security and Private Investigation in Miami, Florida, to learn such subjects as competitor intelligence, industrial espionage, electronic eavesdropping, bugging, de-bugging, advanced firearms training and many other skills. The difference is that the knowledge passed on for use in private investigation comes not from gumshoes but from lecturers with CIA and intelligence backgrounds.

The man who runs the academy has a wealth of experience. G. Gordon Liddy, the former Wall Street attorney, FBI agent and White House special aide, who was jailed for his part in the Watergate burglary, has an impressive business card. Beneath his name, it reads: 'For the Unusual'. On the reverse is a list of services provided, ranging from anti-terrorism to sophisticated corporate security.

The four years he spent in jail proved no handicap to his career. On the contrary, Liddy's refusal to break his silence about Watergate made him widely admired. 'I don't know of any American who was raised by his parents to be a snitch or to admire tattletales,' he said. 'I've had plenty of people, including Democrats, come up and say: "I don't like your politics, but I like the way you handle yourself."'

Liddy is a relaxed but very tough character with a steel will which surfaces in most things he undertakes, from a TV chat show which was taken off the air, to his own SAS-style unit, called the Hurricane Force, which offers to go anywhere and do anything for the right price. Anyone considering taking advantage of the opportunity is advised to have between £333,000 and £666,000, depending on the equipment required and the risk involved.

The team, which is closely linked to the work of the academy, says it will not do anything to embarrass any law enforcement agency. But Liddy adds: 'We won't call the Government every time we get involved in anything.' Two former SAS men are said to be members of the unit. One of them, who referred to himself only as John, told journalist Philip Finn of the *Daily Express* in 1986: 'This is not a mercenary outfit that jumps into action for anyone who has the need or the cash. I don't think we'd be inclined to rescue a drug dealer who was imprisoned in Mexico by Mexican authorities. We want to help legitimate people who have been victimised.'

The skills of the team are also passed on to students at the academy. Courses, held in different locations around Miami, are booked up months in advance. 'The only way to get similar training,' Liddy said, 'would be to become an FBI agent or work for the CIA.' At the end of each session Liddy himself flies in from his mountain home to deliver a final lecture and hand out diplomas.

At the Nick Harris Detective Academy, the same system of full-time professionals working alongside students prevails, but with more of a hard-nosed private eye approach than James Bond indulgences. Marcus Joseph was not half-way through his day when other cases were making demands on his time. Twelve files on his desk awaited attention, all in colour-coded folders indicating insurance fraud, bank assignments, missing persons and skip traces.

Before arriving at the office, he had been out at 7.30 a.m., staking out a company that was being wound up. 'They were ripping off their own merchandise as fast as they could. We had them under surveillance to find out how the products were being taken out and where they were being warehoused.'

That had taken care of breakfast. By 1 p.m., with no time for lunch, he was heading down the San Diego Freeway to the home of a movie star who was worried that details of a business deal had been leaked to rival parties. Marcus lifted a briefcase of sophisticated de-bugging equipment from the boot of his car and trotted up the sweeping steps of a palatial villa in the Hollywood Hills. Back at the detective academy, students were struggling with the complexities of similar equipment. Alongside, on a workbench, were drug samples in glass phials for identification training, electronic eavesdropping equipment and fingerprint lifting kits.

After acquiring one client of psychic persuasion, Marcus found he had another. By 7 p.m., when the evening class was filing in, he was visiting a woman who was selling her home. She believed it was haunted and wanted the Nick Harris Agency to verify its supernatural attractions. In Los Angeles, it seems that the unlikeliest detail can enhance a sale. Marcus resigned himself to a night away from his wife and young son.

'There are some things you can prove,' he smiled. 'Others, well, who knows? Private investigation is an information business. We have moved out of heavy metal into high technology. Everyone wants access to information and the private eye is becoming the conduit. By the 1990s the age of the private investigator will have finally arrived.'

The agency's five case directors, helped by field agents scattered throughout greater Los Angeles, handled a varied turnover of work. A big burger restaurant was worried that its rival down the block was selling more quarter-pounders and wanted an undercover agent to find out why. Valley residents wanted to sue a chemical company for toxic fumes leaked into the already polluted atmosphere. Cocaine-addicted employees had taken to pilfering company goods. An insurance firm suspected a back-injury claimant of attending aerobics classes. A crazed Japanese woman demanded that the Nick Harris Agency murder her husband. By the time the pale sun broke over Van Nuys again, Marcus was red-eyed and ready for another day.

Nick Harris training paid off for the agency's proprietor, Milo Speriglio. He completed the course as a student, diploma in hand, and walked to the detective agency side of the company to ask for a job. There were no vacancies and he was referred by the academy to West Coast Detectives. The novice PI was assigned to routine field cases and, within five months, chalked up so many successes that he was appointed chief investigator. Within a year of graduating, he became their general manager.

'I'll never forget my first case,' he told *Working World* magazine in 1988. 'I was assigned to track down a former sweetheart for a client. She had been missing for nineteen years. After a week of turning over stones, one at a time, I found her. Surprisingly, the subject lived less than a mile from my client. The two probably crossed paths many times without recognising each other.'

After more than four years directing the fortunes of West Coast Detectives, Milo was offered the post of director of the Nick Harris Agency and chief administrator of the training academy. Within two years of accepting he was elected chairman of the board. Since then he has set examples for his students to follow by investigating a number of celebrity cases. His first star client was Elizabeth Taylor, who retained him to discover who was using her name on clothes without permission. Based on his evidence, a court injunction was granted in her favour.

He investigated the death of Jayne Mansfield, decapitated in a car accident, and discovered that she was a member of the Church of Satan. Her lover, who was driving the car at the time, had had a curse put on him by the High Priest. Milo believed it resulted in eight car accidents, the last of which claimed his life. Marlon Brando asked Milo to find out who was leaking secrets about his private life to the press. The culprit turned out to be the wife of one of his best friends. Natalie Wood's drowning off Catalina Island, in the Pacific, while climbing into a dinghy from her husband Robert Wagner's yacht is another case on the Speriglio files. As a result of his findings, coroner Thomas Noguchi asked for the case to be reopened.

His most noted case, however, was what *Celebrity Plus* magazine described as 'the mystery of the century'. The death of Marilyn Monroe fascinated Milo, who investigated it over a fifteen-year period, with help from many former graduates of the Nick Harris Academy.

'We proved beyond a shadow of doubt,' he told *Working World*, 'that Miss Monroe did not take her own life, as reported. Sergeant Jack Clemmons, acting Watch Commander of the Los Angeles Police Department, was the first to investigate. "It was murder," he told me. The deputy coroner's aide said: "I was forced to sign the death certificate. I think she was killed."

'The official report states that Marilyn Monroe swallowed forty-seven Nembutal sleeping capsules. Yet no drinking vessel was found in her locked room – the water in the house was turned off – the plumbing was being changed. No residue of the pills was found in her stomach lining. This indicates she did not swallow the capsules. The drug was found in her blood, establishing the cause of death. How did Marilyn die? She was injected by the liquid form of Nembutal. Dr Noguchi discovered a bruise on her hip – was it the injection site? Miss Monroe had a love liaison with President Kennedy, then with his brother, Attorney General Robert Kennedy. Just prior to her untimely death, the actress had an abortion. Bobby refused to talk to her, and she threatened to call a press conference to "tell all". All, if exposed, would have threatened national security and ended the careers of two of America's most powerful men.

'Her red diary recorded historical events the Kennedy brothers told her, including the CIA/Mafia role in the plot to assassinate Fidel Castro. It was stolen from the safe in the coroner's office forty-eight hours after her death. Jimmy Hoffa had Marilyn's phones tapped and her rooms bugged. She did not die at home, as reported. Walter Schaefer, president of Schaefer Ambulance, told me: "We took Marilyn to the Santa Monica Hospital. She was comatose, close to death." He said she died there. Someone stole her body and returned it to her Brentwood home – and the cover-up began. These are only a few of the hundreds of facts uncovered during the investigation into the mysterious death of Miss Monroe. Private eyes have many tales to tell; most of the time we cannot make them public.'

Many results of his research appeared in his books, *Marilyn*

Monroe: Murder Cover-up (1986) and *The Marilyn Conspiracy* (1987).

Milo Speriglio is right in that every private eye does have his secrets. Some he keeps to himself, while others he passes on as valuable experience to train others. At seminars in America and Britain, knowledge is shared on all aspects of investigation, especially skills which are frequently demanded in the work.

The test of a private eye is ultimately the success or failure of his inquiry; however, there are those who may not necessarily have achieved their objective but who have nevertheless furthered the status of their profession by the way they have handled a case – like, for instance, private detective Jim Lyness. When 5000 police-men were involved in the long and costly hunt for the Yorkshire Ripper in 1975, Lyness, a rugged Ulsterman who has since retired to Spain, was hired by the parents of victim Barbara Leach to find their daughter's killer. A year after embarking on his daunting task, Jim Lyness showed the same dedication and enthusiasm for the case as the day he took it on.

Around this time, in 1980, there was a sign behind his desk in his Oldham office which read: 'The impossible we can do at once. Miracles take a little longer.' The joke had taken on a hollow ring as, each day, Lyness found his one-man operation making little headway. He followed leads and sifted scraps of information, however small, with a growing determination that he would not rest until he had brought the Ripper to justice. Colleagues and the public thought that he had no chance of success, with little more than hunches to go on. The official police bill, at the time, was running at £3 million and seriously stretching resources.

Lyness covered his office walls with large-scale maps of the murder spots and photographs of the Ripper's victims so that the purpose of his operation never left him. As word spread about his involvement he began to receive calls from the public offering help. There were also the usual share of crank calls and, what began to intrigue him, a long series of silent calls.

'I have had twelve calls in an afternoon,' Lyness said at the time. 'They go beyond the stuff you get used to from cranks. Hoaxers can never resist saying something, just to provoke a reaction. These are different. The calls are completely silent. Whoever is on the other end is trying to pluck up courage to talk.'

Lyness, who had twenty-one years' experience as an investigator, received more than 3000 telephone calls from ordinary people wanting to help him. In public relations terms, it gave people a sympathetic picture of the working private eye. The police, on the other hand, firmly regarded the case as their territory. They made it clear that Lyness would not be allowed access to any information or given co-operation in any way. The private eye shrugged it off.

'Although it is the crime of the century, it has never seemed a mammoth case to me. It never enters my mind. I have just one end in view and work towards it. I have never contacted a newspaper or sought publicity. I was working on the case for a month even before my secretary knew. About a month after the murder, Mr Leach rang me one night from his home in Kettering. I had never met the man before. He asked me over and I agreed immediately to take the case. A personal friend of mine in the States, an investigator, was pulled in by police to help on the Boston Strangler case. Here, they said I would not be allowed access to anything – and I hadn't even asked.'

Jim Lyness's inquiries took him to Spain, on a tip-off from a Swedish girl who had been dated on holiday by a suspicious Englishman. Anna Rogulskyj, the only Ripper victim to escape with her life, telephoned Lyness's office daily, dredging her memory for any clues which might have helped him. In the end, the chance arrest of Peter Sutcliffe curtailed the private eye's efforts. With hindsight, Lyness probably had little hope of apprehending the Ripper, but the support he received from the public captured something of the enthusiasm for private detection which is rarely seen outside America.

Such a level of acclaim for the work of an investigator had not been seen since 1956, when Italian private eye Tom Ponzi arrived in Terrazzano di Rho, a grimy industrial town outside Milan, to tackle a situation which made international headlines. Ponzi, whose Milan business was one of the biggest private investigation agencies in Europe, had no client, only an instinctive impulse to offer his help when two psychopaths held a hundred children and three teachers hostage in their local school.

The men, brothers Arturo and Flavio Santano, arrived at the school by motorbike and sidecar at 10 a.m. and began unloading boxes of explosives and weapons. By the time they had finished, two carboys of sulphuric acid, 88 pounds of gelignite, four pistols and a thousand rounds of ammunition had been stacked inside the school entrance. Classes continued and the strange activity of the two men went unnoticed. They even managed to barricade the front and rear entrances with heavy furniture while lessons were in progress.

Then they ran into the classrooms, herding the terrified children and women staff into one room overlooking the town square. Children were clubbed and acid was poured onto the floor to warn teachers what would happen to their faces if they resisted. The scene inside the school was one of terror and hysteria as the Santanos prepared to make their demands. They fired a shot at a passer-by and told him to fetch the local mayor.

By this time a hysterical crowd of parents and townspeople had gathered, surging forward towards their children crammed into the upstairs window. The Santanos demanded a hundred million lire from the mayor and threatened to detonate the school if it was not delivered. Pandemonium ensued. Within fifteen minutes 800 armed carabinieri were drafted in, together with a battalion of infantry troops, six tanks and a field artillery battery. They were followed, almost as quickly, by an army of radio, press and television crews.

The world watched and waited as the mayor made a path through the crowd to lay the ransom money on the ground. Siege tactics were in their infancy in those days and, as soon as the brothers saw the money, they demanded more – a billion lire (about £1 million) in cash. To underline their point they threatened to kill one child for every minute that elapsed over their three-hour deadline. As time passed, the Santanos became increasingly agitated and clubbed one child in front of millions of horrified television viewers. His frightened screams stunned the parents, press and troops in the square to silence.

Ponzi was in a meeting with a client when news of the siege was broadcast. Without thinking what he could do, he instinctively shouted for a colleague and took off in his Alfa for Terrazzano di Rho. By the time he reached the square, the brothers were ranting into a microphone which had been passed to them to facilitate communications. Ponzi noticed that they were standing back from the window, behind the children, and their line of vision was slightly blocked. This, coupled with an open window at the side and a disused ladder lying nearby, gave him an idea. A journalist friend, who had been receiving feedback from a team of psychiatrists watching the brothers, tipped him that, within a few minutes, they would be completely out of control. Ponzi, afraid that violence was imminent, edged his way towards the ladder.

A local man, Sante Zennaro, tugged his arm and offered to help. He was soon joined by several others anxious to save the children. 'Ponzi grasped the sides of the ladder, planted a foot on the bottom rung and started up,' wrote his biographer Bela von Block. 'The rung broke under his weight. He fell, half-sprawling. Sante Zennaro, who'd been right beside him, didn't wait. He shoved Tom aside and scrambled up the ladder himself.'

An amateur was the last thing Ponzi wanted. Zennaro reached the top, hoisted himself over the window ledge and ran screaming for the classroom. The brothers dropped the microphone and opened fire on him. A bullet caught Zennaro in the shoulder, spinning him off his feet and almost bringing down Ponzi who was right behind him. The detective, ducking and weaving, charged Flavio Santano and knocked him unconscious. The brother ran back into the classroom, clubbing his way through a mass of children to reach the gelignite he had primed ready for detonation.

Ponzi, who had a flesh wound to the wrist, brought him down within a few feet of the explosives and a terrible fight ensued. Children ran screaming in confusion. Arturo Santano punched and clawed at the investigator's eyes in maniacal fury. Ponzi fought back as they rolled nearer the explosives and finally managed to batter him unconscious with blows to the face.

Zennaro, meanwhile, had staggered to the door and managed to pull down the barricade. As he stood there, covered in blood, waving in the troops, they tragically mistook him for one of the brothers and gunned him down. The picture of Ponzi, with Flavio's gun in hand, calling the police up the ladder, was flashed around the world. He became a hero and, back in his Milan office, thousands of letters and telegrams, cheques and donations poured in from grateful members of the public. The money was used to open a fund for Zennaro's family and the children of Terrazzano di Rho. Many years later, when the hostage children had become adults, von Block visited the town and found that candles were still being lit in the local church by townspeople for their favourite private eye.

Cases of dogged detection are less dramatic, and the investigator quietly going about solving a complex case is less newsworthy than a have-a-go hero. But Raymond Schindler, one of the greatest private eyes of all time, managed to make headlines wherever he went. This grey-haired, quietly-spoken American solved more than 10,000 cases in a career which began in 1912 in New York and spanned almost half a century.

The most celebrated murder investigation on his files was a case which attracted worldwide newspaper coverage in 1943, one of the few to divert readers' attention from reports of war and make them follow every twist of the mysterious death of British socialite Sir Harry Oakes in the Bahamas.

Oakes was, by all accounts, a vengeful and cantankerous man who made many enemies. When he was found gruesomely murdered in bed, there were many suspects, but suspicion eventually centred on his son-in-law, Alfred de Marigny, a French count, who was staying a short distance away. Because of the coverage and international scandal, the exiled Duke of Windsor, who was Governor of the Bahamas at the time, called in additional help from the Florida police. Two detectives searched the bedroom where Oakes had been murdered and claimed to have lifted a fingerprint from a screen near the bed. It was said to belong to de Marigny.

Oakes's body had been discovered by his daughter Nancy. He had been beaten about the head and attempts had been made to set the room on fire. Bahamian police arrested the Count de Marigny, mainly on the strength of rumours that he had feuded with his father-in-law, and awaited the Florida police. A frantic Nancy contacted Ray Schindler and retained him to prove her husband's innocence.

It seemed an uphill task, particularly as the detectives set out to obtain a conviction with the greatest possible speed. 'They actually destroyed much of the evidence that might have proved him guiltless,' wrote Schindler's friend and biographer Robert Hughes. 'The prosecution forbade de Marigny's attorneys and Ray Schindler access that might controvert the theory of his guilt. When Ray found in various places the imprints of a bloody hand, he was calmly told: "The fingers were stubby and de Marigny's were not, so we dismissed them." They not only dismissed them, but tried to erase them. And succeeded so far that Ray could not use them for the identification of one who seemed to him the far more probable murderer.'

Schindler's investigation, restricted though it was, enabled the defence to prove that the fingerprint could not have been taken from the screen, and de Marigny was acquitted. The detective who claimed to have taken the print should have photographed it *in situ*, but claimed to have 'forgotten' his camera. At the place on the screen from where the print was said to have been lifted, there was no trace of the delicate operation, a fact which can usually be detected. Books and films have since put forward theories as to who the killer might have been. There was no thorough post-mortem at the time, and the trustees of Sir Harry Oakes refused permission for pathologists to exhume the body. The mystery remains unsolved. Schindler, for his part, accomplished the job he was engaged to do and went on to attend to other cases. His involvement drew widespread media attention to the fact that scientific investigation by a private eye might succeed where efforts by the police have failed.

Training and sharing knowledge to encourage high standards of investigation is regarded with great importance in Europe and America. Seminars concentrate on practical aspects of the job and problems which are commonly encountered. The art of mobile surveillance is a common topic of lectures. A special session on the subject was held at the mid-year conference of California Licensed Investigators in 1987. The lecture, conducted by Eddy McClain, of Krout & Schneider, a 60-year-old West Coast investigation agency, illustrates many situations working investigators find themselves in.

'For thirty years I have observed experts and novices attempt surveillance assignments,' McClain said. 'It is harder than it looks. Most people can't follow a friend across a large city when there is no need for secrecy. There is a very fine line between staying with the subject to complete the assignment and either losing him or getting picked off. Inept operators will do both. Instinct is mandatory to tail successfully. Few people have it.

' ... The more surveillance work investigators do, the finer their skills and instincts are honed. Many investigators are called upon to conduct surveillance so infrequently that they never develop their skill level by building on a repertoire of experience and error. The pro who does a lot of surveillance has to fight boredom and laziness – because taking the job for granted will bite your backside just the same as the greenhorn who doesn't know what to do in the first place ... I often hear the uninitiated say, "anyone can follow somebody around and take their picture." Wrong. You have to be smarter and more cunning ... You have to move fast and think faster. You have to be able to drive like Mario Andretti and have the nerve of Evel Knievel. You have to make an accurate record of your observations, be believable to a judge and jury, and suffer long hours with a full bladder and empty stomach. No, it's not easy – but it is a hell of a lot of fun.'

One man who shares that view is Richard Jacques Turner, who runs Paragon Investigations in Hull, Yorkshire, and is president of the World Association of Detectives. 'I really enjoy it,' he said. 'It is something which gets the adrenalin going. I find that there are very few people who can conduct a successful mobile surveillance. It is terribly difficult. I now give driving tests to people who come to me for a job. I ask them to take me from one place to another as quickly as possible to see how they take opportunities in traffic. It is possible to take opportunities without driving dangerously – it is also possible to miss a lot, too, but they are not the drivers I am looking for.

'To me it is a great challenge to be able to stay with somebody because the odds are all on the side of the person you are following. I usually take a trainee with me in the car and point out the sort of distances we keep between a car we are following. In the city centre in the rush hour, the car has to be directly in front of you, or you lose it. On country roads you might sometimes allow four or five cars in between; on motorways it is possible to hang well back, with up to a dozen cars between. It varies enormously and depends, too, on the person you are following. If they are quite a quick driver, you cannot afford to allow them a lot of space. If they are very slow, and every car on the road is overtaking them, you need a few vehicles between, otherwise you are the only car behind them all the time.'

American surveillance has a jargon of its own:

'Op' means the operative, or investigator;

'Hot' or 'Hinky' refers to the subject being cautious or suspicious;

'Picked' – the subject has observed the private eye and is mildly suspicious;

'Burned' – the subject knows he is under surveillance;

'Cool' means that the subject is unaware he is being followed;

'A loose tail' is when the investigator hangs well back to avoid discovery, but ensures that contact is not broken;

'Loose surveillance' involves not keeping the subject in vision at all times, but checking periodically that contact is being maintained;

'Cover' – cars between the investigator and the subject are usually referred to as cover. Similarly, a woman and child in the private eye's car, to throw suspicion, would also be cover.

In a crime-conscious country like America, there are numerous pitfalls for the investigator. Parking outside a store, for example, can easily alert the owner to call the police because he will think a robbery is being planned. Investigators who park outside schools are recommended to tell the headteacher what they are doing in case they are suspected of being child molesters. Following a bus from stop to stop will possibly make the driver think he is about to be robbed and call the police. All these small points, which easily go unnoticed when a subject has to be kept in view at all times, are stressed to trainees.

Additionally, the subject may be as good as the PI himself, and run checks to see if he is being followed. Experience has taught that there are set patterns for this. Some can be anticipated; for others, there is no alternative but to give up and return to the office.

The following avoidance techniques were passed on by Eddy McClain, an old hand at the game, to Californian investigators:

1. The subject stops abruptly and looks for cars behind him.
2. He casually looks behind him as he turns a corner.
3. He makes a U-turn and retraces his route. In this case the surveillance usually has to be abandoned.
4. He circles the block to see if he is being followed.
5. He enters a shopping precinct car park and drives to another exit.

6 He stops abruptly after turning a corner.

7 He uses friends to spot investigators.

8 The subject is seen using his rear-view mirror
too much.

9 He starts to pull away, then stops, to see who
else is pulling away.

Most of these points are known to investigators the world over. In
Britain the average working private eye uses surveillance, video,
sound recordings and photographs to compile evidence. They are
part of the daily routine of investigators like Steve McLoughlin,
whose Manchester-based parent company, Archer Investigations,
covers most of the north of England. Business for McLoughlin was
expanding at such a rate that he moved to bigger premises in 1989,
away from the Corn Exchange, with its Victorian Heath-Robinson
lift and tiled walls which gave the corridors a mixed feeling of law
court and public lavatory.

Steve McLoughlin is small and well-dressed, in double-breasted
suit and matching tie, more the self-made businessman than
gumshoe. The desk before him looked like the scene of a burglary. A
35mm camera balanced precariously on a heap of court writs.
Photographs of a white Toyota climbing a moorland track spilled
towards an ashtray heaped with cigarette ends. Phone books,
letters, documents bearing legal seals, and cuttings from newspapers covered every inch of desk space.

Steve McLoughlin owned the most rapidly-expanding agency in
the north of England which he founded in 1977 – a combination of
good investigator and shrewd businessman, with an eye for buying
small agencies from retired private eyes and absorbing them into
the fold of his growing empire.

'It doesn't look very glamorous,' he gestured at his desk, 'but I
could never give it up. Detection is like heroin to me. I'm hooked. I
have an understanding wife, too, which helps enormously.'

McLoughlin is a study in stress control: a man who could say a
lot, but allows his quiet Lancashire voice to come out in a slow,
controlled drip. His face, too, has acquired the knack of remaining
expressionless. Beneath the well-cut suit, his frame is lean and
hard-muscled. McLoughlin is a detective straight from the pages of
a Dick Francis novel. He was a National Hunt jockey, trained at a

racing stables in the north-east. Then his first marriage fell apart. In the run-up to the divorce, he engaged a private eye to gather evidence, but continued with the investigations he had been making himself. In the course of his enquiries, the gumshoe happened to see the jockey carrying out his own sleuthing and was so impressed that he offered him a job on the spot.

McLoughlin changed horses, but still had racing in his blood. As his own detective agency expanded, he bought a small betting shop and a pony for his children. He still rides himself on the rare occasions that his work allows. In a strange way, his own experience turned the wheel full circle. One day a distraught woman walked into his office and asked him to take on some divorce inquiries for her.

'It was particularly harrowing for her,' Steve McLoughlin said, 'because the husband had invented all kinds of malicious tales about her to cover up an affair he was having.'

The woman, a personal assistant to a managing director, felt a sense of outrage and injustice. As McLoughlin set about his investigation, she found herself unable to rest, and conducted her own research in parallel. The detective was so impressed with the results that he offered her a job. The woman, who was 36, carried out surveillance and observation for him in the evenings when her office work was over. There were two other women investigators – both veteran process servers – one who had been full time for eight years and a colleague who operated part-time in a tough area of Liverpool.

'Process serving is a legal minefield, and often very dangerous,' McLoughlin explained. 'The best qualities for the job are someone who is slightly extrovert, adaptable and has an abundance of common sense. The rest is a matter of learning the ropes.'

The ropes frequently include the extremely complicated process of executing an Anton Pillar, not a gymnastic sequence, but a High Court order to freeze company documents which can only be served in the presence of a lawyer.

'We use it when, for example, an executive has been creaming off clients to form a company of his own. A case we just completed involved weeks of shadowing, legal telephone tapping within the company and discreet inquiries to collect the necessary evidence, before serving the order.'

McLoughlin is one of a growing number of British detectives who are concerned about how the industry is moving into the future. He believes passionately in thorough training, and was himself taught by a woman investigator whom he considers the best in the business. He believes that as his own business expands and the industry develops into the 1990s, the image of the private eye generally has failed to keep pace. Clients already see detectives as therapists: 'They walk into the office looking not only for an investigator but also for someone to share their problems.' McLoughlin wants private eyes accepted as a professional service to the community and there are already some indications that this is happening.

'The trend,' according to a 1989 report in *Today*, 'began in America where, in addition to a lawyer and a therapist, many people retain a PI. Now it has spread to Britain. With salaries in the £30,000 a year league, investigators are swapping their dirty trenchcoats and double bourbons for tailored suits and computerised offices.

'Peter Heims of the Association of British Investigators, says: "It used to be unusual for the public to instruct a solicitor, but not any more. The same has happened in our business."'

There is no doubt that public acceptance of the industry in Britain has improved, despite the misgivings of the past two centuries. In recent years it has made enormous strides in corporate areas, developing both hardware and investigative methods to serve the complex needs of international business. On the domestic front – the face of the private eye conjured by the man in the street – progress still needs to be made. Whenever there is adverse reporting on PIs who have fallen from grace, the industry's fragile relationship with the public slips a little. In America, such stories have little effect, for reasons of history. In Britain they are seen as damaging, and investigators such as Peter Heims have devoted years to containing the rift and nursing the industry through a period of change and challenge.

'Many people use that fateful expression, "when one door closes, another opens", shrugging their shoulders philosophically when another client is lost,' PI James Ackroyd wrote in *The Investigator* (1974), his manual for private detectives. 'This is an impractical attitude to adopt, since in the end all doors will be well and truly closed. Even though apparently impossible, the aim at least should be to retain every client.'

Private investigators in Britain feel that, with lack of adequate outside controls, their growing reputation is being sullied by the conduct of those who operate on the fringe of the profession. Leafing through the pages of any newspaper file on private investigation reveals a preponderance of stories, around 90 per cent, on slipshod gumshoes, falling standards and dirty tricks, with only a small proportion of articles reflecting a true picture of the profession. One handful of cuttings, taken at random, included an ex-policeman, jailed for corruption, who opened his own agency with £40 a week government 'enterprise allowance'; an investigator convicted of child sex offences; another touting for business among the newly bereaved; and the well-publicized activities of Mr Gary Murray, a self-appointed watchdog of the profession, who has devoted considerable time to exposing incompetence and government employment of amateurish sleuths for MI5 'dirty' work.

The newspapers concerned were fulfilling their public duty in reporting the news, but it is against this overall imbalance of presentation that investigators feel they have to struggle to put their case. As Peter Heims explained in an article he wrote in 1972 for *Police Review*: 'One of the ultimate aims of the ABI is to be recognised by professional men as a body of professional men. Our colleagues in the United States of America have attained this status and I feel sure that we will eventually. Let us not deceive ourselves, we still have a long way to go, for many of the public regard us as being in a rather dubious business.'

It is possible to get a glimpse of the private eye untainted by bad publicity from the escalation of events in the Soviet Union since the introduction of *glasnost*.

The Russian public, inured for many years to the idea of State spies, might be forgiven for viewing private detectives with grave suspicion. In fact, the opposite has been the case since the first agency opened its doors in April 1989. 'Alex', a co-operative launched in Leningrad and Moscow by former KGB men, was warmly welcomed by police and public alike. Demand keeps director Valentin Kosyakov working in his office until 8 p.m. or later most nights.

Parents have engaged Alex to check on teenagers who err into drug taking and prostitution, and trace missing relatives. Companies have hired them for counter-industrial espionage which, at first, might appear unnecessary in a country where firms are not generally thought to be in competition with each other. According to Alex, however, there is widespread infighting for access to raw materials, with most companies employing at least one expert whose task is to secure materials at the expense of rivals.

Alex has the blessing of the authorities who faced an overall rise in urban crime of 32 per cent throughout the country in the first half of 1989. According to Western reports, police officers were leaving the force because they could not cope with low pay and the increased danger of organized Mafia-style gangs.

The *Organised Crime Digest*, a Washington-based closed-circulation news sheet issued to law enforcement agencies worldwide, has monitored the rise of organized crime within the Soviet Union and noted with alarm the extent to which it has increased. The *Digest* reported 62 crimes involving firearms in Moscow in the first five months of 1989 – an increase of 326 per cent over the same period for the preceding year. The figure may be misleading because statistics are only beginning to be reported in the more relaxed climate of *glasnost*, but there is little doubt that firearms offences have risen.

The weekly *Moscow News* interviewed a waiter who resigned from the city's Sevastopol Restaurant after claiming that it had been taken over by organized crime leaders and small-time thugs. 'They've been coming to the restaurant for a long time, but in the last two years they have crowded out all other customers,' he said. 'They order expensive things, like brandy, champagne and caviar, and they act brazenly. A waiter's knees start shaking when he sees them at his table: several bosses with their bodyguards and chauffeurs. The guards don't drink, while the bosses go wild. They bring foreign currency and prostitutes from downtown hotels, and they play cards for enormous stakes. They make some of their business deals right at the table.'

The Soviet Union's crime problem is still minor compared with that of many Western nations, but shows signs of growing rapidly. British organized crime researcher Tommy Prior obtained a report in 1989 of a police lieutenant who saw two prostitutes lure foreigners into a taxi while he was on duty outside the Intourist Hotel. 'The lieutenant said two cars pulled up and several thugs jumped out, dragged the foreigners from the taxi, beat them up and robbed them. "I started to pursue them at once," he said. "On Sadovaya Street the criminals opened fire from sawn-off shotguns. They were shooting from both rear windows. It was half past midnight, there was a lot of traffic, and I couldn't return fire for fear of hitting someone in an oncoming car. Driving the car alone at seventy-five to eighty miles per hour, I couldn't take good aim. Besides, policemen can only use firearms in an emergency. You think twice before shooting because of the whole enquiry procedure."'

Alex offers a bodyguard protection service to visiting foreign businessmen, in addition to protecting the flood of small businesses opened since President Gorbachev's encouragement of free enterprise.

'These businesses have become the object of criminal aspirations,' Valentin Kosyakov explained. 'Crooks think businessmen make a lot of money. The State cannot possibly protect every single one. We charge a scale of fees according to the type of work involved. I cannot say what an average case would cost,' he added, tongue in cheek, 'but we are cheaper than Pinkerton's.'

The gangs are becoming bolder and more ruthless. A young journalist, Vladimir Glotov, of the radical magazine *Ogonyok*, was killed while investigating organized crime in August 1989. His body was found beneath a tree outside his home in a Moscow suburb with his skull smashed in and his neck trampled on. Alex offered protection to journalists from its squad of 60 trained security guards in Moscow. 'Most of our work is the fight against crime,' Valentin Kosyakov said. 'We get on well with the police. We fight the same battle. We do not like the term gangs. We talk of criminal groups. They are becoming more consolidated, spreading all over the Soviet Union.'

What is perhaps most interesting about Alex is not the important crime-fighting role it is playing, but the fact that it rarely advertises its services within the Soviet Union. The Russian public has no previous experience of private investigators, and no preconceptions which might influence their opinions.

'The work we are doing is very new in the Soviet Union,' Kosyakov said, 'but the response has been great. We have a good

image and a positive relationship with the public. We are continuing to build a picture through our services, of the private
detective as strong, helpful and professional.' Or, as Mr Kosyakov
put it, 'A man of moral purity.'

Private investigation is expanding at a greater rate, with more
detectives and specialist agencies operating than at any time in the
industry's 150-year history. The deep historical differences in
public attitude to PIs in Britain and America still remain, although,
in the UK, standards set by members of the ABI have done much to
elevate the image of the profession.

There perhaps a lesson
to be learned here from the United States, where the PI's role is
made easier by greater access to information and tough licensing
qualifications. It has not prevented a plethora of renegade operators, but the need to satisfy strict requirements has encouraged a
high degree of professionalism which has cemented good public
relations and co-operation from the authorities.

However, British investigators still lack the means, which can
only be granted by government, to meet the challenge of competing
internationally in the age of information.

British clients have no *Which?* report on which to base their PI
choice, no guarantee that the agency they pick is committed to the
ABI's code of ethics and, more importantly, no assurance that the
PI will carry out his work to the best of his ability for a reasonable
fee. The strict regulations which British PIs have campaigned for
since 1913 would give the industry greater respectability and be to
the advantage of the companies and individuals increasingly hiring
investigators.

There is little logic to the muddled insistence of successive
governments on ignoring the pleas of British private eyes for professional status. The extent to which the media have suggested that
the security services regularly employ cowboy operators to breach
the laws of privacy and discretion, however, might suggest that
change is not in Whitehall's interest. If this is the case, or part of it,
then British PIs can do little more than extend their present efforts
at self-regulation, maintain high qualification standards for ABI
members and hope that closer political unity with Europe will bring
Community-wide legislation in the 1990s.

In the meantime, the jaded spirits of the profession may be lifted by the enthusiasm with which fledgling Russian investigators see their public role. Despite the ghosts of the past, PIs can benefit from each other's experience. Links between detective associations in Britain and America and the Alex agency in Moscow and Leningrad have already been made in the hope that investigators around the world may co-operate and learn from each other's methods. The future of Sam Spade may be in safe hands, after all.

BIBLIOGRAPHY

Ackroyd, James: *The Investigator*, Frederick Muller, 1974

Armes, Jay J.: *Jay J. Armes Investigator*, Macdonald, 1976

Bles, Mark, and Low, Robert: *The Kidnap Business*, Pelham, 1987

Caesar, Gene: *Incredible Detective*, Prentice Hall, 1968

Chesney, Kellow: *The Victorian Underworld*, History Book Club, 1970

Cobb, Belton: *The First Detectives*, Faber & Faber, 1957

Cummings, Sir John: *Bibliography Dealing With Crime*, Patterson Smith (reprint), 1970

Dear, William: *The Dungeon Master*, Houghton Mifflin, 1984

—— *Please . . . Don't Kill Me*, Houghton Mifflin, 1989

Everson, William: *The Detective In Film*, Citadel, 1975

Fleisher, Mark: *Warehousing Violence*, Sage, 1989

Greene, Marilyn: *Finder*, Crown, 1988

Griffiths, Major Arthur: *Mysteries of Police and Crime* (3 vols), Cassell, 1920

Heims, Peter: *Countering Industrial Espionage*, 20th Century Security Education, 1982

Horan, James: *The Pinkertons*, Robert Hale, 1967

Horan, James D., and Swiggett, Howard: *The Pinkerton Story*, Heinemann, 1952

Hougan, Jim: *Spooks*, W. H. Allen, 1979

Hughes, Robert: *The Complete Detective*, Sheridan House, 1950

Kerner, Annette: *Woman Detective*, Werner Laurie, 1954

Knapp and Baldwin: *Newgate Calendar*, Robins, 1824

Lewis, William: *No Time To Eat*, Vantage Press, 1971

Marshall, Herbert: *Memories of a Private Detective*, Hutchinson, 1924

Morn, Frank: *The Eye That Never Sleeps*, Indiana University Press, 1982

Nolan, William: *Dashiell Hammett – A Life at the Edge*, Arthur Barker, 1983

Oughton, Frederick: *Ten Guineas a Day*, John Long, 1961

Parkhurst, William: *True Detectives*, Crown Publishers, 1989

Pileggi, Nicholas: *Blye, Private Eye*, Playboy Press, 1976

Pinkerton, Allan: *Bank Robbers and Detectives*, Dillingham, 1887

Pinkerton, William: 'The Yeggman', paper read to the International Association of Chiefs of Police, 1904

—— 'Forgery', ditto, 1905

—— 'Bank Sneak Thieves', ditto, 1906

Rowan, Richard Wilmor: *The Pinkertons*, Hurst & Blackett, 1931

Ruehlmann, William: *Saint with a Gun*, New York University Press, 1974

Stead, Philip John: *Vidocq*, Staples, 1953

Summer, Anne: *But I Couldn't Do That*, Souvenir, 1968

Symons, Julian: *Bloody Murder*, Faber & Faber, 1972

Thompson, Josiah: *Gumshoe*, Little, Brown, 1988

Tracy, Jack: *An Encyclopaedia Sherlockiana*, Avon, 1977

Von Block, B. W.: *Super Detective,*
    Playboy Press, 1972

Publications

The Private Security Industry, a paper
by Peter Heims; *Sunday Telegraph;*
Leeds Mercury; Sala's Journal; Dallas;
Daily Express; Dallas Times-Herald;
A. B. Bookman's Weekly; Reynolds
News; News Review; Radio Pictorial;
Tit-Bits; Guide and Ideas; Reveille;
Police Review; Daily Mirror; John
Bull; Sunday Pictorial; Newsweek;
Texas Monthly; Washington Post; Los
Angeles Times; Leader; News of the
World; Weekend; Guardian; London
Evening News; Working World;
Sunday Times; Today; Organised
Crime Digest.

INDEX